Vol. XCVI   No. 3

T5-ASM-554

Bible Expositor and Illuminator

SUMMER QUARTER   June, July, August 2024

God's Work Through Women and Youths

UNIT I: Women of Faith

UNIT II: Young People of Faith

Editor in Chief: James M. Leonard, Ph.D.
Managing Editor: Michelle Birtasevic
Edited and published quarterly by
LIFESTONE MINISTRIES
UNION GOSPEL PRESS DIVISION
Rev. W. B. Musselman, Founder
Price: $8.19 per quarter*
*shipping and handling extra
ISBN 978-1-64495-422-5

LOOKING AHEAD

This quarter we will consider how God displays His greatness and glory through unexpected people—in particular through women (unit I) and young people (unit II).

God gave women a prominent place in His plan from the beginning of Creation. The initial absence of woman was the only thing "not good" when He created the world (Gen. 2:18-15; lesson 1).

After Adam and Eve fell into sin, God gave immediate hope by declaring that an offspring of the woman would crush the head of Satan, the deceiving serpent (Gen. 3:15). The Lord continually reinforced this promise throughout the Old Testament by using women as His instruments of deliverance at key points in Israel's history.

The prophetess Deborah mobilized Barak and the army of Israel to deliver God's people from the Canaanites (lesson 2).

Ruth was not an Israelite, but God demonstrated His own faithfulness through her commitment to her mother-in-law, Naomi, and through Boaz's protection of Ruth (lessons 3—5).

Hannah overcame her enemies, not through retaliation or her own willpower, but through *prayer*—a weak instrument from a human perspective, but a strong instrument in the hands of God (lesson 6).

Through Esther, God once again gave Israel victory over their enemies and spared them from being massacred (lessons 7—8).

In the New Testament, women continued to be at the center of God's work, as seen in a sinful woman's display of love for Christ (lesson 9) and Dorcas's quiet but impactful ministry to widows (lesson 10).

God also used young people and children as instruments of His grace (unit II). A prominent example is young David, whom God chose not because of his outward appearance but because of his godly heart (lesson 11).

God foreshadowed the far-reaching power of the gospel when He used the witness of a young servant girl to make Himself known to a Syrian military leader (lesson 12).

Josiah inherited the throne as a young child, but he became one of the best kings Judah had ever known, leading the nation away from idolatrous practices back to God (lesson 13).

As we study these amazing stories, let us take courage in our own ministries. God wants to work through our weaknesses so that His name will be glorified.

—*Matthew Robinson*

Women in the Bible

Tom Greene

Let's get the obvious out of the way: a lot of people outside the church today dislike what the Bible says about women, claiming it is sexist. However, a lot of those same people cannot tell you what a woman is, and many who think they can are not reliable guides to follow. But let's consider what they are saying. What is the biblical view of women? Is the Bible sexist? The answer is a resounding *NO!*

Let's paint a biblical view of womanhood, starting with Creation: "So God created man in his own image, in the image of God created he him; male and female created he them" (Gen. 1:27). This is very important. God created both men and women in His image. Everyone, whether male or female, is equally worthy of respect.

When Eve was created, she was called a "help," or helper (2:18). This does not imply that women are inferior to men: David uses the same word to call the Lord his helper, and no one would say God was David's inferior (cf. Pss. 30:10, 54:4, 89:19). We *do* begin to see a difference in *roles* in Genesis 2, but no difference in importance. When Adam says "This is now bone of my bones, and flesh of my flesh" (Gen. 2:23), he is saying that he and Eve are of same essence. Men and women are equally valuable and loved in the sight of God.

Throughout the Old Testament, we see that the roles of men and women were somewhat different: although both had some legal rights, women could not be priests, (Ex. 29:9) and a husband was considered the head of a household (cf. Num. 30:3-16). Virtually everyone agrees on this (whether they like it or not), so we will not spend a long time here. Instead, we will focus on the status and role of women in the New Testament and among the people of God today.

In the New Testament, we clearly see that Jesus valued women. In a time when women sadly had less social and legal standing than men, Jesus regularly and caringly spoke with women and encouraged them to follow and support Him (Matt. 15:22-28; Luke 8:1-3; 10:38-42; John 4:7-26; 11:20-44). Indeed, when He was crucified, it was primarily women who stayed near the cross (Matt. 27:55-56). All the Gospels record that women were the first witnesses of His resurrection.

Jesus clearly valued women. He was also willing to break social norms; if He had wanted to, He could have appointed a woman as one of His twelve disciples. The fact that He did not do so is telling regarding the unique roles of men and women in ministry.

Men and women have different roles in churches in the New Testament, and women are not permitted to teach in the public gathering of the church (I Tim. 2:11-14). Because Paul is specifically writing about the context of the public worship of the church in I Timothy 2, his commands there should not be taken beyond what he intended. In Acts 18:26, we see both Priscilla and Aquila (a husband-and-wife team) teaching a man in a private setting.

Women are equally intelligent, valu-

(Editorials continued on page 186)

SCRIPTURE LESSON TEXT

GEN. 2:18 And the LORD God said, *It is* not good that the man should be alone; I will make him an help meet for him.

19 And out of the ground the LORD God formed every beast of the field, and every fowl of the air; and brought *them* unto Adam to see what he would call them: and whatsoever Adam called every living creature, that *was* the name thereof.

20 And Adam gave names to all cattle, and to the fowl of the air, and to every beast of the field; but for Adam there was not found an help meet for him.

21 And the LORD God caused a deep sleep to fall upon Adam, and he slept: and he took one of his ribs, and closed up the flesh instead thereof;

22 And the rib, which the LORD God had taken from man, made he a woman, and brought her unto the man.

23 And Adam said, This *is* now bone of my bones, and flesh of my flesh: she shall be called Woman, because she was taken out of Man.

24 Therefore shall a man leave his father and his mother, and shall cleave unto his wife: and they shall be one flesh.

25 And they were both naked, the man and his wife, and were not ashamed.

NOTES

The Creation of Woman

Lesson Text: Genesis 2:18-25

Related Scriptures: Genesis 1:26-31; 3:9-21; 5:1-2; I Timothy 2:12-15

TIME: unknown

PLACE: Garden of Eden

GOLDEN TEXT—"The Lord God said, It is not good that the man should be alone; I will make him an help meet for him" (Genesis 2:18).

Introduction

John J. Davis wrote, "Evolution, as represented in Darwinism and neo-Darwinism, simply asserts that all living organisms arose from one simple, living cell. The origin of that cell is traced to the accumulation of chemical and protein elements brought together over a long period of time by unknown chance factors.

"The concept of spontaneous generation, which is widely accepted and on which evolutionary theory is based, is an a priori assumption that lacks controlled scientific proof" (*Paradise to Prison,* Baker).

Since Christians are often under pressure to balance scientific explanations of origins with belief in God and Creation, many have accepted what is referred to as theistic evolution. This theory states that while God might have directly created the original life forms, He followed that by ordering and directing the evolutionary process through the laws of nature He had established.

It might be tempting to accept such a compromise, but that explanation does not accord with the Bible's description of the creation of man. Scripture clearly attributes the origin of both Adam and Eve to direct creative acts of God.

LESSON OUTLINE

I. **ADAM BY HIMSELF—**
   Gen. 2:18-20

II. **ADAM WITH A COMPANION—**
   Gen. 2:21-25

Exposition: Verse by Verse

ADAM BY HIMSELF

GEN. 2:18 And the Lord God said, It is not good that the man should be alone; I will make him an help meet for him.

19 And out of the ground the Lord God formed every beast of the field, and every fowl of the air; and brought them unto Adam to see what he would call them: and whatsoever

Adam called every living creature, that was the name thereof.

20 And Adam gave names to all cattle, and to the fowl of the air, and to every beast of the field; but for Adam there was not found an help meet for him.

Adam's need (Gen. 2:18). Creation occurred in six days, followed by the day on which God rested. Some speculate that each of the days of Creation lasted for eons, but that interpretation frequently gives greater weight to scientists' assertions of the age of the universe than to direct exegesis of the text. The Bible does occasionally use the word "day" in a non-literal sense, as when the prophets describe the exile of Israel and Judah as a "day" (cf. Jer. 30:7). However, the mention of "evening and morning" at the end of each day in Genesis 1 tells us that the six days of Creation were ordinary twenty-four-hour periods.

{Genesis 1 repeatedly states that what God did was good (vss. 4, 10, 12, 18, 21, 25). In summary, verse 31 says, "And God saw every thing that he had made, and, behold, it was very good." We would expect nothing less, since He is God and is Himself good in every way (Pss. 34:8; 135:3).

When we come to Genesis 2:18, however, we suddenly read, "And the Lord God said, It is not good that the man should be alone."}Q1 Both men and women understand this statement. Men often feel incomplete and inadequate to handle many of the things they face in life. Women know that if it were not for their assistance, men would sometimes fail and fall apart when trying to accomplish certain tasks! God made a good and valid observation here and followed it with a good decision to "make him an help meet for him."

The key word is "meet." It translates the Hebrew word *neged,* which means "in front of" or "counterpart." God did not make someone of lesser quality to be with Adam. He made someone comparable to him. The person God knew Adam needed was someone equal and compatible.

Matthew Henry wrote, "The woman was made of a rib out of the side of Adam; not made out of his head to rule over him, nor out of his feet to be trampled upon by him, but out of his side to be equal with him, under his arm to be protected, and near his heart to be beloved" (*Matthew Henry's Commentary on the Whole Bible,* Hendrickson).

In God's plan, the woman was absolutely necessary. {While many cultures today devalue women and treat them as owned objects or worse, in God's eyes they have always been valuable and loved and deserving of consideration and respect from the opposite sex.}Q2

Adam's decisions (Gen. 2:19). It might be that Adam's assignment from God as described in this verse led to his realization that he was not complete. {One of God's creative acts had been to make animals and birds out of the ground. At some point He brought these creatures to Adam and told him to name them.}Q3 When God decided to create man, He determined that He would give him dominion over the animal world (1:26). So He allowed Adam to exercise his dominion by choosing names for these creatures.

Genesis 2:19 says, "Whatsoever Adam called every living creature, that was the name thereof." The very act of naming God's creation shows that he was an extremely intelligent being. It took a great deal of creativity to accomplish such a momentous task. All we have to do is think through the names of as many animals and birds as we can, and we soon realize that Adam accomplished a great feat.

Since God created the animals and

birds male and female, He probably brought them to Adam in pairs. {We have no idea how long it took him to complete his task, but we have to wonder—when did Adam realize that he was alone while everything in the animal world had a mate to share its life?}Q4

"The plain fact is that Adam needed Eve. Not a single animal God had created could do for Adam what Eve could do. She was a helper 'meet [suitable] for him.' When God paraded the animals before Adam for him to name them, they doubtless came before him in pairs, each with its mate; and perhaps Adam wondered, 'Why don't I have a mate?'" (Wiersbe, *The Bible Exposition Commentary,* Cook). It was God who made the statement that it was not good for Adam to be alone, and only He could do something about it.

Adam's solitude (Gen. 2:20). This verse lets us know that Adam successfully completed the task God had given him. Adam named all the "cattle," "fowl of the air," and "beast[s] of the field." The Hebrew word translated "cattle" usually refers to large, four-legged animals. Sometimes they are thought of as those animals that can be tamed or used to assist people in field work. "Every beast" is often thought of as referring to those that live in the wild and are not generally tamable. Adam named every creature.

The text then notes that among the animals, a "help meet" was not found for Adam. "The English word 'helper,' because it can connote so many different ideas, does not accurately convey the connotation of the Hebrew word. . . . Usage of the Hebrew term does not suggest a subordinate role, a connotation which English 'helper' can have. In the Bible God is frequently described as the 'helper,' the one who does for us what we cannot do for ourselves, the one who meets our needs. {In this context the word seems to express the idea of an 'indispensable companion.'}Q5 The woman would supply what the man was lacking in the design of creation and logically it would follow that the man would supply what she was lacking, although that is not stated here" ("Genesis 2:18," classic.net.bible.org).

Henry M. Morris wrote, "There was clearly no *kinship* in any manner between man and the animals. None was *like* him; none could provide fellowship or companionship *for* him. It is abundantly clear and certain that he had not recently *evolved from* them! If the latter were true, and his body was still essentially an ape's body (or the body of whatever 'hominid' form may have been his immediate progenitor), it seems strange that he could have found nothing in common with either parents or siblings" (*The Genesis Record,* Baker).

Every creature but Adam had companionship; he was the only created being that was truly alone. God had given the command to His creatures to "be fruitful, and multiply" (1:22). At this point in Creation, that was possible for every creature except Adam!

ADAM WITH A COMPANION

21 And the LORD God caused a deep sleep to fall upon Adam, and he slept: and he took one of his ribs, and closed up the flesh instead thereof;

22 And the rib, which the LORD God had taken from man, made he a woman, and brought her unto the man.

23 And Adam said, This is now bone of my bones, and flesh of my flesh: she shall be called Woman, because she was taken out of Man.

24 Therefore shall a man leave his father and his mother, and shall cleave unto his wife: and they shall be one flesh.

25 And they were both naked, the man and his wife, and were not ashamed.

7

God's work (Gen. 2:21-22). God is said to have specifically caused a "deep sleep" to come over Adam. This later happened to King Saul when he was pursuing David (I Sam. 26:12). In order to show Saul that He was with David, God caused such a deep sleep to come upon him that David and Abishai walked into the middle of the military camp, stood beside Saul, discussed whether or not they should kill him, and then walked away with his spear and jug of water! "Deep sleep" thus indicates that Adam was rendered totally unconscious for the upcoming procedure.

Because of this we understand the creation of Eve was done by God without assistance from Adam. She was His gift to Adam. Like him, she was a direct creation of God; unlike him, she was made of tissue from a living being. While Adam slept, God took one of his ribs, then closed him up again. "The woman is formed from the man himself, making her of like nature, the same flesh and blood, a being with equal faculties and likewise 'in the image of God' (1:27)" (Criswell, ed., *The Believer's Study Bible*, Thomas Nelson).

Keil and Delitzsch noted, {"The woman was created, not of dust of the earth, but from a rib of Adam,}Q6 because she was formed for an inseparable unity and fellowship of life with the man, and the mode of her creation was to lay the actual foundation for the moral ordinance of marriage" (*Commentary on the Old Testament*, Hendrickson). It was in this marriage relationship that Adam would be able to fulfill the command of God to be fruitful and multiply.

It must have been an electrifying moment when God brought the newly created woman to the man. Those of us who are married recall the many joyful emotions that accompanied the development of that relationship and its culmination in marriage. What was it like for Adam? One moment he was alone. The next moment he woke up from a deep sleep and was presented with a beautiful companion!

God's will (Gen. 2:23-24). *Nelson's New Illustrated Bible Commentary* says, "'This is now' means 'At last!' ... Adam's wording is poetic and exalted; seeing Eve was a shocking and exhilarating experience because the match was perfect. Here was a mirror of himself, someone just like him, and yet different!" (Radmacher, Allen, and House, eds., Thomas Nelson). Adam then called her "woman," continuing the use of his authority to name the creatures God had created. {The Hebrew word for woman (*isha*) corresponds to the word for man (*ish*). She was "woman" because she was taken out of man.}Q7

Adam recognized that God had literally "built" a woman from the rib He had taken out of him (the meaning of "made" in Genesis 2:22). She truly was "bone of my bones, and flesh of my flesh" (vs. 23). The word for "rib" might refer generally to Adam's "side," not necessarily to an actual rib bone. The point is that God opened Adam's side and took some part of him with which to build the woman. With this understanding we better comprehend Adam's reference to her as his bone and flesh.

Genesis 2:24 is the classic passage on the establishment of the marriage relationship. It begins with the word "therefore," indicating that what had happened in the immediate context led to the conclusion stated in this verse. {The relationship that a man and woman are to have in their marriage is based on this first union between Adam and Eve, which was a union established by God.}Q8 {The emphasis is that a man should leave his parents and make this new relationship his primary one. He is to cleave to his wife.}Q9

The concept of leaving has to do with loosening and relinquishing ties. It does not negate the biblical command that a man should honor his parents; it means that while he continues to do that, his first priority will now be his wife. {The concept of cleaving conveys the thought of clinging and adhering to someone. A man is to conscientiously stick to his wife above all others, including his parents.}[Q10] Husband and wife are considered to be one flesh, that is, so thoroughly joined together as to become one totally unified whole made up of the two persons.

A problem that pastors often have to deal with in marriages is the fact that sometimes this unity becomes fractured after children arrive. Children are a great blessing from the Lord, but a parent should never put a child ahead of his or her spouse. That can be easy to overlook because a child requires so much time and attention. It is important for spouses with children to continue prioritizing each other. The oneness of a husband/wife relationship should never be violated.

The ideal is that both parents will be involved in caring for the children and will operate as a unit. One of the greatest sources of security for any child is the knowledge that Dad and Mom love each other dearly and that nothing will ever separate them or damage their closeness. This above everything else will cause a child to feel loved and secure, for he will never have to worry that his homelife and relationship with his parents might be destroyed.

Man's innocence (Gen. 2:25). It is clear that God's perspective on marriage is that it is between one man and one woman. "Their nakedness (v. 25) suggests that they were at ease with one another without any fear of exploitation or potential for evil. Such fellowship was shattered later at the Fall and is retained only in a measure in marriage when a couple begins to feel at ease with each other. Here the nakedness, though literal, also suggests sinless-

ness" (Walvoord and Zuck, eds., *The Bible Knowledge Commentary,* Cook).

Adam and Eve were innocent, and there was no shame in their relationship. They complemented each other completely. The high standard for marriage had been established once and for all! "Marriage was God's idea. Through a monogamous, heterosexual relationship God planned the procreation of children. The family, based on the creation foundation, was God's plan for a human race that would obey His commands and glorify Him" (Anders, ed., *Holman Old Testament Commentary,* Broadman and Holman).

—Keith E. Eggert

QUESTIONS

1. What does Genesis 1 repeatedly say about Creation, and what was different in Genesis 2?
2. How does God's view of women differ from what is found in many of the world's cultures today?
3. What task did God give Adam soon after the Creation?
4. In what key way did Adam's situation differ from that of all the creatures he named?
5. What does the term "help meet" tell us about Eve in relation to Adam?
6. How was the creation of Eve different from that of Adam?
7. What did Adam name this new creature, and why did he choose that name?
8. Why do we find the classic biblical statement about the establishment of marriage here?
9. What truths are stated in it?
10. What are the implications of the command to "leave" and "cleave"?

—Keith E. Eggert

Preparing to Teach the Lesson

We live in a day when the natural and normal relationship between man and woman has been distorted by society. In particular, the sinful perversion of normal sexual relationships has become very prevalent. This is rightly discouraging to the sincere Christian. We can only recover the right viewpoint by learning how God established the human relationship at the time of Creation. We then can begin to see how to apply God's Creation principles to our own lives. God created us male and female for His purposes and for our good. Like every other good creation of God, our experience of it can be ruined by sin and erroneous thinking. Understanding God's pattern for our relationships is essential in leading fulfilling and rewarding lives.

TODAY'S AIM

Facts: to discover what God did and purposed when He created mankind.

Principle: to bring our thinking and actions into conformity with God's established ways for mankind.

Application: to learn to embrace God's relationship patterns so that we can experience His blessings in life.

INTRODUCING THE LESSON

In our society, it is common to refer to someone as "hot." One would think from common speech that physical beauty is the most desirable characteristic a person can have. Even when one is spoken of as being spiritual, the real meaning of the word is usually distorted to mean soulful or emotional. A true understanding of what makes one spiritual is rare among people today.

When God created mankind as male ~~and~~ ~~fe~~male, He also established their ~~relations~~hip. This was not only the right relationship; it was also the most rewarding and fulfilling of all possible relationships. Although it has been perverted by sin, it is still God's pattern for mankind's life.

DEVELOPING THE LESSON

1. God saw man's need (Gen. 2:18). God created all the animals in pairs as male and female. He gave them the commission to multiply and populate the earth with their kind. God established the same basic pattern of life for the animals as He did for man. Just as an artist's paintings all exhibit certain elements of his skill, so too the works of God show similarities of design. This is not evidence of evolution but evidence of the Great Designer.

God added a new element in the creation of mankind: He "breathed into his nostrils the breath of life; and man became a living soul" (Gen. 2:7). Man was set apart from the animals in that he was a spiritual being. He could breathe the same air, eat (some of) the same food, and live on earth, but he was a spiritual being meant to have fellowship with God.

Other than the natural instincts for food and sleep, Adam probably had no idea what his needs were or what they would be in the future. Adam was alone; he needed someone to share his life with—a suitable helper.

At the conclusion of each day of Creation, God looked at what He had done and saw that it was good. Then He looked at Adam's situation and said, "It is not good that the man should be alone" (Gen. 2:18). He then purposed to make Adam a suitable helper.

2. God helped man see his own need (Gen. 2:19-20). Adam was created as an adult, with no background or experience. God gave him the intellectual experience of naming all the animals. Part of the naming process could have included observing the animals' behavior and the way they interacted. Some were quite social, collecting in large herds, but each had a mate. By observing this, Adam may have seen that he too needed a mate—someone with whom he could share his life.

3. God made provision to fulfill man's need (Gen. 2:21-22). God did not take from the dust of the earth again and create an unrelated being from Adam. Instead, He created the woman from Adam's rib, signifying that they were intimately linked. They were to be partners in life. This was to be the basic unit of mankind—one man and one woman for life. This is the natural and normal course of life for human beings.

It is not considered politically correct today to espouse that view. But it is not physically or spiritually correct to rebel against God's specific plan and order for mankind.

Romans 1:18-32 details what can happen when mankind rebels against God, and one of the results is sexual immorality. God cannot bless sin in any form. He will not bless relationships that go against His clearly expressed wishes.

4. God instituted the relationship between man and woman (Gen. 2:23-25). It was natural for Adam to continue his activity of naming what God had created. He obviously knew what God had done to create the woman, and the fact that he named her woman reflects that. Adam viewed her as an extension of himself—"bone of my bones, and flesh of my flesh"—recognizing that she was one with him. This is the God-ordained human relationship.

The narrative in Genesis 2 switches from Adam's speech in verse 23 to God speaking in verse 24. We then read a historical narrative in verse 25. We know it is God speaking in verse 24 because Jesus attributed it to God in Matthew 19:4-5.

We must understand that one-man/one-woman pairing for life does not depend on social convention, laws, or the whims of love or lust. It is the pattern God set forth both for His glory and for our good.

God points out in this historical narrative that the man and his wife were naked and not ashamed. There were no other people around to see them, and they had no concept of anything sinful. They were completely innocent.

ILLUSTRATING THE LESSON

God's plan for man and woman was good and would bring fulfillment to them both.

CONCLUDING THE LESSON

God knew of Adam's need and provided for it. He also knows each individual's needs and has made every provision for those needs (cf. Matt. 6:31-32). It is wise to acknowledge this and govern ourselves accordingly.

ANTICIPATING THE NEXT LESSON

In the next lesson, we explore the story of the prophetess Deborah and how God used her to deliver Israel from their enemies (Judg. 4:4-10, 12-16).

—*Brian D. Doud*

PRACTICAL POINTS

1. God never intended for man to be alone (Gen. 2:18).
2. Our wise God often allows us to recognize our deficiencies so that we might appreciate His provision and seek Him (vss. 19-20).
3. God's omnipotence is displayed by His ability to create however He chooses (vs. 21).
4. God's provision is always exactly what we need (vs. 22).
5. God designed husband and wife to be in complete unity, as symbolized by the creation of woman out of man's side (vss. 23-24).
6. Only the forgiveness of God can restore man's innocence Gen. 2:25; cf. Gen 3:7; Heb. 10:19-22).

—Don Kakavecos

RESEARCH AND DISCUSSION

1. How does this story of the creation of the woman compare to the account given in Genesis 1? What are the differences and the similarities?
2. Why do you think God waited to create woman, since He already knew it would not be good for Adam to be alone? Does this help us understand why God might delay the fulfillment of our needs and desires?
3. How is God's purpose and design for marriage indicated by His formation and presentation of the woman to Adam, Adam's declaration in 2:23, and the Bible writer's comment in verse 24?
4. In what ways does verse 25 set the stage for what was to happen in chapter 3?

—Don Kakavecos

ILLUSTRATED HIGH POINTS

Help meet (Gen. 2:18)

Man by himself was not complete. He needed a helper, so God provided woman to be his counterpart, his complement, his companion. There is order, however, in that the husband is to lead and the wife is to be submissive. The husband leads in love, and the wife lovingly submits (cf. Eph. 5:22-25). We can look to Christ as our model for both sacrificial leadership (cf. John 13:13-15) and submissive love (cf. John 14:31).

Cleave unto his wife (vs. 24)

The basic concept in the Hebrew word translated "cleave" is that of being joined or stuck together. People in ancient times were familiar with a variety of glues made out of tree sap, tar, and animal bone and hide.

Today we have a variety of adhesives for many applications. Some are of the "superglue" type; others, like rubber cement, are designed so that the joined parts can be separated freely.

God designed marriage to be likened to superglue, not rubber cement. When superglued items are separated, they seldom come apart cleanly.

Were not ashamed (vs. 25)

Mark Twain wrote in *Following the Equator,* one of his many books, that "man is the only animal that blushes. Or needs to." The Christian knows why (cf. Rom. 3:23).

It is interesting to read other people's explanations of man's shame. One person wrote that man should be ashamed because he produces over a billion tons of waste per year. This is probably true, but it is not the ultimate reason man stands ashamed before God. The real reason is that we, like Adam and Eve, have disobeyed God (cf. Gen. 3:1-7).

—David A. Hamburg

Golden Text Illuminated

"The Lord God said, It is not good that the man should be alone; I will make him an help meet for him" (Genesis 2:18).

The golden text is a beautiful declaration from God of man's need for woman. It is amazing to consider that even after all He had made already—the sun, the stars, fish, birds, and plants, as well as Adam—God still was not finished.

Some key things can be learned when we examine the details of this verse. First, God said that it was not good for man to be alone. Adam could not live life as God intended if he was by himself. God's desire was for man to "be fruitful, and multiply, and replenish the earth, and subdue it" (Gen. 1:28). Adam could not fulfill this task without someone who could bear children—namely, a woman.

Second, Adam was given a desire for relationship. The Triune God has existed in relationship from eternity. And He said, "Let us make man in our image, after our likeness" (vs. 26). Agur, the human author of Proverbs 30, wondered in awe at this natural desire for relationship and intimacy built into the fabric of a man's soul (vss. 18-19).

Third, this is the first time in the Genesis account of Creation that God declared something to be "not good." The previous five days of Creation ended with the label "good." Yet even after God miraculously created the first man from the dust of the earth, He could not consider this part completely good yet. The creation of woman would fulfill what was missing.

Fourth, Eve was a helper "meet" for Adam. She would help Adam with the task of subduing the earth and taking care of God's creation. She was created with just the right mixture of physical, emotional, and mental qualities to assist her husband in the profound task to which he had been divinely assigned.

The truths from the golden text present some very important applications for Christians of the twenty-first century. One such application is found in the humanity of the woman. Eve was created as a helper, but she was created just as human as Adam. Indeed, God created both male and female as equal in humanity, although different in roles.

Moreover, both Adam and Eve were created as special beings. They were more than the animals in standing and importance. Such a distinction is vital to understanding the identity of humanity. Many popular scientists, teachers, professors, and textbook writers maintain that men and women are merely animals. They say that people are no better in quality and purpose than an ostrich or an orangutan. This line of reasoning traces the origin of man to biological randomness and happenstance.

This kind of unbiblical thinking is especially dangerous because it ignores God's love for life. God is the Author of Life, as evidenced in the personhood of Adam and Eve at Creation, and He commands His people to honor Him for that special gift. Scripture says that God "giveth to all life, and breath, and all things" (Acts 17:25). Psalm 150:6 reads, "Let every thing that hath breath praise the Lord."

Such is the responsibility of the born-again Christian. One of the best ways to honor God is to live out the gift of life He has given us in honor of Christ. Such a dedication will both honor God and serve as a light to those whose minds are darkened by faulty thinking.

—J. A. Littler

Heart of the Lesson

"There are two human views to the creation of man and woman. One is the man's view; the other is the woman's view. Are you ready? The woman's view of creation is this: God made the man and looked at him and said, 'I can do better than that,' and He made the woman. Now the man's view is: God made the beasts and man and then He rested. And then He created woman and neither beast nor man nor God has rested since" (Swindoll, *Ultimate Book of Illustrations and Quotes,* Thomas Nelson).

This bit of humor hardly matches what the biblical text declares or what the heart of the lesson is. It serves, rather, as a contrast to what God truly intended for man and woman.

1. Adam's need for a helper to do what God gave him to do (Gen. 2:18). When studying Scripture, it is important to pay attention to a verse's context. In this case, Adam had been told what he could and could not eat in the garden and what would result if he did eat of the forbidden fruit. It is unclear if Eve was present when God first gave this command, but she had certainly heard it by the time she conversed with the serpent in chapter 3.

Our first parents had many privileges in the Garden of Eden. There was just one prohibition. The question was whether they would obey or disobey. Adam needed a helper, and God gave one to him. One of the purposes of that helper was to obey God's commandment alongside Adam.

Although we now live in a fallen world, we should still recognize that one of the purposes of marriage is the mutual sanctification and spiritual edification of husband and wife in the service of God.

2. God's creation of beasts and birds (Gen. 2:19-20). God created our world and our first parents and all the beasts of the earth and all the birds of the sky. That is a key element in this week's lesson, and there can be no doubt about it for all who believe the Bible is God's Word.

God gave Eve to Adam as his helper. He also gave Adam the wonderful privilege and solemn responsibility of naming the beasts of the earth and the birds of the air. Whatever Adam named them pleased God.

3. God's creation of Eve from Adam's side (Gen. 2:21-25). Before creating Eve, God first put Adam to sleep. This means, of course, that Adam contributed nothing to the creation of Eve except one rib. In reality, he did not even give that. God took one of his ribs and created Eve from it!

One implication of this marvelous work of God is that God was in charge of Adam and Adam was totally dependent upon God for all his needs. The truth is that we too are in need of acknowledging God's many provisions and blessings toward us.

When God had finished fashioning Eve, He brought her to Adam. Think about that for a minute. Adam was given the first woman on earth. And she was entirely God's work of creation. There they both stood, staring at each other in total amazement. They were literally "made for each other."

Then Adam acknowledged to Eve their unique relationship to each other (Gen. 2:23). God had created them both, and they now had become one flesh and were to cleave to each other. At that time they were both naked and unashamed.

—Robert P. Lightner

World Missions

When God created man, His job was not quite finished. He knew that it was not good for man to be alone. To solve this dilemma, God made woman to be mutually joined to man (Gen. 2:24). They were to love one another, have children, and exercise dominion over the earth (1:28; 2:22-24).

Dominion over the earth included far more than just a physical dominion over all the creatures made by God. Man was to exercise spiritual dominion in this world. The world, the flesh, and the devil all compete for dominion over mankind (cf. I John 2:16). However, through Christ, we can have dominion over all three (3:8). Both within marriage and within the church, man and woman are intended to join forces to minister effectively to a hurting world.

Aquila and Priscilla are a New Testament example of a husband and wife who labored together to reach others for Jesus Christ. They also traveled in evangelistic and missionary endeavors, assisting the apostle Paul.

Paul first met this couple in Corinth after Claudius commanded all Jews to leave Rome (Acts 18:1-3). Their occupation as tentmakers enabled them to meet their financial needs as they sought to tell others about Christ. When Paul left for Ephesus, they followed him and remained there to build the church (vss. 18-19). It was there they met Apollos, a man "mighty in the scriptures" who knew only the "baptism of John" (vss. 24-25). They were able to help him when they "expounded unto him the way of God more perfectly" (vs. 26). This illustrates that great things can be accomplished by yielded lives.

In the modern missionary movement (beginning in the late eighteenth century), remarkable missionary couples emerged who have made a lasting impact on the work of world missions. These have inspired others to give their lives for the cause of Christ.

Charles and Lettie Cowman were faithful missionaries whose whole desire was to reach the people of Japan for Jesus Christ. Before their salvation, Charles was a successful manager of a telegraph office in Chicago. Lettie was a fashionable wife caught up in the ways of the world. All that changed when Jesus Christ became their Lord (Cowman, *Missionary Warrior,* Oriental Missionary Society).

Beginning with their conversion, they threw themselves into Christian work. Charles led seventy-five of his coworkers to Christ in about six months. He preached in churches and missions around the city. Lettie was also faithful in Christian service.

When the call of God came to give themselves to the work of foreign missions, they plunged in wholeheartedly. They arrived in Japan in 1901. Thousands were soon converted, and Bible training schools were opened. Charles organized a massive village campaign to give out gospel portions to all 10,300,000 homes in the country. This was completed with a host of gospel workers in 1918. This plan of evangelism soon expanded to Korea, and another work opened in China in 1925.

Meanwhile, Lettie served in the areas of evangelism, music, correspondence, and writing. She outlived Charles and served as the president of the Oriental Missionary Society from 1928 to 1949.

When God created male and female, He knew that it was not good for man to be alone. He made them for one another to do His work and to lead others to salvation.

—*James O. Baker*

The Jewish Aspect

According to Jewish belief, the statement of the Lord in Genesis 2:18 is the last of the "ten divine utterances by which the world was created" (Nulman, *The Encyclopedia of Jewish Prayer*, Jason Aronson). The other nine are contained in 1:3-29.

With this passage, as with the rest of the Hebrew Bible, rabbis of the Jewish Talmud added to the story and built speculation upon speculation. They believed in an oral Torah, or oral law, that they claim was given to Moses at Sinai besides the written five books contained in the Bible. They purport to be bringing this oral tradition to light in their fanciful interpretations and mythical elaborations—hanging a mountain on a thread, as they say.

In the case of Eve being created from Adam's rib, they say that "the first human being was a hermaphrodite, male and female together. God separated them and turned them 'face to face' so that procreation could occur" (Sherwin and Cohen, *How to Be a Jew*, Jason Aronson). Thus, in Jewish theology, each subsequent human being is half a person who becomes complete through marriage.

The Jewish writers wax eloquent on the subject of sexual relations. The mystics go so far as to say that those who engage in the procreative act are God's partners for all creative acts, drawing down "the divine influx" and fulfilling not only a human need but a divine one as well (Sherwin and Cohen).

The Pharisees came to Jesus asking about marriage—or rather divorce. Keep in mind that the Pharisees likely held very similar beliefs to those of the rabbis mentioned above. Mark 10:3 records the Lord referring them to Moses. Then Jesus gave them a literal interpretation and application of the Creation account: "God made them male and female . . . they twain shall be one flesh" (vss. 6-8).

This guides us in our interaction with Jews today. The lesson is that we should stick to the Scripture itself—and a literal interpretation of it. When we go beyond what is written, we fall into error. The Pharisees fell into error on this issue and others by going beyond what was written, adding to it, and teaching their interpretations as equal to or better than the inspired text.

They still do that. The Jewish scholars refer to Talmudic rabbis and to other famous rabbis, giving one quote after another. We have to avoid being drawn into this morass of conflicting interpretations. We do well to draw their attention back to the Bible passages themselves, without any adulteration. We can give them Bibles and encourage them to read them. Many Jews are ignorant of their Holy Book, typically using the Hebrew scroll only as a talisman and an object of reverence.

They leave the study and liturgy to the rabbis. If we can point out the truth of the Word and get them to look into it—maybe even reading it to them—they will find Christ in it and perhaps will be saved by hearing the Word (cf. Rom. 10:17).

The Holy Spirit can guide us to have marriages that please Him and fulfill the pattern in the Scripture so that our Jewish friends will ask us how we do it. We accomplish what they seek through commandments. The answer is a living relationship with the Creator God.

—Philip J. Lesko

Guiding the Superintendent

"Charles Swindoll mentioned an ad in a Kansas newspaper. It read, 'I will listen to you talk for 30 minutes without comment for $5.00.' Swindoll said, 'Sounds like a hoax, doesn't it? But the person was serious. Did anybody call? You bet. It wasn't long before this individual was receiving 10 to 20 calls a day. The pain of loneliness was so sharp that some were willing to try anything for a half hour of companionship'" (www.sermonillustrations.com).

DEVOTIONAL OUTLINE

1. Unsuitable companionship (Gen. 2:18-20). God Himself revealed that loneliness is not a good state for a person to be in. God desires His people to exist and thrive in relationship. God determined to solve Adam's problem of being alone.

God brought before Adam the smaller and larger land animals and the animals that inhabited the sky. He gave Adam the ability to exercise his dominion and authority over these creatures by giving them names. When Adam finished his assignment, it was determined that no animal creature would be a helpful, appropriate companion for him.

2. Suitable companionship (Gen. 2:21-25). God continued to fulfill His will by providing Adam with a suitable companion. God used a portion of Adam himself to create his helpful partner. God caused Adam to experience a trancelike "deep sleep." God opened up Adam's body, took out one of his ribs, and healed his flesh.

Using Adam's rib, God sovereignly created a unique human being who would be a suitable companion for Adam. God brought the human being to Adam, and he called the person "woman," indicating that she was of the same flesh as man and therefore an appropriate companion.

God's creative activity would have an impact on the most intimate of human relationships—marriage. It would be characterized by a oneness that, in God's eyes, would never experience dissolution. In a context of perfect harmony and innocence, Adam and his wife lived in an unclothed state that did not produce even the slightest measure of shame.

AGE-GROUP EMPHASES

Children: Children should be taught not only that God created them to be unique boys and girls but also that they should experience joy in being in one another's presence. Children need not only times of Bible teaching but also play-oriented times of supervised social interaction.

Youths: Young people are feeling the pressure of growing up in a gender-neutral culture that blurs the God-created uniqueness of being male or female. Young people are confused about how to enjoy and celebrate what it means to be a man or a woman. They often experience abnormal fear and shame when relating to the opposite sex.

Sunday school should provide a biblical forum for learning and discussion that upholds the joy and holiness of male and female relationships and the sanctity of the relationship of marriage.

Adults: In the confused world that adults now live in, they need encouragement to be biblical role models of godly maleness or femaleness and to show how those God-ordained personalities should exist in holy relationship—especially the marriage relationship. Encourage your adults to be salt and light by celebrating their uniqueness either as godly singles or as committed husbands and wives.

—*Thomas R. Chmura*

SCRIPTURE LESSON TEXT

JUDG. 4:4 And Deborah, a prophetess, the wife of Lapidoth, she judged Israel at that time.

5 And she dwelt under the palm tree of Deborah between Ramah and Beth-el in mount Ephraim: and the children of Israel came up to her for judgment.

6 And she sent and called Barak the son of Abinoam out of Kedesh-naphtali, and said unto him, Hath not the LORD God of Israel commanded, *saying,* Go and draw toward mount Tabor, and take with thee ten thousand men of the children of Naphtali and of the children of Zebulun?

7 And I will draw unto thee to the river Kishon Sisera, the captain of Jabin's army, with his chariots and his multitude; and I will deliver him into thine hand.

8 And Barak said unto her, If thou wilt go with me, then I will go: but if thou wilt not go with me, *then* I will not go.

9 And she said, I will surely go with thee: notwithstanding the journey that thou takest shall not be for thine honour; for the LORD shall sell Sisera into the hand of a woman. And Deborah arose, and went with Barak to Kedesh.

10 And Barak called Zebulun and Naphtali to Kedesh; and he went up with ten thousand men at his feet: and Deborah went up with him.

12 And they shewed Sisera that Barak the son of Abinoam was gone up to mount Tabor.

13 And Sisera gathered together all his chariots, *even* nine hundred chariots of iron, and all the people that *were* with him, from Harosheth of the Gentiles unto the river of Kishon.

14 And Deborah said unto Barak, Up; for this *is* the day in which the LORD hath delivered Sisera into thine hand: is not the LORD gone out before thee? So Barak went down from mount Tabor, and ten thousand men after him.

15 And the LORD discomfited Sisera, and all *his* chariots, and all *his* host, with the edge of the sword before Barak; so that Sisera lighted down off *his* chariot, and fled away on his feet.

16 But Barak pursued after the chariots, and after the host, unto Harosheth of the Gentiles: and all the host of Sisera fell upon the edge of the sword; *and* there was not a man left.

NOTES

Deborah Encourages Barak

Lesson Text: Judges 4:4-10, 12-16

Related Scriptures: Judges 4:17-24; II Kings 22:14-20;
Exodus 14:23-28; 15:18-21

TIME: 1237 B.C.　　　　　PLACES: Ephraim; Mount Tabor; Megiddo valley

---

GOLDEN TEXT—"And Deborah said unto Barak, Up; for this is the day in which the Lord hath delivered Sisera into thine hand: is not the Lord gone out before thee?" (Judges 4:14).

Introduction

Joshua had fought with King Jabin of Hazor and defeated him (Josh. 11:1-10). In the time of the judges, another regional despot from Hazor with the same dynastic name oppressed Israel for twenty years. Jabin's rule was enforced by his chieftain Sisera of Harosheth.

Deborah is the only woman among the judges raised up by God to deliver Israel. She was already a prophetess serving in the hill country of Ephraim when she challenged Barak to revolt against the Canaanites. She herself joined Barak in the assault against Sisera's army and joined with him in celebrating the victory.

Deborah was already held in high esteem for her work as a settler of civil disputes. Perhaps that is why fearful Barak insisted that Deborah go with him to battle.

Another woman involved in the drama of that day was Jael, wife of Heber the Kenite. Inviting the fleeing Sisera into her tent, she hid him under a blanket while he rested from exhaustion. Then she dispatched him with a hammer and a long nail while he slept.

LESSON OUTLINE

I. PROPHETESS—Judg. 4:4-5

II. PROCRASTINATOR—Judg. 4:6-10

III. PROPHECY—Judg. 4:12-16

Exposition: Verse by Verse

PROPHETESS

JUDG. 4:4 And Deborah, a prophetess, the wife of Lapidoth, she judged Israel at that time.

5 And she dwelt under the palm tree of Deborah between Ramah and Beth-el in mount Ephraim: and the children of Israel came up to her for judgment.

Judging (Judg. 4:4). Deborah was the wife of Lapidoth, a Hebrew name meaning "torches" or "lightning flashes." Her name means "bee," although there is little in the text that indicates any relevance in the name.

{Deborah is depicted as serving God as a prophet and as a judge.}^Q1 We are not told whether there was a direct connection between her role as a prophetess and her role as a judge in Israel. Prophet and judge are connected in that Deborah was a leader. More relevant is that "judge" is used here in settling disputes rather than delivering the oppressed.

Journeying (Judg. 4:5). Lapidoth and Deborah lived on the border between the territories of the tribe of Benjamin and the tribe of Ephraim. She apparently held court under a palm tree named after her at a location between Ramah and Bethel in Mount Ephraim. She was strategically positioned on a popular road north of Jerusalem. This location made easy for Israelites to easily access one of God's appointed judges when it was necessary to consult one.

The text notes that Israelites brought disputes to her, implying that she was wise and just. {Because she was centrally located in Israel, people journeyed to her where she ministered under "the palm tree of Deborah" (vs. 5).}^Q2

PROCRASTINATOR

6 And she sent and called Barak the son of Abinoam out of Kedesh-naphtali, and said unto him, Hath not the Lord God of Israel commanded, saying, Go and draw toward mount Tabor, and take with thee ten thousand men of the children of Naphtali and of the children of Zebulun?

7 And I will draw unto thee to the river Kishon Sisera, the captain of Jabin's army, with his chariots and his multitude; and I will deliver him into thine hand.

8 And Barak said unto her, If thou wilt go with me, then I will go: but if thou wilt not go with me, then I will not go.

9 And she said, I will surely go with thee: notwithstanding the journey that thou takest shall not be for thine honour; for the Lord shall sell Sisera into the hand of a woman. And Deborah arose, and went with Barak to Kedesh.

10 And Barak called Zebulun and Naphtali to Kedesh; and he went up with ten thousand men at his feet: and Deborah went up with him.

Challenge (Judg. 4:6-7). Deborah takes the initiative and delivers the divine command to Barak to take ten thousand men from the tribes of Naphtali and Zebulun and go to Mount Tabor. The command is emphatic: "Hath not the Lord God of Israel commanded" (vs. 6).

Barak, whose Hebrew name means "lightning," was the son of Abinoam of Kedesh-naphtali. Barak's home was located about eighteen miles north of the Sea of Galilee. After Joshua conquered Kedesh-naphtali (Josh. 12:7, 22), the community was designated a city of refuge where individuals accused of criminal activity could shelter safely while awaiting trial (Josh. 20:1-7; 21:32).

{Deborah summoned Barak and emphatically declared that God had called him to take a force of ten thousand men to assault Sisera and his army at Mount Tabor (Judg. 4:6-7).}^Q3 Mount Tabor was where the tribal borders of Issachar, Zebulun, and Naphtali converged, southwest of the Sea of Galilee.

God had said that He would draw Sisera and his nine hundred iron chariots and infantry to the river

Kishon. This stream flowed out of Mount Tabor and Mount Gilboa westward through the Plain of Esdraelon, or Valley of Jezreel, to the Great Sea (Mediterranean) at the Bay of Acre north of Mount Carmel.

Sisera's large army and powerful chariots no doubt struck terror into the hearts of opponents (vss. 3, 7, 13). It is no wonder that Barak was apprehensive about going up against them with only ten thousand infantrymen and no mention of chariots to counterbalance those belonging to Sisera.

Compromise (Judg. 4:8-9). {Barak sent a reply back to Deborah that must have startled her—"If thou wilt go with me, then I will go: but if thou wilt not go with me, then I will not go."}[Q4] Men traditionally led military campaigns. Why, then, would Barak insist that Deborah go with him before he agreed to go? More important, why did Barak refuse to obey God's command if Deborah would not join him?

Surely Barak considered himself more suited to feats of strength, hardship, and military combat than any woman. The notion of a woman leading his army must have been quite humiliating for him. Why would he make the request? Knowing that Deborah was a prophetess endorsed by God, perhaps Barak sought her presence to assure victory against the superior forces of Sisera.

We can well imagine that perhaps Deborah did some serious thinking about Barak's proposal and that she prayed about it to determine the will of God in this matter. It would mean leaving her regular ministry and involving herself in something for which she had no previous experience. She might even have considered Barak a coward and wondered whether he would cut and run if the coming battle went badly for Israel.

Deborah replied to Barak that she would surely go with him. However, this military journey would not produce honor for Barak himself. {Deborah said that the Lord would give Sisera into the hand of a woman.}[Q5] She did not say she was referring to herself. In fact, the woman would be Jael, wife of Heber the Kenite. More will be said about her later in this lesson.

Deborah left Mount Ephraim and traveled up to Kedesh in order to join Barak. It would appear that this was a compromise. She needed to get him to go, and he would not go without her; so they agreed to go together.

The story is similar to Moses' pleas after the golden calf incident when Moses insisted that God not send Israel forward without the divine presence (Ex. 33:12-17). In this case, Deborah, as the prophet of God, represented God's empowering presence.

It appears in this account that Barak is a mere shadow in the presence of the great show of faith that Deborah displays. However, the book of Hebrews lists Barak in the hall of faith (11:32). Despite his unwillingness to go to battle if Deborah will not go with him, his valiant attack against the better equipped army led by Sisera shows us that he indeed has faith in the Lord—certainly drawing from Deborah's example.

Call (Judg. 4:10). From Kedesh Barak sent out calls to the tribes of Zebulun and Naphtali to come to him. In the absence of a standing army, Barak and Deborah had to depend on citizen-soldiers to engage the Canaanite forces. These volunteers would come in weakness, brining their own rudimentary weapons, bedding, and other meager provisions.

Since there was no training program these volunteers would be expected to know how to fight and obey orders. After the military campaign ended, they would be free to return to their homes.

When the volunteers arrived at Kedesh, they were met by Barak and Deborah. Ten thousand men followed at their heels as they moved toward Mount Tabor, as the Lord had directed (vs. 6). The men in the ranks must have wondered why a woman was going with them, but many probably knew Deborah by personal contact or by reputation because of her work as a judge in Ephraim. They may have felt confidence in knowing that God's representative was there with them.

PROPHECY

12 And they shewed Sisera that Barak the son of Abinoam was gone up to mount Tabor.

13 And Sisera gathered together all his chariots, even nine hundred chariots of iron, and all the people that were with him, from Harosheth of the Gentiles unto the river of Kishon.

14 And Deborah said unto Barak, Up; for this is the day in which the LORD hath delivered Sisera into thine hand: is not the LORD gone out before thee? So Barak went down from mount Tabor, and ten thousand men after him.

15 And the LORD discomfited Sisera, and all his chariots, and all his host, with the edge of the sword before Barak; so that Sisera lighted down off his chariot, and fled away on his feet.

16 But Barak pursued after the chariots, and after the host, unto Harosheth of the Gentiles: and all the host of Sisera fell upon the edge of the sword; and there was not a man left.

Chariots (Judg. 4:12-13). The report came to Sisera that Barak had come to Mount Tabor. {Sisera immediately gathered together all of his nine hun-dred iron chariots. According to verse 15, Sisera himself was a charioteer. These horse-drawn, metal, rolling vehicles must have been the ancient equivalent of tanks. Facing them on the move must have been a frightening experience.}[Q6]

The chariots, with supporting infantry, moved out from Harosheth of the Gentiles. This city was located in northern Israel near the Kishon River.

Confidence (Judg. 4:14). Barak's army probably arrived at Mount Tabor in time to set up camp for the night and get some rest from the long march. But they needed more than rest if they were to be ready for battle. In order to inspire confidence and courage for what was to come, Deborah told Barak that this was the day in which the Lord would deliver Sisera into his hand. {With great emphasis, she pronounced to Barak that it was the Lord who, in effect, had already broken camp and was leading the Israelites into battle, echoing the rally cry that the Lord goes before them (cf. Ex. 23:23; 32:34; Deut. 1:30; etc.).}[Q7]

{Barak mustered his forces into marching order and headed down from Mount Tabor.}[Q8] The tramp of ten thousand men could be heard. No one knew whether he would survive the battle and be able to go home again, but each was committed to the military objective. Deborah's presence must have been good for the men's morale. They were anxious to see what God would do for them that day.

Conquest (Judg. 4:15-16). Deborah's claim that God was going before the Israelites is followed by the notice that the Lord discomfited (that is, routed, confused, troubled) Sisera and his army by the edge of the sword. In fact, it was the Lord who was leading Barak and his army against the Canaanites (vss. 14-15). The Lord was not wielding a literal sword Himself, but He aided the soldiers of Israel, who wielded their swords, terrorizing the enemy soldiers. {The text in Judges 4 does not detail the Lord's assault, although Judges 5 poetically describes the rise of a storm and the sudden flooding of the Kishon River as sweeping the enemy away, similarly to the drowning of Pharaoh's army at the Red Sea (Ex. 14:23-28).}Q9

Sisera saw that things were going against him and his men. Consumed by cowardly self-interest, he jumped out of his chariot and fled on foot. Confident Sisera turns fearful when confronted by God.

Exhilarated by his victory on the battlefield, Barak might have stopped, celebrated with his troops, and headed home; instead, he pursued the charioteers and the foot soldiers all the way to Harosheth. He thoroughly dealt with the enemies of Israel by hunting down and killing every Canaanite. God had heard the cries for justice prayed by the oppressed Israelites and now was executing his just sentence.

There was one individual who managed to escape the carnage, and that was Sisera. For that information, read ahead to verses 17-21 and 5:24-27.

Heber the Kenite, previously mentioned in Judges 4:11, had a wife named Jael. She was at her tent when Sisera came running by, and she invited him to come in and not be afraid. She implied that she would protect him from the pursuing Israelites. Jael covered him with some sort of thick blanket. He asked her for water to drink, but she gave him milk before covering him again.

Sisera told Jael to stand at the door of the tent. If anyone were to ask if anyone was in the tent, she was to say no. {As exhausted Sisera slept, however, Jael sneaked in and used a hammer to drive a long spike into his temple, pinning his skull to the ground.

This fulfilled Deborah's words that the Lord would deliver Sisera into the hands of a woman (vs. 9).}Q10 Barak may have assumed that Deborah was referring to herself, but he was soon to learn that she was referring to Jael instead. As he chased after the fleeing Sisera, Barak was met by Jael and told to come into the tent to find the man he was pursuing. It was then that Barak saw what had happened to Sisera.

Most biblical exploits seem to be concerned with what men have done, but this episode in ancient Israel highlights the work accomplished by two women through God's help.

—Gordon Talbot

QUESTIONS

1. What were Deborah's two ministerial callings?

2. Why did people from all over Israel come to Deborah in the territory of Ephraim?

3. What message did Deborah convey to Barak in Kedesh-naphtali?

4. How did Barak react to Deborah's message?

5. How did Deborah respond to Barak's proposal?

6. Why did the Israelites have cause to fear Sisera's army?

7. What advantage did Deborah indicate that Israel had over Sisera?

8. Where did Barak's army engage the Canaanite forces under Sisera?

9. What did God use to help Israel defeat the Canaanites?

10. How did Jael fulfill the prophecy made in Judges 4:9?

—Gordon Talbot

Preparing to Teach the Lesson

This week's lesson opens a new dimension of thinking. God can use any person He wants to fulfill His plans and purposes in this world. Once He chose to use a woman who was a leader and a prophetess. There were thirteen judges in all who led Israel in times of crisis. Deborah was one of them, chosen by God for such a time as this.

TODAY'S AIM

Facts: to see how God chooses leaders when they are needed.

Principle: to emphasize willingness to be led by God.

Application: to prepare students to be servants willing to follow God's call.

INTRODUCING THE LESSON

The lesson opens with the Israelites under Canaanite oppression since they had turned to do what was "right in their own eyes" after their prior deliverance through Ehud. Israel had forgotten God and had strayed from Him. In their crisis, God intervened. This time He sent a woman handpicked for His purpose.

DEVELOPING THE LESSON

1. Deborah introduced (Judg. 4:4- 5). Prepare to meet Deborah. All we are told is that she was the wife of Lapidoth and that she was already recognized as a prophetess in the nation. As a judge, she was considered to be a wise woman, and people came to her to have their disputes settled. She did this under what came to be known as the Palm of Deborah between the cities of Ramah and Bethel in the hill country of Ephraim.

Even in the church today, we ought to recognize believers who have the wisdom of God. They can help resolve many of the conflicting issues in our churches in a manner that will please God.

In ancient Israelite culture, it was unusual for a woman to take up a leadership position of the kind Deborah held, let alone to go into battle with the men. It is obvious from the text that the Spirit of God in her had made her acceptable to the people in the land. They respected her for her godly wisdom.

2. A word from God (Judg. 4:6-7). Deborah received a special word from God for Barak. The name "Barak" means "lightning." We are only told that he was the son of Abinoam and lived in Kedesh in the land of Naphtali. Barak was instructed to go to battle against Sisera and his army and was assured of victory.

Here is a lesson for us. If we receive assurance from God as we make our choices in life, we will be blessed by Him. This tells us that we ought to consult God before we make our moves. Where God leads, He certainly will always bless.

3. Deborah with Barak (Judg. 4:8-10). Barak had a condition for his acceptance of the word from God. He said that he would go into battle only if Deborah would go with him. On the surface, this seems to be a simple request. After all, Deborah was a woman of God. On closer examination, however, we see that Barak did not take the word of God as it was in trust. He wanted the reassurance of Deborah to go with him into the battle. For that wrong choice, Barak got no honor for the victory. The battle would be won at the hands of a woman. Deborah marched with the armies of Barak.

The lesson for us is that when God gives us a word of assurance, we are to trust Him without qualification. What

He has promised, He will certainly fulfill. We can count on that. Discuss with the students the difficulties they have faced in recognizing the voice of God and how they have trusted for the outcome.

4. Sisera prepared for battle (Judg. 4:12-13). Jabin's army, under the leadership of Sisera, heard the news that Barak was coming after them. They prepared for battle. Sisera got his nine hundred chariots ready for action along with his mighty men and moved to the banks of the Kishon River. We can picture the world coming against the believer, prepared to fight any person who stays close to God. When God is on our side, though, nothing can defeat the child of God.

Deborah played a key role in the life of her people. Not only was she a prophetess, but she was also a judge. Now she prepared to go with the army as it fought God's enemies. From this we learn that God can use all kinds of people at any time. He is not limited to our little plans but is able to use unexpected people, by the world's standards, to bless His children—and at the time we need Him the most.

In everyday situations, believers would be wise to trust God's wisdom, and not their puny human strength and meager resources. While Barak trusted Deborah's words from God, he certainly failed in this particular area of relying on God fully. After all, he had already been assured of divine victory in the battle.

5. Deborah prepared Barak for victory (Judg. 4:14-16). This historical narrative closes with Deborah encouraging Barak to expect great things from God. After the battle, Sisera was defeated. He left his chariot and ran on foot and escaped with his life, but all his warriors were killed. We are assured of victory when we know that God is on our side.

ILLUSTRATING THE LESSON

God is not limited by our standards. He can work with all kinds of people, in any circumstances. His plans cannot be thwarted.

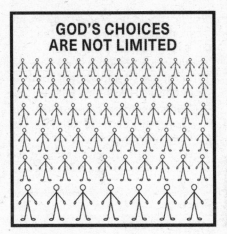

GOD'S CHOICES ARE NOT LIMITED

CONCLUDING THE LESSON

This week we have seen that God is not limited in His resources to deal with crisis situations in our land or in our personal lives. He can use anyone He wishes.

In a lesson like this, the question of women preaching, teaching, and pastoring is bound to arise. God is not against using great women of faith. History certainly proves this. The apostle Paul, however, commanded that the women in Ephesus are not to "usurp authority over the man" (I Tim. 2:12). This has always been a controversial issue in the church, but when we stick to God's principles, we will be safe. We are certainly called to fully acknowledge God's gifts and the way God works uniquely in each individual.

ANTICIPATING THE NEXT LESSON

In our next lesson, we will explore the faithfulness of Ruth to her mother-in-law and to God.

—*A. Koshy Muthalaly*

PRACTICAL POINTS

1. The obedience of a large number of people is often involved in God's will being accomplished (Judg. 4:4-7).
2. We should not unduly rely on human support if we know the Lord is with us (vss. 8-10).
3. When we act in obedience to the Lord, we should expect that the enemy will be alerted (vss. 10, 12).
4. God's enemies can put forth an impressive show of strength, but that is no real obstacle (vss. 13-14).
5. When the Lord gives victory, we must follow up on it diligently (vss. 15-16).

—*Kenneth A. Sponsler*

RESEARCH AND DISCUSSION

1. What qualified Deborah to be a judge and prophetess for God (Judg. 4:4; cf. Ex 4:15-16; 7:1-2)? What qualifies any of us to speak for God?
2. What kind of character was Barak, in your estimation? Would you have entrusted such an important mission to him? Why or why not?
3. Why did Barak's request to have Deborah accompany him cause him to forfeit the honor of the victory (Judg. 4:8-9)? What motive was behind the request?
4. What is significant about the mention of the nine hundred chariots possessed by the enemy (vs. 13)?
5. What did Deborah see in the circumstances before them that perhaps Barak and others did not (vs. 14)? How is she an example for us?

—*Kenneth A. Sponsler*

ILLUSTRATED HIGH POINTS

Is not the Lord gone out before thee? (Judg. 4:14)

A U.S. military chaplain worked with a fellow chaplain who could not hold himself together in the sometimes gruesome environment of service in Iraq. Although the two men discussed his fears and prayed together, he sank into such a state of apprehension that he struggled just to perform his duties.

Ultimately, the man received a challenge from his fellow chaplain, who told him that if he was scared, he had to recognize that God has everything under control. The formerly timid chaplain was able to fulfill his responsibilities with confidence, because the Lord's strength is made perfect in weakness.

There was not a man left (vs. 16)

He had superior military training. He had the might of the U.S. Cavalry that could come to his aid. He had distinguished himself as a very courageous fighter in battle. These things did not matter, however, when George Custer led his men into battle against an encampment of Cheyenne and Sioux Indians on June 25, 1876.

Custer's group was soon surrounded on a barren hillock while Indian warriors poured in a devastating hail of arrows and bullets. The fighting there probably did not last more than an hour. When it was over, not one of Custer's detachment of 210 men was alive.

Americans of that time were stunned to think that such a famous and fearless military hero could be annihilated so quickly by supposedly "uncivilized" Indians. The power of Sisera, with his nine hundred chariots, was also astonishing; so the fact that women played a large role in defeating him must have dumbfounded all who heard it.

—*Todd Williams*

Golden Text Illuminated

"And Deborah said unto Barak, Up; for this is the day in which the Lord hath delivered Sisera into thine hand: is not the Lord gone out before thee?" (Judges 4:14).

Once again Israel sinned against God and was oppressed by another nation. Jabin, the king of Canaan, and the general of his army, Sisera, cruelly oppressed God's people. But God did not forget His people. He sent Deborah with a message for their deliverance.

Deborah was a prophetess and a judge. Being a judge in Israel meant that she was respected and decided disagreements between people. As a prophetess, Deborah delivered messages from God to the people of Israel. In Deborah's interaction with Barak, we see an excellent example of how to disciple those who are weak in faith.

Deborah sent a message to Barak to come hear the message God had given her. God had chosen Barak to command an army to deliver Israel from Jabin and Sisera. Barak was to gather 10,000 men from the tribes of Israel and go to Mount Tabor. Once he was there, God would deliver Sisera and his army into Barak's hand.

The text doesn't mention that Barak had any special abilities or skills. Israel's victory would not come because of better leadership, better soldiers, or better weapons. In fact, Sisera's army was better equipped. They had 900 chariots. Israel had none. Sisera had a huge advantage from a human perspective.

Sisera's defeat would come because God would fight for His people. He would use an inferior army to defeat a powerful force.

Despite hearing Deborah's message from God, Barak did not have confidence to go into battle. He told Deborah that unless she was willing to go with him to Mount Tabor, he would not go, either.

It is never a good idea to disobey God. Certainly, Barak heard the stories about Moses defeating the powerful Egyptians, and of Joshua defeating the tribes that lived in the Promised Land. Even with a promise from God that he would be victorious, Barak was unable to look beyond the obstacles that kept his people from gaining freedom.

At this time of Barak's great weakness, Deborah provided the strength that he needed. She did not deride him for his weakness, nor belittle him before others. She supported his role as a leader according to God's intention that he should command the army of Israel.

She acquiesced to Barak's request that she accompany him to Mount Tabor. Deborah had the confidence that God would fulfill His promise of victory.

Nevertheless, Barak's weak faith did have a personal cost. He would not receive the glory for defeating Sisera. Instead, a woman would receive the glory.

Deborah provides an excellent example of Christian discipleship for those who are weak in faith. Deborah was by Barak's side to encourage him when he most needed the support. She directed him to trust God with his decisions. When it was time for battle, Deborah explained that the Lord was already leading. It was time for Barak to follow God to victory. May we have wisdom like Deborah did as we disciple others who are struggling in their faith.

—*Glenn Weaver*

Heart of the Lesson

God often works in ways that seem strange to us. He uses people who appear to be unlikely leaders for mighty works.

In the time of the judges, God told Israel there would be trouble because of their disobedience. This lesson explores a major example of God's mercy toward His people. Even though they had been unfaithful to Him, He had not forgotten them. He heard their cry for help against the Canaanites.

1. Deborah agrees to lead with Barak (Judg. 4:4-10).

God called Deborah as a judge and prophetess to lead His people. It must have been unusual for a woman to be a leader in that day. Deborah was well-respected, though, and regularly settled disputes that people brought to her.

The Canaanites had been oppressing Israel for twenty years. The people finally cried out to the Lord. In His loving-kindness, God heard and answered their cries. He instructed Deborah to send for Barak and command him to lead the ten thousand soldiers into battle.

Deborah obeyed God. She told Barak of God's plan. God had even promised victory in battle. What more could a leader want?

Barak wanted Deborah to go with him. We do not know whether Barak wanted her there as an assurance of God's presence in the battle or whether he was afraid. He showed a lack of trust in God, though.

Deborah knew God would be displeased, as was she. She agreed to go into battle with Barak, but she also prophesied that he would not get the honor for winning this battle. Instead, honor would go to a woman.

2. God wins the battle (Judg. 4:12-16).

Deborah told Barak that God would lead Israel into battle. Sisera gathered together his nine hundred chariots and all his soldiers for a massive battle. He was ready to wipe out Israel.

By all rights, humanly speaking, Sisera should have won this battle. Israel, with no chariots, was hopelessly outmatched.

Deborah ordered the army to go, though, and Barak led them into battle. Suddenly, God sent a big storm, which caused flooding on the battleground. Mud bogged down the chariot wheels. Soldiers fled on foot. Now, with things more even, Israel routed their enemy, killing every single soldier.

Sisera, who commanded the Canaanites, managed to escape on foot. He thought he would be safe hiding in a nearby tent, but God had prepared the heart of Jael, a woman, to deceive the exhausted leader and kill him.

This battle was a major victory for Israel. God had once again come through for them, for He is faithful. God used an unlikely leader—a woman—at a time when women were not turned to for leadership. Were there no men who had a heart for God at that time?

For whatever reason, God chose Deborah. He knew she had faith in Him. She willingly agreed to do what He told her to do.

How strong is your faith? Do you believe God and follow what He tells you to do? Do you trust Him to come through, even when the situation seems impossible?

God loves to do seemingly impossible deeds. He glories in showing His power so that we, in turn, can give Him glory for all He does in our lives.

—Judy Carlsen

World Missions

God gave a ruthless enemy "into the hand of a woman" (Judg. 4:9). In more recent times the Lord has given whole peoples into the hands of godly women missionaries.

Today, South Korea has more Christians per capita than almost any other nation in Asia. In 1884, however, Korea was a dark, dangerous land. Horace Underwood and his wife, Lillias, went to Korea as pioneer missionaries. They spent their honeymoon penetrating the Korean countryside, where no foreigner, certainly no woman missionary, had ever gone before.

Lillias used her medical and nursing training to gain a foothold for the gospel. The couple dispensed medicine and the good news all the way to the Manchurian border. They found that the ancient gods no longer appealed to the Koreans. A religion based on veneration for ancestors, it had few dedicated followers.

In peril from bandits, rampant diseases, inadequate provisions, and harsh weather, the Underwoods treated seven hundred people and won thirty-three people to Christ.

One of the most satisfying encounters Lillias Underwood had in Korea was with the queen. The queen had a full retinue of male doctors, but because of Korean etiquette, they could not see or touch her. To take her pulse, a line was attached to her wrist. It ran out into an adjacent room. To have her tongue examined, she had to stick it through a hole in a partition. Lillias gave her special care, along with the message of salvation. (Mathews, *Dauntless Women,* Friendship Press).

After long service, the Underwoods went home, sick and weak. Reverend Underwood died within a year. Lillias died soon after. But where Christ was once unknown, there are now successive generations of believers because of the Underwoods.

Other women such as Amy Carmichael and Ida Scudder have played an important role in the evangelization of south India. A mission hospital opened in the important city of Bangalore in 1974. There were few patients then, but now the hospital has sixty beds, serving the 52 million people spread over 33,000 villages where three hundred different languages are spoken. In thirty years, some 700,000 have been treated.

The real measure of the worth of the hospital is seen in the effects of the gospel that is dispensed with the medications. There are eighty churches in Bangalore alone.

Losing a patient is never easy. The hospital recently learned of a family that had lost a father years before. The staff gave the wife a Bible. She returned home and read it to her family. All came to faith in Christ (*Commission Magazine,* International Mission Board, 2004).

Women also have had a big role to play in the rain forest on the Venezuelan border. This is difficult country, but the people must be reached. The government has a policy of restricting evangelization of indigenous people by foreigners. In 2005, the president ordered the expulsion of a large number of missionaries. The burden for the lost is somewhat hampered by regulations that require special permits. We should pray for the evangelistic efforts of native Venezuelan Christians, who can freely do more than foreign missionaries.

—*Lyle P. Murphy*

The Jewish Aspect

On the afternoon of November 29, 1947, the United Nations voted to partition Palestine into two states: Israel, the Jewish state, and Palestine, the Arab state. The Arabs of Palestine and other Arab countries declared they would not abide by this decision. They wanted Palestine to be an Arab nation where Jews could live as a protected minority. After living two thousand years as a persecuted minority in Gentile nations, the Jews said no thank you to this idea. World leaders at that time agreed with the Jews.

In the winter of 1948, Israeli leadership met in Tel Aviv. Eliezer Kaplan, the finance minister, had just returned from the United States. He told Israel's governing council that they could count on five to ten million dollars of support from the Jewish community of America. The five to ten million dollar figure struck the Israelis like a bolt of lightning. They were about to fight a life and death struggle. They were confident they could beat the Palestinians, but they doubted they could defeat the armies of Syria, Lebanon, Iraq, Jordan, and Egypt—all backed by the tremendous growth of Saudi oil revenues.

Israel needed twenty to forty million dollars to buy bombers, fighters, tanks, artillery, machine guns, and all the other equipment needed to build a modern army. After World War II, these weapons were readily available on European arms markets. Israel had already sent agents to Paris and Prague to shop for these weapons. They just did not have the money to buy them.

David Ben-Gurion, the leader of Israel, exclaimed that he needed to go to the United States at once and explain to the American Jewish community how desperate Israel's situation was. At this point a woman's voice was heard. Golda Meir calmly pointed out to Ben-Gurion, "What you are doing here I cannot do; however, what you propose to do in the United States I can do" (Collins and Lapierre, *O Jerusalem!* Simon & Schuster). Ben-Gurion was hesitant, but the other leaders of the Jewish Agency voted to send Golda.

Golda arrived in America at just the right time, for many of the leaders of American Jewry were meeting in Chicago. The very men and women with whom she needed to talk would be gathered in one place, but could she convince them to help?

When it was her time to address the convention, Golda said with the courage of Deborah, "A Jewish state will exist in Palestine. We shall fight for its birth. . . . We shall pay with our blood. . . . But what is equally certain is that our morale will not waver no matter how numerous our invaders may be."

She reminded her audience that the invaders were coming to destroy Israel with an arsenal of modern weapons. To stop them Israel needed modern firepower, and she needed it immediately. "My friends," Golda said, "we live in a very brief present. When I tell you we need this money immediately, it does not mean next month, or in two months. It means now."

Golda Meir got it "now." The American Jewish Community donated fifty million dollars to the Israeli defense fund. When she arrived back in Tel Aviv, Ben-Gurion told her, "It will be recorded that it was thanks to a Jewish woman that the Jewish state was born" (Collins and Lapierre).

—*James Coffey*

Guiding the Superintendent

When one considers the role of an Old Testament judge as being a warrior-leader, one most likely thinks of a male individual to fill that role. In fact, all the other judges recorded in Israel's history were men. When it comes to providing leadership for His nation, however, God does as He sees fit.

In this week's lesson text, the Bible describes a unique time in Israel's history. When the Israelites were in bondage to the idolatrous Canaanites who were led by King Jabin, they cried to the Lord for deliverance. God heard their cry and used a female judge, Deborah, to guide them toward freedom.

DEVOTIONAL OUTLINE

1. The consent to accompany Barak into battle (Judg. 4:4-10). When the Israelites were oppressed by the mighty Canaanites under the leadership of King Jabin, God sovereignly chose the Prophetess Deborah, wife of Lapidoth, as Israel's judge.

During her judgeship, Deborah called Barak to hear God's words. Deborah told Barak that God had chosen him to lead ten thousand men from the tribes of Naphtali and Zebulun into a guaranteed victorious battle against Sisera, the leader of King Jabin's army.

Barak told Deborah that he would obey God's revelation only if she would accompany him into battle. Deborah agreed to Barak's condition; however, she told him that his conditional obedience would not bring him honor.

2. The great victory over Sisera and his army (Judg. 4:12-16). Sisera learned that Barak and his warriors had moved into fighting position; so he responded by gathering together his fighting men, along with nine hundred chariots.

Before the battle had begun, Deborah reassured Barak that he would be victorious. During the battle, God thoroughly defeated Sisera's army. As a result, Sisera fled the battlefield, while Barak pursued the leaderless Canaanite soldiers to the city of Harosheth. By the end of the battle, the only surviving Canaanite soldier was the fleeing Sisera.

AGE-GROUP EMPHASES

Children: One children's song from the 1800's contains these words: "Jesus loves the little children, / All the children of the world. / Red and yellow, black and white, / They are precious in His sight. / Jesus loves the little children of the world" (Woolston).

We definitely wouldn't call anyone red or yellow anymore. However, it is important to teach children about God's love for all people (perhaps using a different song.) God loves His people so much that He will use anyone with an obedient heart to do His will.

Youths: Use this week's lesson text to teach the young people about God's awesome sovereignty. Even when an individual responds to the Lord with conditional obedience, God will configure events so that His plan will be accomplished.

Have your teachers encourage the young people to humbly submit to their sovereign God and embrace His will for their young lives.

Adults: In the twenty-first century, gender roles are not as defined as they used to be. This fact causes difficulties and must be handled with great care by the church.

Help the adult men celebrate God's sovereign acceptance of and use of godly women to accomplish His awesome will.

—*Thomas R. Chmura*

SCRIPTURE LESSON TEXT

RUTH 1:1 Now it came to pass in the days when the judges ruled, that there was a famine in the land. And a certain man of Beth-lehem-judah went to sojourn in the country of Moab, he, and his wife, and his two sons.

2 And the name of the man *was* Elimelech, and the name of his wife Naomi, and the name of his two sons Mahlon and Chilion, Ephrathites of Beth-lehem-judah. And they came into the country of Moab, and continued there.

3 And Elimelech Naomi's husband died; and she was left, and her two sons.

4 And they took them wives of the women of Moab; the name of the one *was* Orpah, and the name of the other Ruth: and they dwelled there about ten years.

5 And Mahlon and Chilion died also both of them; and the woman was left of her two sons and her husband.

6 Then she arose with her daughters in law, that she might return from the country of Moab: for she had heard in the country of Moab how that the LORD had visited his people in giving them bread.

7 Wherefore she went forth out of the place where she was, and her two daughters in law with her; and they went on the way to return unto the land of Judah.

8 And Naomi said unto her two daughters in law, Go, return each to her mother's house: the LORD deal kindly with you, as ye have dealt with the dead, and with me.

9 The LORD grant you that ye may find rest, each *of you* in the house of her husband. Then she kissed them; and they lifted up their voice, and wept.

14 And Orpah kissed her mother in law; but Ruth clave unto her.

16 And Ruth said, Intreat me not to leave thee, *or* to return from following after thee: for whither thou goest, I will go; and where thou lodgest, I will lodge: thy people *shall be* my people, and thy God my God.

NOTES

Ruth Follows Naomi

Lesson Text: Ruth 1:1-9, 14*b*, 16

Related Scriptures: Judges 2:11-19; Matthew 19:27-30

TIME: between 1130–1120 B.C.   PLACE: Moab

GOLDEN TEXT—"Ruth said, Intreat me not to leave thee, or to return from following after thee: for whither thou goest, I will go; and where thou lodgest, I will lodge: thy people shall be my people, and thy God my God" (Ruth 1:16).

Introduction

The family is the basic unit of a community. When family units suffer, the whole community suffers.

Heartbreaking stories of family tragedy permeate newspapers and newscasts today. We hear not only of house fires, traffic accidents, and neighborhood shootings that claim children's lives, but also of horrible dysfunctions within family units. Spouses divorce and fight for the children; former spouses kidnap children; disturbed parents beat, molest, or even kill unwanted or disabled children.

Ironically, out of such wretched conditions come some unlikely stories of success and love. God bestows grace so that the selfish, abusive, poor, handicapped, and abused can be transformed and may yet glorify Him and bless their communities with good deeds.

Such is the outcome of the biblical account of Naomi and Ruth. It begins as a family tragedy, but it ends in a way that brings blessing to Israel and all mankind. Our lesson unfolds the beginning of this remarkable account.

LESSON OUTLINE

I. A FAMILY MIGRATION—
   Ruth 1:1-2

II. A FAMILY TRAGEDY—
   Ruth 1:3-5

III. A FAMILY PARTING—
   Ruth 1:6-9

IV. A FAMILY LOYALTY—
   Ruth 1:14b, 16

Exposition: Verse by Verse

A FAMILY MIGRATION

RUTH 1:1 Now it came to pass in the days when the judges ruled, that there was a famine in the land. And a certain man of Beth-lehem-judah went to sojourn in the country of Moab, he, and his wife, and his two sons.

2 And the name of the man was Elimelech, and the name of his wife

Naomi, and the name of his two sons Mahlon and Chilion, Ephrathites of Beth-lehem-judah. And they came into the country of Moab, and continued there.

The famine in Judah (Ruth 1:1a). The events in the book of Ruth occurred "in the days when the judges ruled." Politically, these were chaotic days when Israel had no central government. Spiritually, there was frequent apostasy, and God chastised His people through foreign invasions.

{The book of Ruth, in contrast to Judges, portrays a local community of those times undisturbed by warfare. It reveals peaceful contacts between Israelites and their Moabite neighbors. And it shows that even in a time of apostasy, some still strongly trusted the Lord.}[Q1]

Conditions were not ideal, however, for the land was under a severe famine. We are not informed about its cause, though inadequate rainfall usually was to blame. We also do not know whether it was local or widespread throughout Israel. We are not explicitly told whether God brought about this famine as a punishment for sin or for some other reason. It is merely mentioned as the cause for a family's departure from the land.

The migration to Moab (Ruth 1:1b-2). The family at the center of this narrative lived in Bethlehem in the tribe of Judah. Ironically, Bethlehem means "house of bread," and its name reflected the bounty of the region. {But now even Bethlehem experienced scarcity. So the man and his family, identified in the next verse, left Israel for the land of Moab.}[Q2] He intended to "sojourn" there—that is, to stay temporarily until the famine ended.

{Moab was a country southeast of Israel on the opposite side of the Dead Sea. Its people were the descendants of Lot through his oldest daughter's incest with him (Gen. 19:37). During Israel's journey to Canaan, the king of Moab had resisted them by hiring Balaam to curse them (Num. 22:1-6).}[Q3] Because of this, Moabites were barred from participating in Israel's national life (Deut. 23:3-6). Nevertheless, some persons of these nations had friendly relations.

The persons in the migrating family are identified in Ruth 1:2. The head of the household was Elimelech, whose name means "my God is king." His wife was Naomi, whose name means "pleasant" or "delightful." The names of their two sons may hint at physical problems: Mahlon ("weak," "sickly") and Chilion ("wasting," "pining"). These people are called "Ephrathites." Ephrath was the original name for Bethlehem (cf. Gen. 35:19; Mic. 5:2). Thus, an Ephrathite was simply an inhabitant of Bethlehem, though this older designation may indicate that they were descendants of one of the older established families of the area.

To migrate, even temporarily, to a foreign land was a drastic measure, and Elimelech has been criticized for doing so. Why could he not trust God to supply his family's needs in Bethlehem? Others apparently stayed there and survived. Were not the hardships that followed this family evidence that they were out of God's will? Yet the text does not condemn or praise Elimelech, and we must take care not to reach hasty conclusions.

A FAMILY TRAGEDY

3 And Elimelech Naomi's husband died; and she was left, and her two sons.

4 And they took them wives of the women of Moab; the name of the one was Orpah, and the name of the other Ruth: and they dwelled there about ten years.

5 And Mahlon and Chilion died also both of them; and the woman was left of her two sons and her husband.

The death of Elimelech (Ruth 1:3). This family escaped the famine only to suffer more severely. First, Naomi's husband died. With only this bare statement, we do not know how long they had been in Moab when this occurred or what their economic condition was at the time. But we do know that the words "and she was left" carried serious implications. The death of a family head would have been a severe blow even in Bethlehem, for it would deprive her of all livelihood. How much worse when it happened in a foreign country!

Naomi was left with her two sons, which in her circumstances was more a blessing than a burden. They were probably young adults at this time and could work to support themselves and their mother. Naomi could also take comfort that despite their father's death, they could perpetuate the family name.

The marriages of the sons (Ruth 1:4). We might expect Naomi and her sons to return to Bethlehem after the death of Elimelech. There they would at least have the support of their community. Instead, they put down roots more firmly in Moab when the young men married Moabite women. The names of the two wives were Orpah and Ruth. This text does not tell us which wife married which man. We only learn in 4:10 that Ruth was married to Mahlon.

Although the Mosaic Law does not specifically forbid intermarriage with Moabites, it does strongly imply that it was ordinarily sinful (cf. Deut. 7:1-6; 23:3-6). Nehemiah confirmed this when he pronounced a curse on Israelites married to Moabites (Neh. 13:23-27). {Such intermarriage posed a spiritual danger since Moab worshipped a false god (Num. 21:29). In fact, it was Moabite women who seduced Israel to worship Baal-peor in the wilderness (25:1-3).}[Q4]

These marriages entailed perils that were best to avoid. Boaz's marriage to Ruth may be the only recorded lawful marriage to a Moabite in the Old Testament. (Israelites could marry converts.)

After this Naomi and her sons continued to live in Moab. "About ten years" (Ruth 1:4) could refer to either the time after they arrived or the time after the marriages. In either case, the intended land of "sojourn" had seemingly become a permanent residence.

The deaths of the sons (Ruth 1:5). {Now, without explanation, the deaths of the two sons are reported. This left Naomi in a most pitiable condition. The family had disintegrated; the only ones left were three widows, and the two young women could be of little help to Naomi.}[Q5]

She was deprived of all income and faced a future of poverty. {In that time, a woman without a man's support was destitute, for economic life centered around the family. Naomi also faced the end of the family name, for she was too old to bear more sons.}[Q6] With the utter hopelessness of her situation must have come questions: Was there any meaning in this? Why did God allow it to happen? Was she in any way responsible for all this?

A FAMILY PARTING

6 Then she arose with her daughters in law, that she might return from the country of Moab: for she had heard in the country of Moab how that the LORD had visited his people in giving them bread.

7 Wherefore she went forth out of the place where she was, and her two daughters in law with her; and they went on the way to return unto the land of Judah.

8 And Naomi said unto her two daughters in law, Go, return each to her mother's house: the LORD deal kindly with you, as ye have dealt with the dead, and with me.

9 The LORD grant you that ye may find rest, each of you in the house of her husband. **Then she kissed them; and they lifted up their voice, and wept.**

The decision of Naomi (Ruth 1:6-7). At least one piece of good news reached Naomi at this time: "the Lord had visited his people in giving them bread." In His sovereignty, He had ended the famine in Judah.

{Naomi therefore decided to return to Bethlehem. Moab had no further attraction for her, and she had reasons for wanting to escape its hold on her life and her memories. She would be better off among her relatives in Bethlehem.}^Q7

As she made her way homeward, her daughters-in-law accompanied her. They no doubt considered it their duty to do so. By marrying into an Israelite family, Orpah and Ruth had severed some ties with their own people. But now that their husbands had died, they were in an awkward situation. In a sense, they were women without a country, since their family ties on both sides had been dissolved. For the moment, Naomi was their only point of identification; so they went with her.

Their willingness to break ties with their homeland and to enter an alien culture also gives evidence of a close bond of loyalty. They apparently loved Naomi and refused to let her face the future alone. Their affection speaks well of their character. It also speaks well of Naomi, whose godly virtues had attracted such loyalty. Here, then, were three women united by a common grief and facing an uncertain future. But they determined to face it together.

The parting of the women (Ruth 1:8-9). Naomi recognized the difficulties Orpah and Ruth would face in Israel. They were young, with hopes of remarrying and rearing families. But their prospects of finding husbands in Bethlehem were slim because of cultural barriers. So she released them from any obligation to her. "Go, return each to her moth-er's house," she said. We might have expected her to say "father's house," but she was referring to the women's quarters of their homes. There their mothers could comfort them, and they could prepare for another marriage.

Naomi prayed that the Lord would deal kindly with the two women. It is noteworthy that she invoked the kindness of the Lord of Israel, not Chemosh, the false deity of Moab. Naomi had been away from her homeland for ten years, but she still held firmly to her faith in the Lord. Apparently she had also imparted an understanding of her faith to her daughters-in-law.

Furthermore, in using the expression "deal kindly," or "show kindness" (vs. 8), Naomi used the Hebrew word that refers to the loyal love established by a covenant. It is often used to describe God's covenant dealings with Israel, but here she prayed that He might extend this covenant love to foreigners as well. She had seen evidence of this same kindness in them, which they had displayed to their husbands and to her.

She then invoked the Lord's favor on these young women a second time: "The Lord grant you that ye may find rest, each of you in the house of her husband" (vs. 9). "Rest" here refers to the security a woman had through marriage. In their case it meant a release from the worries and troubles their widowhood would bring. It was unlikely that they could experience this in Bethlehem; their Moabite culture could provide greater opportunities for remarriage.

{Naomi kissed Orpah and Ruth as she anticipated a final parting, but this merely stirred their emotions. They broke out into loud weeping. As they wept, they protested that they would indeed stay with Naomi.}^Q8 But she discouraged them, arguing that she would have no more sons for them to marry. Why should they stay with someone whom God had forsaken?

A FAMILY LOYALTY

14 And Orpah kissed her mother in law; but Ruth clave unto her.

16 And Ruth said, Intreat me not to leave thee, or to return from following after thee: for whither thou goest, I will go; and where thou lodgest, I will lodge: thy people shall be my people, and thy God my God.

Ruth's decision (Ruth 1:14b). After more tears, Orpah made her decision. She kissed Naomi goodbye and turned back. Naomi's advice sounded sensible; if she ever wanted to remarry, this was apparently the way to achieve it. {Having been forced to examine her values, Orpah decided that becoming a wife again was more important than remaining a daughter-in-law to Naomi.}^Q9

Ruth, however, cleaved to her mother-in-law. She had counted the cost no less than Orpah and had reached the opposite conclusion. {Her life would henceforth be with Naomi, whatever the sacrifice. The Hebrew term for "cleave" indicates the closest possible loyalty and affection.}^Q10 It is the word used to describe the ideal relationship between husband and wife (Gen. 2:24). Ruth's identity would be tied to Naomi.

Ruth's dedication (Ruth 1:16). One last time Naomi tried to dissuade Ruth (vs. 15). She reminded her that Orpah had returned to her people and gods, and she urged Ruth to do likewise. This was bad spiritual advice, but Naomi was thinking only of the earthly happiness Ruth would gain.

Ruth was adamant, however. She begged Naomi to stop entreating her to return. She declared that she would go where Naomi went and lodge where she lodged. Both along the way and back in Judah, she would share the circumstances of Naomi's life.

But she went even further: "Thy people shall be my people." Ruth would cease being a Moabite and would identify with a new society with new customs and laws. This inevitably entailed a new spiritual identity—"and thy God my God." Ruth had seen a spiritual dimension in this Israelite family that she wanted for herself. She trusted the Lord and would worship Him.

Ruth declared that she would stay with Naomi until death separated them. And even then she would be buried at the same place. She concluded with a solemn oath to the God of Israel.

Ruth's example remains a challenge for every subsequent generation to imitate. She had seen in a family a miniature of the community of faith in Israel, and she desired to be part of it. So she made a choice and commitment that altered her life and Naomi's.

—*Robert E. Wenger*

QUESTIONS

1. How does the portrayal of life in Israel differ in the books of Judges and Ruth?

2. Where did Elimelech and his family live? Why did they go to Moab?

3. Who were the Moabites? How had they dealt with Israel?

4. What peril attended the marriage of Israelites to Moabites?

5. What tragedies befell this Israelite family in Moab?

6. What kind of future did Naomi face after her husband and sons died?

7. What factors led Naomi to decide to return to Bethlehem?

8. How did Naomi's daughters-in-law initially respond when she urged them to remain in Moab?

9. Why did Orpah return to her home?

10. What level of commitment is expressed in Ruth's "cleaving" to Naomi?

—*Robert E. Wenger*

Preparing to Teach the Lesson

Our lesson this week focuses on two women—Naomi and Ruth—and their loyal love for one another.

TODAY'S AIM

Facts: to show how one young woman from Moab found refuge in a family who knew the true God.

Principle: to affirm that our families can be places of refuge and safety if we follow God's order for them.

Application: to show how we can make our families places of community when we leave behind our old life and choose to follow Christ.

INTRODUCING THE LESSON

Have you ever been in a foreign country and felt all alone? You were far away from home and did not know the customs and traditions of the land. It would have been even worse if you did not know the language or how to communicate in strange surroundings. Sometimes even the symbols we are used to at home are very different from those used in the other land, which can be frustrating to a foreigner.

Then you come across a family that takes you under its wing and cares for you, and you feel safe. A sense of belonging and community emerges from this newfound relationship. Ruth was a young Moabite who had such an experience, and through it she found the God of Israel. Our lesson this week shows us how a family can be a shelter from the unfamiliar and can become home to the stranger.

DEVELOPING THE LESSON

1. Family disruption (Ruth 1:1-5). Natural disasters have a way of disrupting one's normal way of life. Hurricanes, for example, are notorious

for this. In biblical times, especially during the time of the events of the book of Ruth, it was famine that was a source of disruption. Famines are mentioned over and over again in the Bible. One cannot forget the great famine that lasted seven years during Joseph's time (Gen. 41:28-30).

It is interesting that in times of famine, food was often available in foreign lands and the people of God had to go there to get it. This would be a good time for the class to discuss whether famines are a judgment of God on His people in times of disobedience. Although we are not given any indication of that in the text about this particular famine, Deuteronomy 28 does indicate that famines in Israel were a curse for disobedience (vss. 15-22). And, of course, sin is the ultimate cause for all evil and suffering in the world. However, since the church today is not a national entity, we should not understand natural disasters as always a direct punishment for specific sins of the church or of a certain nation.

Here is another interesting fact. Elimelech's family came from Bethlehem. The name Bethlehem means "house of bread," and yet they were facing a shortage of bread. "Bread" is often used as a generic term for food.

We are told that over a period of ten years, Elimelech and the two sons, Mahlon and Chilion, died, leaving Naomi with her two daughters-in-law, Ruth and Orpah. It was a time of total disruption in the family, but Naomi knew the God of Israel, and she could rest assured that He would take care of her.

2. Return home (Ruth 1:6-9). Families disrupted by natural events (or any other disaster, for that matter) are hard to put back together. But we read that the Lord God had restored good harvests to Judah, the area from which Elimelech's family had come. Naomi and her daughters-in-law decided to go home.

Going home holds a joyful prospect for most people, but if you have experienced death and bereavement and do not even know what that return will be like, it can be painful. For Naomi, there had been many years of famine in Judah since she first left. Now all she had as family were two Moabite women. Going home was no longer what she thought it would be when she left. So much had happened.

Get the class to enter into this kind of experience in their own minds, and allow them to talk about what community would mean at such a time. Remind them that Naomi and Ruth discovered this together in the new family that God Himself had brought together. Note that Naomi tried to convince her two daughters-in-law to go back to their own homes because of the disruption the death of her husband and two sons had caused.

3. Newfound community (Ruth 1:14b, 16). The two daughters-in-law were given the choice to return to their own homes. Orpah returned to Moab while Ruth stayed with Naomi. Help the class wrestle with the decision that Ruth and Orpah had to make. Ask what they would have done and why. Why did Ruth value her family tie with Naomi so highly and Orpah did not? What can we learn from this to make our families places of wholeness? Were there other factors Ruth considered?

Here we see that Ruth had the opportunity to find community in her new family with Naomi. She embraced that opportunity with all her heart. What is amazing about this is that it was the first step that led to Ruth's inclusion in the messianic line from which Jesus was born. Here we see the extreme grace of God to one who did not belong to His people but who was given a place of honor in that society and would be remembered forever.

ILLUSTRATING THE LESSON

Ruth, a foreigner, chose to find a home with Naomi in Bethlehem. God invites all to accept a place in His own family.

CONCLUDING THE LESSON

There is a wonderful lesson for all of us here. We were once outside the realm of God's kingdom, but through His grace He has invited us back inside its borders where we are now part of His family. We did not deserve it, but God in His mercy forgave our sins in Christ and made us His very own.

Just as Ruth found a new family with her mother-in-law, Naomi, so we have found a new home in Jesus and what He did for us on the cross of Calvary. It is now our calling to help others find new community in the family of God. When God becomes our Heavenly Father, we are brought into a new relationship with all others who love Him. People in some other religions have no concept of the fatherhood of God, but it is vital for us as Christian believers.

ANTICIPATING THE NEXT LESSON

In our lesson next week, we will see a picture of Christ's redemption in God's provision for Ruth and Naomi.

—A. Koshy Muthalaly

PRACTICAL POINTS

1. God's people are not automatically exempt from the difficulties of life (Ruth 1:1-2).
2. Sometimes God chooses to allow circumstances that leave Him as our only hope (vss. 3-5).
3. The wise person recognizes that every good thing is from God (Ruth 1:6; cf. Matt. 5:45; Jas. 1:17).
4. No matter how difficult or how uncertain the outcome, take the next biblical step (Ruth 1:7).
5. Our own difficulties should never preclude our desire for God's blessing on others (vss. 8-9).
6. Following God involves sacrifice but also the hope of His sure provision (vss. 14, 16).

—Don Kakavecos

RESEARCH AND DISCUSSION

1. Some say that Naomi's family was wrong for going to Moab. Are there biblical grounds for thinking this? (On the one hand, see Genesis 26:1-3 and Deuteronomy 23:3, but on the other see Genesis 12:10 and 45:4-11.)
2. How does a believer's response to tragedies in his life indicate his views of good and evil and of the promises and character of God (cf. Ruth 1:3-5)? What must we remember about God at such times (cf. Num. 23:19)?
3. Why is it often difficult to seek the good of others when we ourselves are experiencing tragedy or grief?
4. What promises help us obey God in difficult times (cf. I Cor. 10:13; Phil. 4:13, 19; Heb. 13:5)?

—Don Kakavecos

ILLUSTRATED HIGH POINTS

Intreat me not to leave (Ruth 1:16)

One day a rabid wolf wandered into a native village in northern Canada. There were about 250 sled dogs in the village—more than a match for one sick wolf. Yet the intruder killed many dogs and injured others. How could this be?

In order to keep the dogs from fighting among themselves, the villagers had tied them to wooden stakes spaced far enough apart to prevent them from reaching each other. Because of this, the wolf walked freely among the dogs, killing and maiming many.

In isolation, the dogs were no match for the wolf. Christians need to unite against an even worse foe.

Ruth's entreaty of Naomi was born of a desperate need. She yearned for a real family. Ruth had come to know that Naomi represented life instead of spiritual death. She wanted to belong to a family like that.

Whither thou goest, I will go (vs. 16)

I hold services in several prisons each month. In one prison a woman was particularly responsive to the gospel message. One day after a service, she said, "I would like to go to your church when I get out." I assured her my congregation would be happy to welcome her.

This made me think of Ruth and her yearning to join herself to a new family in Israel.

Many never go to church to find out for themselves what is good and true. Whenever we sense a hungry soul reaching for fellowship, we should do all we can to introduce him to our church.

My prisoner friend will no doubt be self-conscious when she first comes to worship with us. But with prayer and kindness, she may come to experience a blessing—as Ruth did!

—Ted Simonson

Golden Text Illuminated

"Ruth said, Intreat me not to leave thee, or to return from following after thee: for whither thou goest, I will go; and where thou lodgest, I will lodge: thy people shall be my people, and thy God my God" (Ruth 1:16).

One of the great confessions of faith throughout all history, Ruth's testimony to her mother-in-law of her conversion to the one true God of Israel should be an inspiration to all believers down to the present day. It captures the timeless essence of true faith in the eternal God. None of us are born believers by nature. We must all come to the point of throwing over our entire old, sinful natures and forsaking them in order to follow a new and foreign way, the way of righteousness as defined by God alone. Until we make such a surrender, as Ruth did, we have not been converted.

We live in a world that honors cultural relativism rather than absolute truth. Ruth's confession turns our modern world on its head, as all true faith must. Culture, no matter how dear, must be abandoned for the sake of embracing absolute truth whenever the two are found to conflict with one another.

That principle has become a very unpopular one in our modern world. Today, a person's culture is considered almost sacred, while the actual truths of his religion are often considered to be merely some quaint, optional subset of his broader cultural milieu. Thus, any expectation that a person must change some aspect of his culture in order to fulfill his discipleship as a Christian has fallen into low repute.

The fact is that many cultural practices may be subject to censure when examined under the light of the gospel. Practices such as idolatry, polygamy, and incest seem obvious. Depending upon the culture, there may be many others to question. Some of these may come to light only after prayerful reflection and meditation on God's Word.

Paul gives our commission for this great work of reforming culture in II Corinthians 10:5: "Casting down imaginations, and every high thing that exalteth itself against the knowledge of God, and bringing into captivity every thought to the obedience of Christ."

It is safe to say that Ruth felt none of her cultural rights violated when she committed herself to following Naomi's God. She forsook her country, her religion, and her culture. Why? Because she realized what many today so glibly overlook: that God is worth it!

Of course, expecting converts to Christianity to forsake one worldly culture merely to embrace another, as if it were somehow inherently superior, is an abuse of the sacred commission of the gospel. This error was at one time quite common among some European missionaries as they encountered cultures they reacted to as being "primitive" or "barbaric." However, in avoiding one error, we should be careful not to embrace another, that of unquestioning acceptance.

Let us always examine culture in the eternal light of God's truth.

—John M. Lody

Heart of the Lesson

The book of Ruth testifies clearly of God's gracious faithfulness. Chapter 1 demonstrates that faithfulness even as people dealt with severe disappointments.

1. Disappointments in tragedy (Ruth 1:1-5). The opening verses of Ruth present three significant, tragic events.

A tragedy of desperation is described in the opening sentence of the book. Famine struck the land of Israel. For an agricultural economy, famine was a devastating occurrence. Countries around the world can be afflicted with terrible famines. To make matters worse, it appears that no other nations came to Israel's aid, as so frequently occurs today.

A tragedy of decision occurred as the family of Elimelech left Bethlehem and headed for the greener territory of Moab. The text does not say it explicitly, but this decision may have betrayed a lack of trust in God, as they left the Promised Land for Moab (cf. Gen. 26:1-3).

Once in Moab, the tragedy of death struck the family, not once but three times. Death is always a tragic event; when a person is far away from home and family, it is even more grievous. First Elimelech died, but this was bearable since Naomi still had her sons. Later, however, both sons also died. Naomi was left with her two daughters-in-law, neither of whom had borne a child. Naomi now faced old age with no Social Security and no welfare.

At this point, God's gracious faithfulness has not been observed. The scene was being set, however, for what was to come.

2. Disappointments in trials (Ruth 1:6-9, 14*b*, 16). God works in ways that His people do not always understand. Imagine the trial of Naomi's heart when she heard that the famine was over and prosperity had returned to her homeland. We can easily imagine her disappointed wish that they had never left, just as we often regret past decisions (sinful or not) that have brought unexpected trials to our lives.

At this juncture, another trial arose—a trial of choices. Naomi started back to Judah with Orpah and Ruth as her companions. As they journeyed, Naomi realized that Orpah and Ruth were leaving their homeland with seemingly no hope for any viable future. She confronted the young women with the facts and encouraged them to return home to find husbands and security, suppressing her own fears at having to return home alone.

A desire for safety, prosperity, and security is natural. We seek assurances from our employers on these very matters. We eagerly watch our pensions and 401(k) plans.

A new trial now arose involving personal decisions. Naomi's expressed desire that God bless her daughters-in-law showed that she had shared the knowledge of the Lord with them. The two young women then made diametrically opposed decisions. Orpah's decision was to return "unto her people, and unto her gods" (Ruth 1:15). Ruth made a radically different decision. The first recorded words that Ruth spoke are so memorable and significant that they are widely quoted today, often in marriage ceremonies. She declared full and lasting commitment to her mother-in-law, complete dedication to the people of Israel, and total acceptance of the living Lord of Israel. This remarkable woman continues as an example for all believers today.

—R. Larry Overstreet

World Missions

"Just because you sold your soul to the Devil doesn't mean you're taking the kids with you." With these bitter words, the Iranian mother hurled defiance at her husband, pastor of the Iranian Christian Church of Sunnyvale, California.

The husband was a formerly devout Muslim and a veteran of the Iranian Revolution, a conflict that included the seizing of the American embassy in Tehran. Migrating to the United States, the young man became an even more devout Muslim following the 9/11 attack, which spurred considerable anti-Arab sentiment. Then, by grace, he began to search the New Testament and slowly came to the truth of the gospel.

Hungry for fellowship, the young believer joined an Arab Christian church in Chicago. The members were suspicious of recent converts. Next he tried eight different house churches, all of which failed. He finally formed a Bible study, which grew into the Sunnyvale Iranian Christian Church. The church is believed to be the largest former Muslim fellowship in the world (Lewis, "Looking for Home," *Christianity Today,* September 2008).

In our study this week we learn that Naomi heard "that the Lord had visited his people in giving them bread" (Ruth 1:6). That statement looked forward to a greater provision in Christ Himself. In Jesus, God has provided bread, the bread of life, for those in need.

Since 9/11, Americans have often viewed the Muslim people in their midst with suspicion. While we may have become used to Muslim women wearing the traditional head covering, what have evangelical Christians done to reach this growing minority?

We met a Muslim woman in our home-to-home visitation evangelism program. She told us that we had come at the right time. Her husband, a non-Muslim, had just walked out on her. She added that her Muslim relatives were pressuring her to return to the faith of the Prophet Muhammad. We endeavored to minister first to her broken heart. Then we presented God's plan of salvation and urged her to trust in Christ as the first step toward dealing with her marital problems. This woman was born again.

Islam is a mystery to most Christians. As a result, we may have omitted Muslims from our plans to spread the gospel. We need to correct this as the number of Muslims in the world is growing faster than the number of Christians, including in American prisons.

The rise of new technology has opened up more avenues to reach the Islamic world with the good news of Jesus Christ. The Sunnyvale Iranian church is reaching the exploding house-church movement in Iran itself. The church beams a daily salvation message by satellite into secret fellowships of believers and seekers in Iran. This is the passion of the former Muslims of this congregation. Seventy-five percent of their Iranian audience is under age twenty-five.

In our community, the doughnut shop is owned and operated by a man from Pakistan. He closes every Friday for the Islamic holy day. One of our physicians is also a Pakistani. The leading investigative reporter on our favorite news channel is a Muslim. We must see that they have been placed within sight and sound of faithful Christians in order that they may be reached with the gospel. Start your own Muslim ministry by inviting a Muslim to your church. If you are timid, make it an invitation by mail. The Holy Spirit will use you.

—Lyle P. Murphy

The Jewish Aspect

The book of Ruth is read by the Jews on Shabuoth, a day of thanksgiving for the spring grain harvest, because of the book's depiction of the harvest. In Leviticus 23:15-21, the Lord gave Israel detailed instructions for celebrating Shabuoth. In verse 22 the Lord commanded the Hebrew farmers not to harvest the corners of their fields but to leave them for the poor. Jews love Ruth because Scripture shows her benefiting from this Torah practice.

After Pesach (Passover), the Jews count a sabbath of weeks (seven weeks), or forty-nine days. On the fiftieth day they celebrate Shabuoth. Christians celebrate Pentecost as the fulfillment of Shabuoth and count the fifty days after Easter.

In 2007 Reform Jews came out with a new prayer book. The older prayer book, which is still widely used, is called *The Gates of Prayer*. The new prayer book actually has a Hebrew title. It is called *Mishkan T'filah,* which means "tabernacle of prayer." (Reform Jews today stress the use of Hebrew much more than they used to.)

The reason for replacing *The Gates of Prayer* was not that it was antiquated. Instead, the Reform rabbis replaced it because they wanted to have a more gender neutral prayer book. *The Gates of Prayer* had already updated the previous prayer book's older English usage and changed most pronouns to be gender neutral. However, the creators of *Mishkan T'filah* took it a step further, going to great lengths to use gender neutral language in theological contexts. For example, *Mishkan T'filah* does not refer to God in any masculine way. Not even the English term "Lord" is used in referring to God.

Mishkan T'filah is useful, however, in its descriptions of Jewish festival practices. One section introduces readers to Shabuoth. It refers to the counting of the fifty days as *S'firat Ha'Omer,* or counting of the omer (a measure of grain). *Mishkan T'filah* then makes reference to Leviticus 23:15: "And from the day on which you bring the omer offering—the day after the day of rest—you shall count off seven weeks. They must be complete."

The prayer book then explains, "Pesach and Shavuot are respectively the times of harvesting barley and wheat. Torah therefore called for sacrifices of thanksgiving for the seven weeks in between. 'Omer' denoted the measure of grain being offered. The Rabbis designed a ritual of counting the days, a practice that has been interpreted as bringing to consciousness our people's movement from slavery to Sinai. The purpose of freedom is not simply freedom from servitude but freedom to devote ourselves to God's purposes" (*Mishkan T'filah,* Central Conference of American Rabbis).

I have been attending a Judaism class for about two years. One beautiful spring day when I came to class, there was a note on the door from Rabbi Winn telling us to meet in the sanctuary. Rabbi Winn told us, "Today is Shabuoth." Then he spent the rest of the class explaining the holiday.

After his lesson, he opened the Torah ark, and we began to study the Torah from the Hebrew manuscript. Rabbi Winn explained to us that over the centuries, rabbis have developed the tradition that God gave Moses all five books of the Torah on Shabuoth. This tradition comes from the Talmud rather than the Bible.

Jews not only read the book of Ruth on Shabuoth; they also devote the day to the study of the Torah.

—James Coffey

Guiding the Superintendent

Many definitions may be found for community, but perhaps there is none better than "family." In our lesson this week we will learn that a community is a family—not bound by bloodlines but by love.

Our passage this week demonstrates that principle through the family bond of an Israelite with a Moabite.

Most Sunday school students are familiar with the great stories of King David, both his great exploits and his great transgression. But how many people can tell the story of where David's family came from?

A person might naturally think that David was a pure Israelite by birth, but he would be wrong. David was, in reality, part Moabite. This is a story of how love is thicker than blood.

DEVOTIONAL OUTLINE

1. Move to Moab (Ruth 1:1-2). The story of David's family is truly a love story—the love of a husband and wife, the love of parents for children, and the love of in-laws for each other. Even though the word "love" is only found once in Ruth (4:15), it is a central theme.

The story starts simply enough. "There was a famine in the land" (1:1). Next we are introduced to a man, his wife, and two sons. They decided to leave Bethlehem and journey to Moab to find food.

2. Misfortune in Moab (Ruth 1:3-5). We are told the husband died and the two sons married women of Moab. Within ten years, tragedy struck the family again. The two sons died, and then there were three widows alone to face a cruel world.

3. Return to Bethlehem (Ruth 1:6-9). Two different decisions confronted Naomi when she heard that God had brought food back to her homeland of Judah. Decision number one was that she would return to the land of her origin. This led to decision number two: she would not take her two daughters-in-law with her. After all, it would be easier for them to find husbands in their own country than in foreign Israel.

With deep emotion, Naomi hugged and kissed them goodbye as she headed back to her homeland. She sent them on their way with the blessings of Israel's God.

4. The road back (Ruth 1:14b,16). One of the younger women, Ruth, did not want to return to Moab. The text tells us she "clave" unto Naomi. She was glued to her mother-in-law. She pledged to journey back to Israel with her. Ruth would go with Naomi, live with her, adopt her nationality, and worship her God.

This great love story points us to an even greater one: God's love for the church, which led Him to give up His own Son to reconcile us into His family.

Truly, a community is a family bound by love and not just by blood.

AGE-GROUP EMPHASES

Children: Sadly, many children today do not have a loving, stable family. Teach them that the church community of believers can be their family by love.

Youths: Our text this week deals with the results of choices that several people made. Like many choices, some were good, and some were regrettable for all involved. Choices have consequences—some for a lifetime and beyond.

Adults: This lesson will help adults remember what really is important in life—family, especially the family of God.

—*Martin R. Dahlquist*

SCRIPTURE LESSON TEXT

RUTH 2:8 Then said Boaz unto Ruth, Hearest thou not, my daughter? Go not to glean in another field, neither go from hence, but abide here fast by my maidens:

9 *Let* thine eyes *be* on the field that they do reap, and go thou after them: have I not charged the young men that they shall not touch thee? and when thou art athirst, go unto the vessels, and drink of *that* which the young men have drawn.

10 Then she fell on her face, and bowed herself to the ground, and said unto him, Why have I found grace in thine eyes, that thou shouldest take knowledge of me, seeing I *am* a stranger?

11 And Boaz answered and said unto her, It hath fully been shewed me, all that thou hast done unto thy mother in law since the death of thine husband: and *how* thou hast left thy father and thy mother, and the land of thy nativity, and art come unto a people which thou knewest not heretofore.

12 The LORD recompense thy work, and a full reward be given thee of the LORD God of Israel, under whose wings thou art come to trust.

13 Then she said, Let me find favour in thy sight, my lord; for that thou hast comforted me, and for that thou hast spoken friendly unto thine handmaid, though I be not like unto one of thine handmaidens.

14 And Boaz said unto her, At mealtime come thou hither, and eat of the bread, and dip thy morsel in the vinegar. And she sat beside the reapers: and he reached her parched *corn,* and she did eat, and was sufficed, and left.

15 And when she was risen up to glean, Boaz commanded his young men, saying, Let her glean even among the sheaves, and reproach her not:

16 And let fall also *some* of the handfuls of purpose for her, and leave *them,* that she may glean *them,* and rebuke her not.

17 So she gleaned in the field until even, and beat out that she had gleaned: and it was about an ephah of barley.

18 And she took *it* up, and went into the city: and her mother in law saw what she had gleaned: and she brought forth, and gave to her that she had reserved after she was sufficed.

NOTES

Ruth Meets Boaz

Lesson Text: Ruth 2:8-18

Related Scriptures: Ruth 2:1-7; Leviticus 19:9-10;
Deuteronomy 24:19-22; I Timothy 6:17-19

TIME: between 1130–1120 B.C.   PLACE: Bethlehem

GOLDEN TEXT—"The Lord recompense thy work, and a full reward be given thee of the Lord God of Israel, under whose wings thou art come to trust" (Ruth 2:12).

Introduction

We have a good God who is in control of all our circumstances; and when good things happen for us, it is because He has orchestrated it.

The first chapter of Ruth begins with three widows stranded in Moab. Two traveled from there to Judah, the home of the older woman, Naomi. The entire first chapter sets the scene for the major events of the book that are about to unfold. Two important facts prepare the way for what follows. First, the women arrived in Judah at the time of barley harvest (vs. 22). Second, Naomi had a wealthy relative named Boaz (2:1). These form the basis for all that follows.

Naomi and Ruth were destitute; so to help meet their needs, Ruth requested and received permission from Naomi to go out into neighboring fields to glean. God providentially led her to the fields of Boaz, who inquired about her upon returning from town. His servants gave him a good report about Ruth and her work.

LESSON OUTLINE

I. GENEROSITY FROM THE WEALTHY—Ruth 2:8-13

II. PROVISION FOR THE NEEDY—Ruth 2:14-18

Exposition: Verse by Verse

GENEROSITY FROM THE WEALTHY

RUTH 2:8 Then said Boaz unto Ruth, Hearest thou not, my daughter? Go not to glean in another field, neither go from hence, but abide here fast by my maidens:

9 Let thine eyes be on the field that they do reap, and go thou after them: have I not charged the young men that they shall not touch thee? and when thou art athirst, go unto the vessels, and drink of that which the young men have drawn.

10 Then she fell on her face, and bowed herself to the ground, and said unto him, Why have I found grace in thine eyes, that thou shouldest take knowledge of me, seeing I am a stranger?

11 And Boaz answered and said unto her, It hath fully been shewed me, all that thou hast done unto thy mother in law since the death of thine husband: and how thou hast left thy father and thy mother, and the land of thy nativity, and art come unto a people which thou knewest not heretofore.

12 The LORD recompense thy work, and a full reward be given thee of the LORD God of Israel, under whose wings thou art come to trust.

13 Then she said, Let me find favour in thy sight, my lord; for that thou hast comforted me, and for that thou hast spoken friendly unto thine handmaid, though I be not like unto one of thine handmaidens.

Boaz taking care of Ruth (Ruth 2:8-9). When Boaz came to the fields, he immediately noticed Ruth. Wiersbe creatively imagines, "No sooner had Boaz greeted his workers than his eye caught the presence of a stranger in the field, and a lovely stranger at that. I get the impression that when he saw her, it was love at first sight; for from that point on, Boaz focuses his interest on Ruth and not on the harvest. Though an alien, Ruth was an eligible young woman whom the young men of the town would notice (3:10)" (*The Bible Exposition Commentary: Old Testament,* Victor).

The good report Boaz received about Ruth from his workers (Ruth 2:6- 7) was what really impressed him. {He had already heard about her (vs. 11); so he knew she was a loyal woman of integrity. He also knew she was related to him through marriage; so he had a special concern for her welfare.}[Q1] When he approached her, the first thing he did was get her full attention: "Hearest thou not, my daughter?" (vs. 8). We might say, "Please listen carefully." What he had to say was important enough that she must not miss it.

By addressing Ruth as his daughter, Boaz was probably making reference to the age difference between them, as well as to the fact that they were indirectly related. He was probably closer to Naomi's age than Ruth's. There is a hint of this in the next chapter, where Boaz mentions that Ruth could have gone after younger men than he. His particular instruction at their initial meeting was that she remain in his field and do all her gleaning there.

Boaz's mention of his maidens refers to the young women who worked for him alongside the reapers. The reapers were young men who cut the grain using hand sickles, after which the young women tied up the sheaves. {Gleaners were never employees of the owner. Rather, they were the poor, who were permitted to gather whatever was left behind by those gathering. Boaz was telling Ruth she should stay in his field and close to the young women employed by him. This was a very generous proposition that would give her an advantage over other gleaners.}[Q2]

Boaz added two other words of encouragement. He knew the young men who worked for him would be prone to take advantage of an attractive young foreign woman; so he assured Ruth that he had given specific instructions to them to leave her alone. That would relieve any stress that might have arisen from unwanted attention and allow her the freedom to concentrate on her work. His other instruction was that she should feel free to drink from the vessels of water drawn by his young men for his employees.

Ruth wondering why (Ruth 2:10). {Everything that had happened up to that point in Ruth's life reveals that she was not a proud woman but a sincerely humble one.}[Q3] When Boaz gave these instructions and reassurances that she was welcome not only to glean in his field but also to receive the benefits of his employees, she was understandably humbled and grateful. She bowed clear down to the ground and asked Boaz why he should give her such attention, especially since she was not an Israelite but a Moabite.

It might be that Naomi had been treated negatively in Moab, as foreigners often were, and perhaps Ruth had expected the same now that she was in Judah. She might have approached the whole thought of gleaning with a sense of dread, knowing she could easily be rejected by many of the local people. Boaz's generous, thoughtful treatment was a pleasant surprise to her, and she could not understand why it was being granted to her. Both her actions and her words communicated a deep sense of gratitude.

Boaz explaining his actions (Ruth 2:11-12). Boaz's response was to let Ruth know that he had heard detailed reports about her previous actions toward her mother-in-law since the death of her husband. {Specifically, he said that he had heard that she had left her own parents and the land of her birth to accompany Naomi back to her homeland, which was for Ruth a foreign land.} Q4 He recognized that for her to do that meant she had come to a people she had never known before. It was a statement of sympathetic understanding.

Boaz made it clear to Ruth that he knew what she had done was not easy. He appears to have been genuinely moved by her sacrificial actions. This led him to pronounce a blessing upon her. Boaz expressed his desire that God would reward Ruth for what she had done. He desired God's richest blessings on her life because she had put her trust in Him. She had done what Paul later said the Thessalonians had done when they "turned to God from idols to serve the living and true God" (I Thess. 1:9).

{Boaz pronounced a benediction upon Ruth for her loyalty to Naomi and her deceased husband, asking the Lord's protection for her, as a bird's wing protects her chicks.}Q5

The likening of God to a bird conveys that God keeps his children warm and safe. Psalm 36:7 reminds us, "How excellent is thy lovingkindness, O God! therefore the children of men put their trust under the shadow of thy wings." Nothing can harm us without God's specific permission, as demonstrated in the example of Job. Satan could not touch him unless God allowed it (Job 1-2). Boaz was acknowledging that Ruth would be safe and provided for under God's care.

Ruth expressing appreciation (Ruth 2:13). John W. Reed writes, "Though Boaz's words could have stirred her to pride, Ruth continued to respond in humility. Naomi had given no words of encouragement to Ruth, but this man spoke comforting words that warmed her soul. She mentioned her gratitude for his favor (cf. vv. 2, 10), comfort, and kind words, and hoped they would continue. She felt she was less important than Boaz's servant girls" (Walvoord and Zuck, eds., *The Bible Knowledge Commentary,* Victor).

{Wiersbe writes, "Ruth's response to Boaz was one of humility and gratitude. She acknowledged her own unworthiness and accepted his grace. She believed his promises and rejoiced in them.}Q6 There was no need for Ruth to worry, for the wealthy lord of the harvest would care for her and Naomi. How did she know he would care for her? He gave her his promise, and she knew he could be trusted." There is an obvious parallel in these thoughts with the way we can trust the Lord to care for us.

Ruth's statement was a combination of gratitude and confidence about her future. Her desire to find favor in Boaz's eyes was an expression of her desire to continue to please him and not become a disappointment. She had been comforted and encouraged by his kind words, and she wanted to remain worthy of his goodness to her. What amazed her the most was that he was doing all this for her in spite of the fact that she was not one of his hired maidens.

PROVISION FOR THE NEEDY

14 And Boaz said unto her, At mealtime come thou hither, and eat of the bread, and dip thy morsel in the vinegar. And she sat beside the reapers: and he reached her parched corn, and she did eat, and was sufficed, and left.

15 And when she was risen up to glean, Boaz commanded his young men, saying, Let her glean even among the sheaves, and reproach her not:

16 And let fall also some of the handfuls of purpose for her, and leave them, that she may glean them, and rebuke her not.

17 So she gleaned in the field until even, and beat out that she had gleaned: and it was about an ephah of barley.

18 And she took it up, and went into the city: and her mother in law saw what she had gleaned: and she brought forth, and gave to her that she had reserved after she was sufficed.

Boaz's invitation to Ruth (Ruth 2:14). When lunchtime came, Ruth got another surprise. It is doubtful she had taken any food with her; she had no idea where she would end up and possibly just planned to get through the day without eating until she got back home. Poverty creates situations in which necessity takes over, and one has to adjust accordingly.

{Boaz unexpectedly invited Ruth to eat lunch with him and the reapers.}[Q7] This is another indication of the large-hearted character of Boaz. He was personal with his employees and sat to eat with them—something that many owners may not have done.

If there was any reluctance on the part of the reapers about having Ruth working among them and then being invited to eat with them, it must have disappeared when Boaz himself served Ruth some food. He had invited her to eat the bread and dip it in the vinegar right along with everyone else. The vinegar was a sour beverage into which the hard bread was dipped, making it easier to eat. Some form of roasted grain was also available. Boaz personally served this to Ruth.

Ruth was able to eat as much as she wanted. We cannot help imagining that this must have been quite a luxury to her, after prolonged famine and hard times in Moab. While Ruth 2:14 indicates that she ate until satisfied and then left, a comparison with the end of verse 18 reveals that she had some food left over, which she kept and took home for Naomi. It was quite obvious to her and all those around her that Boaz had become her protector and provider. Little did he know at that point how much farther God would take him in being this protector.

Boaz's command to his servants (Ruth 2:15-16). Apparently Ruth did not linger after the meal but returned immediately to her work. In this we see her diligence and commitment to what she knew needed to be done. The more she gleaned, the more she and Naomi would have for their sustenance. She obviously was not a lazy person. Ruth was not one of those people who expect others to always be meeting their needs. Some folks are givers, and others are takers. Ruth was not a taker but was willing to work for what she received.

The Mosaic law required farmers to allow for gleaners. Leviticus 19:9-10 says, "And when ye reap the harvest of your land, thou shalt not wholly reap the corners of thy field, neither shalt thou gather the gleanings of thy harvest. And thou shalt not glean thy vineyard, neither shalt thou gather every grape of thy vineyard; thou shalt leave them for the poor and stranger: I am the Lord your God." This is repeated in Leviticus 23:22 and again in Deuteronomy 24:19-21, with the added promise that God would bless the one who obeys this. Boaz diligently obeyed this law.

{As soon as Ruth had returned to her work, Boaz gave further instructions to his reapers. What he told them went far beyond the norm when it came to the treatment of gleaners. Instead of being kept to the perimeters of the fields and behind the reapers, Ruth was to be allowed among the reapers themselves and was not to be scolded when she went there. Furthermore, Boaz's reapers were instructed to occasionally drop some stalks of grain on purpose for her to pick up.}[Q8] There was certainly nothing like this included in the law!

Boaz was demonstrating great compassion for Ruth and Naomi in his determination to meet their needs. His obvious respect for Ruth and his concern for his relatives motivated him to take extreme measures toward them.

Ruth's results from her work (Ruth 2:17-18). Ruth worked all day long, right up until evening. {After she finished her gleaning, she beat out the grain from the stalks and ended up with almost an ephah of barley grain. This would have been a little over half a bushel of grain, an unheard of amount for one day's gleaning.}[Q9] {It is certainly a tribute both to Ruth's diligence in working and to Boaz's generosity in making extra provision for her.}[Q10] This amount of grain would have been sufficient for Ruth and Naomi for a good many days.

When Ruth returned home with her grain, she immediately showed it to her mother-in-law and gave her the food she had saved from the lunch with Boaz (vs. 18). We can only imagine Naomi's relief when she saw that her daughter-in-law was safe after being gone all day. We can certainly imagine Ruth's weariness after spending hours working in Boaz's field. Naomi and Ruth rejoiced together over the way God had cared for them and met their needs. This is evident in verse 19, where we read of their excited conversation about the day.

—Keith E. Eggert

QUESTIONS

1. What had Boaz already heard about Ruth before he met her?
2. What did Boaz tell Ruth about where to glean, and what advantage did this give her?
3. What does Ruth's response to Boaz reveal about her and what she might have expected?
4. Why did Boaz say he had taken notice of Ruth?
5. How do we explain the concept of being under God's wings (Ruth 2:12)?
6. How did Ruth express gratitude to Boaz for what he was doing for her?
7. What surprising events happened for Ruth at lunchtime?
8. What did Boaz command his reapers, and why was this unexpected?
9. What were the results of Ruth's day of gleaning?
10. What does Ruth's large harvest say about Ruth's character and the character of Boaz?

—Keith E. Eggert

Preparing to Teach the Lesson

Kindness is a trait that must mark the Christian. Our lesson this week teaches us to show kindness to those who are less well-off than we are.

TODAY'S AIM

Facts: to learn how Boaz took care of the needs of poor Ruth and showed kindness to her.

Principle: to affirm that God blesses those who take care of those who are poor and needy.

Application: to urge students to take care of the less well-off and to show kindness to them.

INTRODUCING THE LESSON

I come from a land where the poor are everywhere. People cannot go anywhere in India without the stark reality of poverty hitting them in the face. There is a sharp distinction between the rich and the poor. When we see great poverty all the time, it is easy to become callous and hard-hearted and to lose our sensitivity to other people's pain and plight. Our lesson this week shows us how Boaz, a rich man, saw poor Ruth and took care of her needs, going out of his way to help her.

The Levitical law strictly commands that God's people take care of the poor. Boaz knew what the law taught, and he faithfully followed it.

DEVELOPING THE LESSON

1. Showing kindness to a stranger (Ruth 2:8-9). When Ruth went into the fields to glean—that is, to pick up the grain left behind by the harvesters—Boaz quickly spotted her. He saw something special about this woman, and he took a liking to her and helped her. He told her to stay in his field and not go to the other fields. He told her to stay with the women who worked for him and work with them. He also gave instructions to the young men not to trouble her. The water provided for his workers was hers for the taking when she was thirsty.

Ruth was in a new land and did not know anyone. Help the class understand what it feels like to be in a foreign country looking for work. You do not know the customs, the language, or the cultural norms; you are basically feeling your way around. What you need is a close friend who knows the local culture. God sent Boaz to help Ruth and to show her kindness.

Nothing happens to the child of God by accident. When we need something, God will open up "all His resources" for us because He loves His children so much.

2. Sharing the goodness of God (Ruth 2:10-14). Notice that after thanking Boaz, Ruth sought an explanation for his kindness to her, a stranger. Notice also how quickly Boaz pointed her back to the God of Israel. We too must use every opportunity to point others to our God, especially when God uses us to help others in times of need.

Boaz told Ruth that he had heard how she loved her mother-in-law and showed her kindness after Ruth's own husband had died. Boaz commended her for her courage in coming to live in a foreign land to help her mother-in-law. He then prayed that the God of Israel, who had sheltered and protected her, would also reward her. Ruth had now become part of God's people. She would soon learn how much the God of Israel loved His own, which now included her.

Note that God brings into His own community those who are willing to make that crucial choice to follow Him. Ruth is an example for all those who wish to join the community of God's people. Emphasize to the students how very different the God of Israel was from the gods of Moab. The Lord has a close relationship with those who join Him in His community. Ruth certainly had not known this kind of unique relationship with God before.

Ruth continued to thank Boaz for his unusual kindness, and when it was time for lunch, he invited her to come and share in the food and drink and to eat with all those who worked in his fields. Show the class that Boaz's kindness to Ruth may be seen as a picture of God's love for us. He goes to great lengths to bring us into His community and family.

3. Telling of grace and kindness received (Ruth 2:15-18). When Ruth went back to work in the field, Boaz told his young men to deliberately drop some of the stalks of grain so that she would have plenty to pick up and take home. They were also to let her work beside them without any disruption.

When Ruth got home, she showed Naomi the large amount of grain she had gleaned from the harvest. She also shared how Boaz had been so kind to her.

Help your students think through the events of Ruth's life so far. She had made a very tough—but correct—choice to follow her mother-in-law to Bethlehem and become part of Naomi's people. And here we see how God divinely planted Boaz in her path to take care of all her needs. When God sees us making a right choice for Him, He will take care of every need we have, and sometimes He uses the most extraordinary people to do so.

Clearly, God demonstrated His love and providential care for Ruth as she trusted Him, making her a part of the community of God's people. We can expect our almighty God to do the same for us when we honor Him by standing up on the side of all that is right.

ILLUSTRATING THE LESSON

God rewarded Ruth's decision to follow Him. She entered into a personal relationship with a personal God, who provided for her through Boaz and made her a part of His community. He always rewards faith and faithfulness.

CONCLUDING THE LESSON

Was it worth it for Ruth to join the community of the faithful on the side of the God of Israel? Her experience certainly shows us that it was. She came to the land of Israel and found the God of the universe. She discovered a God who has a close relationship with His people. She became part of His community, and God sent Boaz to help her in her time of need. We must remember that nothing we do in the name of our God will ever go unnoticed. Our God watches us and in His own time provides ample reward.

ANTICIPATING THE NEXT LESSON

In our next lesson in this series, we learn how to care for one another in a wonderful lesson about the kinsman-redeemer. It is also a picture of our Lord Jesus, our Messiah and Redeemer.

—A. Koshy Muthalaly

PRACTICAL POINTS

1. The godly person does what he can to help the poor and needy (Ruth 2:8-9; cf. Matt. 25:34-40).
2. The grateful respond in humility and not with a sense of entitlement (Ruth 2:10).
3. Be kind to others; God is watching and will reward your faithful obedience (Ruth 2:11-12; cf. Luke 6:35; Eph. 6:2).
4. God supplies all we need, when we need it (Ruth 2:13-14; cf. Ps. 23:1; Phil. 4:19).
5. The godly person both gives and keeps his word (Ruth 2:15-16).
6. God blesses us and others through our diligent work (vss. 17-18).

—Don Kakavecos

RESEARCH AND DISCUSSION

1. How does Boaz's generosity to Ruth demonstrate a godly response to the poor? What are the criteria for whom and how much one should help (cf. Prov. 14:21; Matt. 5:42; Jas. 2:14-17)?
2. Is a demanding spirit of entitlement something one should expect to see in a grateful Christian?
3. How do the words of Boaz in Ruth 2:12 encourage you to be kind to others? Must they be worthy of it or be willing to return the kindness (cf. Rom. 5:8)? What should be the Christian's manner of giving to the poor (cf. Matt. 6:1-4; I Cor. 13:1-3)?
4. How should the Christian approach his or her work (cf. Gen. 2:15; I Cor. 10:31; Col. 3:23)?

—Don Kakavecos

ILLUSTRATED HIGH POINTS

Found grace (Ruth 2:10)

In June 2007, Fred, a young man with muscular dystrophy, approached a street corner and began to cross a few feet in front of a towering truck. When the light turned green, somehow the driver failed to see Fred's wheelchair—even when it became wedged in the truck's front grille. The truck pulled ahead, the wheelchair trapped against it. The heavier vehicle soon reached fifty miles an hour, with the driver still unaware of Fred. Finally, after two terrifying miles, the driver pulled into his company parking lot. By God's grace, Fred was unharmed.

Power is not wrong. In fact, God gives people power and commands that they use it carefully and responsibly to show others grace.

Lord recompense thy work (vs. 12)

In intense turmoil, Martin Luther penned his most famous hymn. The year was 1527, one of the most trying of his life.

In August of that year, the plague struck Wittenberg. As fears mounted, many townspeople fled. But Luther considered it his duty to remain and care for the sick. His house was transformed into a hospital.

He wrote his comrade Melancthon during this period, "I have just spent more than a week in death and hell. My entire body is in pain and I still tremble. But through the prayers of the saints, God had mercy on me and pulled my soul from death."

During this awful time, Luther encouraged his soul with these words: "And tho this world, with devils filled, / Should threaten to undo us; / We will not fear, for God hath willed / His truth to triumph through us" ("A Mighty Fortress Is Our God").

—Ted Simonson

Golden Text Illuminated

"The Lord recompense thy work, and a full reward be given thee of the Lord God of Israel, under whose wings thou art come to trust" (Ruth 2:12).

People living in a foreign land face an uncertain life. Customs are different, and they may not understand the language. Friends and family are left behind. Work prospects may be unclear.

Indeed, Ruth experienced many of these realities. Her husband died. Her sister-in-law returned to her people. But Ruth left her people in Moab while she went with her mother-in-law, Naomi, to the land of Israel. She knew no one there except Naomi. No friends, no husband, no clear way to make a living, and no certainty of a future. All she had was Naomi and Naomi's God.

But God was directing Ruth's steps. Naomi returned to Bethlehem, the area of her relative Boaz. It was in that region that Ruth sought work gleaning in the grain fields to obtain a little food for her and Naomi. Would she be turned away? Or worse, would she be harmed? God protected Ruth by directing her steps to a field that Boaz owned (Ruth 2:3). And it was at that very moment that Boaz arrived at the field.

Boaz saw Ruth and asked his servant about her. The servant told Boaz that this was Ruth, the Moabitess who returned with Naomi. He explained how she had asked permission to work in the field and had worked hard all morning.

Ruth's exemplary character spurred Boaz to respond in kind. He implored her not to leave his fields but to stay and glean with his female servants for her care and protection. He instructed his servants to treat her kindly and invited her to drink water from his water jars (vss. 8–9). Later in the day, Boaz asked Ruth to eat with him and his servants. She ate as much as she wanted and saved the rest of her meal to take to Naomi. Boaz instructed his servants to pull some grain from the bundles and leave it for Ruth to gather for herself (vss. 15-16).

The kindnesses that Boaz extended to Ruth shocked her. She bowed to the ground in gratitude before Boaz and asked why she deserved this gracious attention, since she was a foreigner.

Boaz responded by explaining that he understood her plight and the difficulties that she had experienced. Ruth had demonstrated her good character through her care for Naomi. And even more importantly, she had chosen to serve, worship, and trust the God of Israel. She had turned her back upon the gods of Moab (1:16).

At this point, Boaz pronounced a blessing on Ruth, asking God to reward her for the faith that she had placed in Him. He recognized that Ruth had come to trust the Lord to care for her and Naomi and to provide for their needs (2:12).

God turned Ruth's heartbreaks, trials, and uncertainties into a magnificent account in Israel's history. He showed His loving care toward someone with no claim to being one of God's people. Later God would extend His gracious offer of salvation to all the Gentiles through Jesus Christ.

As for Ruth, her trust in God resulted in great blessings. God provided her with a good husband (Boaz) and children. And she, a poor Moabite woman, found herself included in the greatest lineage of Israel, as her descendants included King David, the ancestor of Jesus Christ.

—*Glenn Weaver*

Heart of the Lesson

The needy are always the objects of God's concern. In His law for Israel, God instructed the owners of fields to allow the poor to glean grain after the reapers had done their work. In fact, they were told not to "wholly reap the corners" of their fields, leaving these areas for the poor (Lev. 19:9; cf. 23:22). While the needy would have to work for their food, at least sustenance would be available for them.

When Ruth and her mother-in-law, Naomi, arrived in Bethlehem, it was "the beginning of barley harvest" (Ruth 1:22). As widows, Ruth and Naomi were destitute, but Ruth seemed to be aware of God's law and asked Naomi to let her go glean in the fields after the reapers (2:2).

Of course, many people ignored God's laws and would not welcome the poor into their fields; but Ruth came upon the fields of Boaz, a godly man who was related to Elimelech, Naomi's late husband. God, in His providence, led her to this place. When Boaz saw the young widow in the field, he took notice.

1. An invitation to reap (Ruth 2:8-12). When Boaz learned the identity of Ruth, he told her not to go elsewhere but to continue to reap in his fields. Boaz instructed his men to leave her alone and told her to drink of the water for his workers when she became thirsty.

Ruth was amazed by the reception and asked why she had found grace in the eyes of Boaz. No doubt Boaz was impressed by Ruth's work ethic (Ruth 2:7), but he also explained that he had heard of how she had left her home and family to accompany Naomi to a place and people unfamiliar to her. Boaz recognized that this was evidence of her faith in Israel's God (vs. 12), and he was eager to welcome and reward her.

2. An invitation to eat (Ruth 2:13-14). Not only did Boaz welcome Ruth into his fields, but he also invited her to eat with him and his workers. This was a privilege not afforded to all those who gleaned and was further evidence of the grace Ruth had found in Boaz's eyes.

3. An abundant reward (Ruth 2:15-18). Boaz made sure Ruth had plenty of grain to take home with her that evening. He instructed his workers to let her glean "even among the sheaves," not just following behind them. In addition, they were to purposely leave some stalks for her to pick up.

As a result of Boaz's generosity, Ruth returned to Naomi that evening with an abundance of grain. It was far more than what any gleaner could normally hope to acquire in a day's work.

This precious account of Boaz and Ruth is part of the larger love story that is recounted in the book of Ruth. But this is a love story with many lessons for God's people.

God demonstrated love for the needy by providing for them in His law for Israel. Ruth demonstrated love for Naomi by seeking to provide for her by diligently gleaning where it was permitted. Boaz demonstrated compassionate love for all the needy by opening his fields for them—and particularly for Ruth by extending to her even greater privileges. And the Lord showed love for all concerned by providentially bringing Boaz and Ruth together at just the right time.

—Jarl K. Waggoner

World Missions

Ruth was a young woman who made a personal sacrifice to embrace and further the relationship she had as Naomi's daughter-in-law. Ruth's sacrifice included a powerful promise of commitment that said, "Whither thou goest, I will go; and where thou lodgest, I will lodge: thy people shall be my people, and thy God my God: where thou diest, will I die, and there will I be buried: the Lord do so to me, and more also, if ought but death part thee and me" (Ruth 1:16-17).

As a result of Ruth's sacrificial promise and faithful commitment to Naomi, God showed Ruth much favor. A part of His favor involved leading Ruth to become acquainted with a man named Boaz. Boaz showed Ruth great favor by allowing her to glean in his fields, producing for Ruth and Naomi a bountiful harvest of food.

In missionary terminology, the term "harvest" refers to the numerous people of the world who do not yet have a personal relationship with Jesus Christ by faith. Jesus said that the harvest is great, but the laborers are few. He urged then that his followers pray for the Lord of the harvest to send more workers (Luke 10:2).

John 4:35 reads "Say not ye, There are yet four months, and then cometh harvest? behold, I say unto you, Lift up your eyes, and look on the fields; for they are white already to harvest." These New Testament verses reveal God's heart toward spiritually lost people. Both texts promote a sense of spiritual need and urgency. Both are powerful indicators that God is "not willing that any should perish, but that all should come to repentance" (II Pet. 3:9).

Let us, therefore, ask the often-taken-for-granted questions: Why missions? Why should I be concerned about the global harvest of souls? The Bible is full of both explicit and implicit references to God's will for world evangelism. Most believers are familiar with the Great Commission (cf. Matt. 28:18-20); however, the Great Commission is only one reason for God's people to be involved in the ongoing Christian effort of spreading the gospel.

Let us examine just a few biblical references to encourage a clear and bold vision for people who are in need of a personal Saviour. Second Kings 19:15 reads, "O Lord God of Israel, which dwellest between the cherubims, thou art the God, even thou alone, of all the kingdoms of the earth; thou hast made heaven and earth." In our pluralistic culture, lost people need to hear that the one, true, living, Creator God exists and wants a salvation relationship with His creation.

Psalm 67:1-2 reads, "God be merciful unto us, and bless us; and cause his face to shine upon us; . . . That thy way may be known upon earth, thy saving health among all nations." The phrase "among all nations" encourages and teaches God's people to develop a global vision for missions, fulfilling the biblical command to be evangelistic witnesses "unto the uttermost part of the earth" (Acts 1:8).

In Acts 13:47, Paul and Barnabas referenced Isaiah 49:6, proclaiming, "I have set thee to be a light of the Gentiles, that thou shouldest be for salvation unto the ends of the earth." Let us embrace the truth that Jesus Christ is the only Way, the only Truth, and the only Life and that no one comes to the Father but through Him (cf. John 14:6).

—*Thomas R. Chmura*

The Jewish Aspect

Boaz is introduced in Ruth 2:1. Four basic facts about Boaz are important to the narrative in Ruth. First, he was a relative of Naomi's husband and therefore could potentially be a kinsman-redeemer, though that is not yet stated. Second, he was a man of great "wealth." The term also can mean valor or strength. Third, he was from the clan of Elimelech, which was a subdivision of the tribe of Judah. Fourth, as to his identity, "his name was Boaz."

Ruth 2:2 deals with Ruth's plan and begins, "Ruth the Moabitess said unto Naomi." Ruth is still called a Moabitess, even after her conversion. She is never called a Jew or Jewess or an Israelite, since she is only a proselyte. This shows that some considered Jewishness a matter of national identity in descent. Ruth was now a believer in Judaism, but she was not ethnically a Jew.

Ruth offered to go out to the fields and glean grain. This would relieve Naomi of the humiliation of gleaning—picking up the grain left behind by the harvesters. This was the means the law afforded for the poor to provide for their needs (Lev. 19:9; 23:22; Deut. 24:19).

The rabbinic interpretation of Ruth 2:2 is that while extreme poverty forced Ruth to pick the fields like any pauper, this was no coincidence but a foreshadowing of that poor man, riding on a donkey (Zech. 9:9), who would descend from her—the Messiah. This interpretation gives the verse a messianic implication by way of rabbinic typology. Also, it shows that Zechariah 9:9 was interpreted as a messianic prophecy.

Three basic observations can be made concerning Ruth 2. First, Ruth found grace in the eyes of Boaz on one level but also in the eyes of God on a higher level. Her loyalty to Naomi in chapter 1 was now being paid back by both God and man. Second, Boaz and Naomi never meet in this chapter; Ruth served as an intermediary between them. If Naomi's childlessness were to be resolved, Ruth would necessarily be involved. Third, God began His payment of Ruth's wages; the generosity of Boaz was only the down payment.

Examining the issues behind Naomi's plan helps shed light on all that was involved. Elimelech had possessed a portion of land in Bethlehem—property that Naomi was forced to sell or was about to sell due to poverty (Ruth 4:3). Naomi hoped that Boaz, a relative of Elimelech, would fulfill the duty of a redeemer both to ransom the property and to marry Ruth, the widow of the rightful heir of Elimelech's land. This marriage would establish the name of her deceased husband, Elimelech, as well as her son Mahlon, upon his inheritance.

Ruth 3 shows an answered prayer and develops major themes of the book. By the end of this chapter, Naomi's prayer in 1:9 was about to be answered: Ruth would find "rest" in marriage. Poverty and hunger would no longer be a factor, since Boaz's gift assured the women of plenty to eat. Ruth no longer identified herself with her lower status but with her own name. "I am Ruth," she told Boaz (3:9). She was no longer simply the Moabitess.

The focus in Ruth 2 and 3 is on human activity through the providence of God. God is clearly the one bringing all these plans and events together. The provision for an heir for Elimelech has been given new hope. Ruth will get additional wages from God in terms of the provision of marriage, and she has moved closer to being integrated into the commonwealth of Israel.

—*Arnold G. Fruchtenbaum*

Guiding the Superintendent

This lesson focuses on both Boaz and Ruth. Because of Ruth's need, her admission of that need, and the provision of her need, she becomes a picture of those outside of God's family who find grace in the eyes of the God who helps.

Having arrived safely in Bethlehem, the hometown of Naomi and Ruth's dead husbands, the two destitute women picked up their lives again. Because Ruth was much younger than Naomi and had a sense of responsibility toward her mother-in-law, she asked permission to go glean in the fields since it was harvest-time. Naomi accepted Ruth's offer and sent her off with a blessing.

The leading of God's Spirit is not explicitly mentioned, but clearly the hand of the Lord was upon Ruth, leading her to the place where she would find food for herself and Naomi.

DEVOTIONAL OUTLINE

1. Ruth's benefactor (Ruth 2:8-16). Right away the owner of the field is brought into the biblical account. As God would have it, the man, Boaz, was a relative of Naomi's husband. After greeting his crew, he spied Ruth nearby and asked his foreman about her. From that moment onward, Boaz showed unconditional love toward Ruth and set out not only to welcome her to glean in his field but also to offer special treatment while there.

Boaz told her to not even consider gleaning in another field. She would be safe among his workers. Not only that, but she would be given food and water in the field as the day wore on. Though he had not seen her before, he had heard of her and her kindness to Naomi and was duly impressed. Her reputation had preceded her.

Per the law of Moses, reapers were not to reap every stalk of the field. They were to leave some for the poor, who would be allowed to glean after them (cf. Lev. 23:22). Ruth was allowed to do this, but the reapers were also instructed to allow her to gather from the very sheaves themselves—something unheard of. She was indeed special in Boaz's eyes.

In all of this there emerges the picture of God's love being poured out on the needy—in this case to someone outside Israel. The Lord casts a loving eye upon us and provides for us in ways that are designed to attract us to His grace. All of this, of course, is intended to draw us to Him so that He may enter into a holy relationship with us. The lavish expressions of care extended to Ruth by Boaz dramatically depict the riches of Christ being bestowed upon those who cry out to Him.

2. Ruth's reward (Ruth 2:17-18). The near-term result of all this and her reward for the time being was a huge amount of barley, roughly two-thirds of a bushel in today's terms. She and her mother-in-law would not need to be concerned about what they would live on, for Ruth had been led by the grace of God to the place where He would bless them.

AGE-GROUP EMPHASES

Children: Guide children to see that the Lord knows their needs and will lead them and provide for them.

Youths: Lead them to understand that God has a plan and a purpose for His own and that they can trust His leading.

Adults: Lead them to see in Boaz's actions the beautiful picture of Christ wooing His bride-to-be.

—Darrell W. McKay

SCRIPTURE LESSON TEXT

RUTH 4:1 Then went Boaz up to the gate, and sat him down there: and, behold, the kinsman of whom Boaz spake came by; unto whom he said, Ho, such a one! turn aside, sit down here. And he turned aside, and sat down.

2 And he took ten men of the elders of the city, and said, Sit ye down here. And they sat down.

3 And he said unto the kinsman, Naomi, that is come again out of the country of Moab, selleth a parcel of land, which *was* our brother Elimelech's:

4 And I thought to advertise thee, saying, Buy *it* before the inhabitants, and before the elders of my people. If thou wilt redeem *it,* redeem *it:* but if thou wilt not redeem *it, then* tell me, that I may know: for *there is* none to redeem *it* beside thee; and I *am* after thee. And he said, I will redeem *it.*

5 Then said Boaz, What day thou buyest the field of the hand of Naomi, thou must buy *it* also of Ruth the Moabitess, the wife of the dead, to raise up the name of the dead upon his inheritance.

6 And the kinsman said, I cannot redeem *it* for myself, lest I mar mine own inheritance: redeem thou my right to thyself; for I cannot redeem *it.*

7 Now this *was the manner* in former time in Israel concerning redeeming and concerning changing, for to confirm all things; a man plucked off his shoe, and gave *it* to his neighbour: and this *was* a testimony in Israel.

8 Therefore the kinsman said unto Boaz, Buy *it* for thee. So he drew off his shoe.

9 And Boaz said unto the elders, and *unto* all the people, Ye *are* witnesses this day, that I have bought all that *was* Elimelech's, and all that *was* Chilion's and Mahlon's, of the hand of Naomi.

10 Moreover Ruth the Moabitess, the wife of Mahlon, have I purchased to be my wife, to raise up the name of the dead upon his inheritance, that the name of the dead be not cut off from among his brethren, and from the gate of his place: ye *are* witnesses this day.

NOTES

Ruth Marries Boaz

Lesson Text: Ruth 4:1-10

Related Scriptures: Ruth 3:1-18; 4:11-22;
Deuteronomy 25:7-10; Jeremiah 32:6-15

TIME: between 1130–1120 B.C.   PLACE: Bethlehem

GOLDEN TEXT—"If thou wilt redeem it, redeem it: but if thou wilt not redeem it, then tell me, that I may know: for there is none to redeem it beside thee; and I am after thee" (Ruth 4:4).

Introduction

The book of Acts describes a beautiful situation: "And the multitude of them that believed were of one heart and of one soul: neither said any of them that ought of the things which he possessed was his own; but they had all things common. . . . Neither was there any among them that lacked: for as many as were possessors of lands or houses sold them, and brought the prices of the things that were sold, and laid them down at the apostles' feet: and distribution was made unto every man according as he had need" (4:32, 34-35).

What a wonderful example of believers caring for one another! Some had more material goods than others, and some apparently were very poor. Those with plenty made certain that those with little had enough. What made this even better was that this was voluntary sharing and not something commanded by the leaders of the church. God put it in the hearts of His people to care for one another. It was a living demonstration of the love God's children should have for each other, as Boaz had for Ruth.

LESSON OUTLINE

I. BOAZ'S PROPOSITION—
Ruth 4:1-6

II. BOAZ'S ACQUISITION—
Ruth 4:7-10

Exposition: Verse by Verse

BOAZ'S PROPOSITION

RUTH 4:1 Then went Boaz up to the gate, and sat him down there: and, behold, the kinsman of whom Boaz spake came by; unto whom he said, Ho, such a one! turn aside, sit down here.

And he turned aside, and sat down.

2 And he took ten men of the elders of the city, and said, Sit ye down here. And they sat down.

3 And he said unto the kinsman, Naomi, that is come again out of the

country of Moab, selleth a parcel of land, which was our brother Elimelech's:

4 And I thought to advertise thee, saying, Buy it before the inhabitants, and before the elders of my people. If thou wilt redeem it, redeem it: but if thou wilt not redeem it, then tell me, that I may know: for there is none to redeem it beside thee; and I am after thee. And he said, I will redeem it.

5 Then said Boaz, What day thou buyest the field of the hand of Naomi, thou must buy it also of Ruth the Moabitess, the wife of the dead, to raise up the name of the dead upon his inheritance.

6 And the kinsman said, I cannot redeem it for myself, lest I mar mine own inheritance: redeem thou my right to thyself; for I cannot redeem it.

A meeting of the town council (Ruth 4:1-2). {Ruth 3 describes what happened between Boaz and Ruth that led to his pursuit of becoming her permanent protector and husband. Naomi had shown Ruth how to indicate to Boaz that she desired this relationship.}[Q1] Boaz was flattered that Ruth wanted this. His response was "Blessed be thou of the Lord, my daughter: for thou hast shewed more kindness in the latter end than at the beginning, inasmuch as thou followedst not young men, whether poor or rich" (vs. 10).

Ruth's appeal was for Boaz to become her kinsman-redeemer. Boaz informed Ruth that there was one kinsman more closely related to her than he was, and that person would have to be given the first opportunity to perform that duty (vss. 12-13). The very next morning, Boaz began the process of obtaining the right to become the kinsman-redeemer for Ruth. It was a legal transaction that required the witness of some of the elders of the city. Such legal matters were usually carried out in the gates of the city.

{Boaz went to the city gate of Bethlehem the next morning and waited for the other kinsman to appear. When he did, Boaz invited him to stop and sit down with him. He then gathered ten of the city's elders and asked them to sit down too.}[Q2] "This was now a man's world where a public decision was to be made on an important matter that profoundly affected the women who had brought it to this point" (Walvoord and Zuck, eds., *The Bible Knowledge Commentary,* Victor). The scene was set for the legal procedure.

Boaz had spent the night guarding his grain (Ruth 3:7, 14), so this legal process took him away from his normal duties. He was a man of his word, however, so he immediately did what he had promised Ruth (vs. 13). The matter before him was now urgent. Ruth had specifically requested that he become her redeemer: "I am Ruth thine handmaid: spread therefore thy skirt over thine handmaid; for thou art a near kinsman" (vs. 9). She referred to herself as his handmaid, revealing a completely submissive attitude toward him.

Earlier, Boaz had pronounced a blessing upon Ruth, mentioning that she had placed herself under the "wings" of God (2:12). This figure of speech indicated protection and shelter, just as the wings of a mother bird protect her young ones. In Ruth's request for Boaz to become her redeemer, she was asking him to take her, his maidservant, under his wing of protection and provision. It was a clear request that he understood immediately.

A redemption proposal (Ruth 4:3-4). Leviticus 25:23-25 explains what Boaz was trying to do: "The land shall not be sold for ever: for the land is mine; for ye are strangers and sojourners with me. And in all the land of your possession ye shall grant a redemption for the land. If thy brother be waxen poor, and hath sold away some of his possession, and if any of his kin come to redeem it, then shall he redeem that which his brother sold."

The piece of property in question once belonged to Elimelech. Naomi had become the owner of her husband's property and probably because of her poverty-stricken position was being forced to sell it. It evidently had not produced any kind of income for her, perhaps because an older woman would not be able to work the land by herself. It was the kind of society where men were dominant and women remained in submissive and less public roles. Owning a piece of property, therefore, had not helped Naomi with the financial needs she and Ruth had encountered. She apparently had no other options.

However, the land could be redeemed by a near kinsman, and that would keep the property in the family, as God intended. As a matter of fact, when property like this was sold outside the family, it reverted back to them in the Year of Jubilee, every fiftieth year (Lev. 25:8-16). This is what is meant by "The land shall not be sold for ever: for the land is mine" (vs. 23).

{Boaz explained the situation to this unnamed kinsman, saying that since he was a closer relative than Boaz, he had the first right to redeem the land.}Q3 Boaz made certain that this relative understood that a legal transaction was taking place. {He referred to the witnesses he had gathered for this occasion: "Buy it before the inhabitants, and before the elders of my people" (Ruth 4:4).}Q4

Jeremiah 32:6-15 explains a similar situation in Jeremiah's day, when he redeemed the land of his cousin. In that case too, everything was done in the presence of witnesses, giving finality to the transaction. Boaz was serious about this matter and handled it by the details of the law.

Upon hearing the proposition, the unnamed relative said that he would redeem the property. He apparently thought that it would be to his advantage to have it, perhaps for additional income for himself. Boaz was probably expecting this response, but he was ready with more information about the proposal.

The kinsman's inability to redeem (Ruth 4:5-6). It is somewhat unclear how Boaz managed to present the rest of the situation the way he did. He seemed to be saying the kinsman would be responsible to fulfill the levirate marriage law. This can be seen in the phrase "to raise up the name of the dead upon his inheritance."

Deuteronomy 25:5-6 explains, "If brethren dwell together, and one of them die, and have no child, the wife of the dead shall not marry without unto a stranger: her husband's brother shall go in unto her, and take her to him to wife, and perform the duty of an husband's brother unto her. And it shall be, that the firstborn which she beareth shall succeed in the name of his brother which is dead, that his name be not put out of Israel." In this way the family name did not die just because the husband did.

In order for Elimelech's name to continue with his sons both already dead, it would have to come through his daughter-in-law Ruth, who had been married to Mahlon. {Boaz therefore linked Ruth with Naomi and explained that if the kinsman redeemed the property from Naomi, he would also have to buy it from Ruth and take her as his wife in order to perpetuate Elimelech's name.}Q5 There is no explicit statement in Scripture linking levirate marriage to the laws of redemption, but it is possible that local tradition or law did specify this kind of agreement.

Boaz's approach in this entire matter might have caused the other kinsman to be temporarily confused about the situation. Whatever he was thinking made him decide that he could not afford to do that. Maybe he shied away from supporting both Naomi and Ruth, or maybe he was afraid that his inheritance would be lessened for his own children. What originally seemed to be a financial benefit to him now appeared to be a liability instead. So he refused to go ahead with the redemption.

In front of the witnesses Boaz had gathered, this kinsman relinquished his right to redeem the property. His response now was "I cannot redeem it for myself, lest I mar mine own inheritance: redeem thou my right to thyself; for I cannot redeem it" (Ruth 4:6). He not only claimed he could not do it but also told Boaz that he could proceed with redeeming it himself. This gave Boaz a clear opening for redeeming the property, since he was the next relative in line for doing so.

BOAZ'S ACQUISITION

7 Now this was the manner in former time in Israel concerning redeeming and concerning changing, for to confirm all things; a man plucked off his shoe, and gave it to his neighbour: and this was a testimony in Israel.

8 Therefore the kinsman said unto Boaz, Buy it for thee. So he drew off his shoe.

9 And Boaz said unto the elders, and unto all the people, Ye are witnesses this day, that I have bought all that was Elimelech's, and all that was Chilion's and Mahlon's, of the hand of Naomi.

10 Moreover Ruth the Moabitess, the wife of Mahlon, have I purchased to be my wife, to raise up the name of the dead upon his inheritance, that the name of the dead be not cut off from among his brethren, and from the gate of his place: ye are witnesses this day.

Sealing the agreement (Ruth 4:7-8). {When the nearer kinsman gave up his right to redeem Naomi's property, He took off a sandal and handed it to Boaz.}[Q6] "The removal of a sandal was part of a legal transaction in ancient Israel (Deut. 25:8-10). It would parallel

the modern custom of concluding a transaction by signing a document or handing over a set of keys. By handing over his shoe, the close relative was symbolically handing over his right to walk on the land that was being sold" (NKJV Study Bible, Thomas Nelson).

This custom apparently had been discontinued before the book of Ruth was written, because the author referred to it as "the manner in former time in Israel concerning redeeming and concerning changing, for to confirm all things" (Ruth 4:7). How long it had been since the practice had been observed is not stated, but the author was aware that readers might not have been familiar with it.

In the levirate law in Deuteronomy 25:5-10, there is also reference to the removal of a sandal. In this case, when the brother of a dead man was supposed to take the widow and have a child to perpetuate the name of the deceased, the one who refused to do so had his sandal removed by the widow, who then spit in his face. This was the humiliation of the man who refused to be responsible for the continuation of his brother's name. It was then said of him, "And his name shall be called in Israel, The house of him that hath his shoe loosed" (vs 10). Although the situation in Ruth 4 is not identical to the levirate law of Deuteronomy 25, a legal transaction took place.

The action of removing a sandal was viewed by the witnesses as confirmation and would be remembered by them if any question arose in the future. {When this near kinsman removed his sandal, he symbolically transferred the right of ownership to Boaz, who could now freely walk on his new property and claim it as his own.}[Q7] It was no longer the right of the other kinsman to walk on that property in that way. He had relinquished that right.

This view of ownership is seen in what God said to Joshua when Israel entered Canaan: "Every place that the sole of your foot shall tread upon, that have I given unto you, as I said unto Moses" (Josh. 1:3). In Psalm 60, when God was speaking of His ownership of certain nations, He stated, "Over Edom will I cast out my shoe" (vs. 8).

The transaction that took place in the gate of Bethlehem that day gave Boaz the freedom to pursue his plans of becoming Ruth's protector, provider, and husband.

Witnessing the transaction (Ruth 4:9-10). Boaz wanted to be certain that the elders witnessing this event understood what they were seeing. He began and ended this declaration with exactly the same words: "Ye are witnesses this day." He spelled out precisely the property involved—namely, that which had once belonged to Elimelech, Chilion, and Mahlon—and that it was Naomi from whom he was acquiring it. These details would make absolutely certain that any future questions were covered.

The witness of the transaction by ten elders was a safeguard for Boaz. It was most unlikely that all ten of them would forget. {There were two events for them to remember from that day. First was the transaction of ownership of the property. Second was the acquisition of Ruth as Boaz's wife.}Q8 It is in verse 10 that we learn for the first time which man Ruth had been married to, namely, Mahlon. When Boaz spoke of not letting the name of the dead be cut off, he referred primarily to Mahlon but indirectly also to Mahlon's father, Elimelech.

It was significant in that culture that a family name not be broken off. That is probably one of the reasons we read so many genealogies in the Bible. The primary purpose of the levirate law was the perpetuation of a family name. {Boaz would be continuing the name of those in his family who had died. In reiterating this to the witnessing elders, he confirmed the importance of the actions he had taken that day and the importance of their witness.}Q9

This was a joyful occasion, as seen in the responses that followed Boaz's actions. {The people gathered in the gate of Bethlehem, along with the witnessing elders, all rejoiced together. All of them were eager to acclaim that they had witnessed the transactions that day.}Q10

"The writer never theologizes on the story he was telling. Yet he may have wanted to suggest that if a mere human being could love an outcast, redeem her, and bring her into fellowship with himself, God could love all the outcasts of the world, redeem them, and bring them into fellowship with Himself" (Gaebelein, ed., *The Expositor's Bible Commentary,* Zondervan).

—Keith E. Eggert

QUESTIONS

1. What happened in Ruth 3 that set up the events of chapter 4?
2. Why did Boaz go to the city gate, and what did he do after he arrived there?
3. What was Boaz's initial proposal to the other kinsman?
4. How did Boaz make certain the other kinsman understood that this was a legal transaction?
5. What additional fact did Boaz explain that caused the kinsman to rescind his offer to redeem Naomi's land?
6. How was the transaction sealed?
7. What did this action mean?
8. What were the two transactions that took place that day?
9. How did Boaz reiterate to the witnessing elders that what they had seen was important?
10. What was the response of those witnessing this event?

—Keith E. Eggert

Preparing to Teach the Lesson

This week we conclude the book of Ruth. Our lesson text challenges us to obey God from the heart and gives us a clear picture of the redeeming work of Christ.

TODAY'S AIM

Facts: to learn how Boaz took over the task of the family redeemer when the first man would not do the job.

Principle: to show that God requires obedience from the heart, not merely from a sense of duty.

Application: to teach that sometimes what is required of us may go beyond what seems possible, but that we should step forward in obedience and do it.

INTRODUCING THE LESSON

Life is full of rules, duties, and obligations. But we should not assume that we have met God's standard when we conform to the bare minimum of these requirements. Certain situations require much more of us, and the difficulty of those situations does not excuse us from doing what is right.

Think of the young husband who finds out a week after getting married that his wife has cancer. Or think of the person who buys a home only to find out that he has been cheated and the home does not have the value he thought it did. Or think of Joseph in the Bible, who found out that his wife-to-be was pregnant. There are, or were, some tough choices to make in each of these situations. As Christians we are called to obey God's will even when it seems like more than we can handle.

In our lesson this week, we learn about Boaz, who not only redeemed Naomi's property but also married Ruth.

DEVELOPING THE LESSON

1. A roadblock removed (Ruth 4:1-6). Read Leviticus 25:23-28 so that students understand the Old Testament concept of a kinsman-redeemer and how it relates to this passage.

Boaz very much wanted to take on the role of kinsman-redeemer for Ruth, but there was a relative who had a prior claim by virtue of closer kinship. Boaz therefore took his seat at the town gate and in the presence of witnesses told the nearer relative that he had the first option to buy the land that Elimelech (Naomi's husband) had left behind. It was the family redeemer's task to buy the land and keep it in the family. Depending on how broadly one applies Deuteronomy 25:5-10, it may have also been his task to marry the widow of his deceased relative to continue the family name. The nearer relative first agreed to purchase the property but then changed his mind when he learned it also involved taking Ruth.

Help the class understand that these laws were designed to preserve the family and the inheritance of property for future generations. They also point out the importance of family roles in ancient Israelite society. It is hard for us in an individualistic society to understand some of these stipulations, but they made perfect sense to the Israelites and had an important purpose.

Ask the students what normally happens today to a person's property and home when he dies. How is this different from the practice of ancient Israel? Notice also that the society of Ruth's time was hierarchical in nature and that the elders of the city saw to it that these Levitical laws were enforced. Focus your class members' attention on the fact that these laws were there to protect the family and the property. God's laws always have a good purpose.

2. A privilege transferred (Ruth 4:7-8). When we look at the Old Testament laws, some may come across as strange and meaningless. But as we have seen, the laws in view here protected the impoverished and the name of those who died without an heir.

Notice that all the transactions were done publicly in front of witnesses. After publicly declining Boaz's offer, the nearer relative took off his sandal and gave it to Boaz. This was a symbol that he was giving up his right as kinsman-redeemer.

The way was now clear for Boaz to buy the land and marry Ruth—both of which he wanted to do. Emphasize that Boaz was willing to do out of love and sacrifice what the other man was unwilling to do. Boaz cared about Ruth and Naomi and what would happen to them. Do we obey God out of mere duty or love?

3. A commitment made public (Ruth 4:9-10). Boaz made a public declaration that he had bought the land that belonged to Elimelech and that he was taking Ruth to be his wife. Now the property could stay in the family, and Ruth could carry on the family name through Boaz. Boaz was the redeemer in this situation. He had kept the family from breaking up and the property from going into strange hands. He provided Naomi's family with the stability that had previously been taken away.

Your students will no doubt recognize that the Old Testament concept of kinsman-redeemer points to Jesus. What Boaz did for Ruth foreshadowed what Christ did for us. Like Boaz, Jesus paid the price that no one else would or could pay, giving even His own life to redeem us.

ILLUSTRATING THE LESSON

Both Boaz and Ruth cared for others. They set an example for us to follow, for they illustrate God's great care for His own.

CARING FOR ONE ANOTHER

GOD CARES FOR ALL

RUTH CARED FOR NAOMI   BOAZ CARED FOR RUTH

CONCLUDING THE LESSON

There are some things in the biblical account of Boaz and Ruth that we cannot ignore. First we need to recognize the love and kindness that Ruth showed to Naomi in providing for her after the loss of Naomi's husband. Then we must note the kindness that Boaz showed to Ruth by paying special attention to her and even doing the duty of the family redeemer when the closer relative declined the privilege and responsibility.

We also need to see how these people followed God's laws, trusting Him to bring about a happy ending to a story of tragedy and hardship. In the lives of Boaz and Ruth we see the working of the great God of Israel, who showed grace to them both.

Before closing the session, remind the class that God blessed this couple by putting them in the lineage that would bring forth the Messiah, our Lord Jesus (Ruth 4:21-22).

ANTICIPATING THE NEXT LESSON

Next week we will study Hannah's prayer after God blesses her with Samuel as her son.

—*A. Koshy Muthalaly*

PRACTICAL POINTS

1. We should do our work for God in a way that is proper and timely (Ruth 4:1-2).
2. Honesty should be the rule of every Christian presentation (Ruth 4:3-4; cf. Eph. 4:25).
3. Wise is the person who listens carefully before speaking (Ruth 4:5-6; cf. Prov. 18:13).
4. Caring for others is seldom without cost to oneself (Ruth 4:6; cf. II Cor. 8:9; Phil. 2:3-8).
5. The wise person gathers witnesses to all important public decisions (Ruth 4:7-10; cf. Matt. 18:16).
6. The Christian should do his godly duty without reservation (Ruth 4:9-10; cf. Col. 3:23).

—Don Kakavecos

RESEARCH AND DISCUSSION

1. Why did Boaz need to call the elders of the city as witnesses to his dealings with Naomi's near kinsman? What does this suggest about the way Christians should transact their business matters today (cf. Titus 2:6-8; I Pet. 2:13-14)?
2. What kinds of things might you need to sacrifice in order to demonstrate true Christian care for others?
3. How does Jesus serve as our perfect example of caring for others (cf. Mark 10:42-45; II Cor. 5:21; 8:9; Phil. 2:1-11)?
4. In what ways does Boaz reflect our Kinsman-Redeemer, Jesus Christ? How are they different (cf. Rom. 5:6-10; I Pet. 1:18-19)?

—Don Kakavecos

ILLUSTRATED HIGH POINTS

Redeem it (Ruth 4:4, 6)

Larry seldom came to church, but his wife was very faithful. She and others prayed every week that church relationships might be established that would bless Larry and lead him to the Lord.

An answer came quickly. Larry's wife announced through tears that her husband had prostate cancer and would soon face an operation and several months of recovery.

The congregation immediately sprang to action. Some pledged fifty or one hundred dollars a month. One family committed to pay for utilities and another for groceries. Still another promised to mow their lawn. All his bills were paid on time.

Larry has since rejoined the congregation. Our actions have the power to visibly demonstrate Christ's own redeeming love for a person.

I have bought (vs. 9)

Shortly after entering prison, Ben had his first visitor—one of the men who had been on the jury during the trial. Ben thought the man was interested in a new trial for him, but he soon discovered his visitor was there simply as a friend.

For seven years the visits continued. Finally, Ben came to Christ through the quiet, persistent witness of this believer.

In the summer of 2003, there was a shocking announcement: the faithful visitor was dying of cancer. In a telephone call, Ben thanked his friend for all the time and prayers given on his behalf.

Ben's change of life was for real. He was released three years earlier than expected because of good behavior. Like Boaz, Ben's visitor went out of his way to put another person's needs before his own. The result was the purchase of a life by Christ's blood. May all of us point to Jesus in a similar way.

—Ted Simonson

Golden Text Illuminated

"If thou wilt redeem it, redeem it: but if thou wilt not redeem it, then tell me, that I may know: for there is none to redeem it beside thee; and I am after thee" (Ruth 4:4).

When Christians hear the word "redeem," they understandably attach deeply spiritual associations to the idea. After all, Jesus Christ is our Redeemer; He paid the redemption price with His own blood to deliver us from the grip of sin and death. We sing glorious hymns extolling the wonder of being redeemed.

No one would likely be moved to sing any hymns about the idea of redemption as it is used in our text here. Boaz was talking about a property transfer. Naomi was selling a parcel of land. To keep the property from falling out of the family's possession, a close relative had the right to redeem it, to buy it back if he could.

Boaz explained what was at stake and then said to Naomi's relative, "If thou wilt redeem it, redeem it." The parcel of land was his if he wanted it and could put up the funds. If he did not want to take it or could not, he needed to say so right away, for Boaz was next in line as a relative to Naomi (and to her deceased husband, Elimelech). When Boaz said, "There is none to redeem it beside thee," he meant that there was no one who could do so aside from the two of them.

This unnamed relative was apparently the only preceding living family member who could exercise the right of redemption, but Boaz was "after" him. Boaz was willing to do it, but he had to give the closer relation the opportunity first. Only if that man waived his right (and responsibility) to do so would Boaz proceed.

As outlined above, this all seems incredibly dry and mundane. But readers of the book of Ruth know there is a little more to it than this. What Boaz really wanted to do was redeem Ruth—that is, exercise his right as a relative of her deceased husband to provide security for her by marrying her. It was what Ruth had requested at Naomi's behest (Ruth 3:1-9), and Boaz was delighted to oblige (vss. 10-11).

Boaz had already shown great admiration for Ruth's virtuous character and sacrificial devotion to Naomi. She was the caliber of woman he would be pleased to have as his wife, even though she was evidently younger. There was only one hitch. Another relative was more closely related and thus would have prior claim to be Ruth's redeemer.

When Boaz met with this relative, however, he initially presented only the property aspect of the redemption. He did not mention marriage to Ruth at the outset. Why? To him, marrying Ruth was the compelling reason for taking on the redemption role; the land was secondary. But he apparently discerned that to the other relative, the property acquisition would be the paramount attraction. Marriage to Ruth, as it turned out, was not desirable to this man.

Perhaps we can see in this a further demonstration of Boaz's integrity. Rather than immediately dampen the relative's interest, he made the deal as attractive as possible, potentially to his own loss. It was only when the man had full knowledge of the benefits to him that Boaz laid out the further obligation. Happily for him (and for Ruth, no doubt), the man wanted no part of that.

—*Kenneth A. Sponsler*

Heart of the Lesson

The events described in the book of Ruth took place "in the days when the judges ruled" (Ruth 1:1). This was a period of great apostasy in Israel, when "every man did that which was right in his own eyes" (Judg. 21:25). It is important to keep this in mind as we study the book of Ruth, for this little book is a ray of sunshine in a dark period of history. Boaz especially stands out as a godly man in an ungodly age.

Boaz showed compassion for the poor and needy by opening his fields to gleaners, as the Law instructed. In particular, he demonstrated loving concern for the young widow Ruth, who had left her homeland to accompany Naomi back to Bethlehem. He had even allowed her to work alongside his workers in the field, and he had fed her as he had his hired men.

Boaz's concern for Ruth and his obedience to God's law are seen in one final incident in Ruth 4. The Law provided for the inheritance of a man who died without a child. A near relative was to take his widow and raise up a son to carry on the dead man's name and inheritance (Deut. 25:5-6). As a relative, Boaz could perform this duty. Yet, as Ruth 3 shows, this was not a burden for Boaz. He was more than willing to take Ruth as his wife and to redeem her dead husband's property, and he made that clear when she presented herself to him at the threshing floor.

One obstacle stood in the way, however; there was another man who was nearer of kin. He would have to relinquish his right to Ruth in order for Boaz to marry her.

1. Boaz's offer (Ruth 4:1-6). Legal proceedings took place at the city gate, and that was where Boaz met the nearer relative and gathered witnesses.

Boaz outlined the situation, and the man was inclined to redeem the property until he learned this would also mean marrying Ruth. He then deferred to Boaz, surrendering his right to redemption.

2. Boaz's action (Ruth 4:7-8). The simple act of removing one's sandal and giving it to another person symbolized the transference of the right of redemption. The kinsman removed his sandal and offered it to Boaz. By receiving it in the presence of witnesses, Boaz was accepting the responsibility to redeem the deceased's property and marry Ruth. Boaz risked losing Ruth by following this procedure, but he was willing to do so in order to follow the Law completely.

3. Boaz's witnesses (Ruth 4:9-10). Boaz then reaffirmed verbally that he was purchasing all the land that belonged to Elimelech and his sons and that he was marrying Ruth and thus raising "up the name of the dead." He reminded those present that they were witnesses to this legally binding act.

Like most legal proceedings, those described in this passage are not very exciting. Yet they remind us that even in the midst of ungodliness and disorder, people who are willing to follow the Lord's way and show compassion and love for others ultimately will be honored by the Lord Himself. The love and concern of Boaz brought lasting joy to Ruth, Naomi, and himself and eventually brought to the throne of Israel the great King David (Ruth 4:17).

Narratives like Ruth's reveal that the genealogy of Messiah is filled with compassion for outsiders that foreshadowed the reconciliation of the world to God.

—*Jarl K. Waggoner*

World Missions

In this week's lesson text the reader is introduced to the biblical concept of the kinsman-redeemer. As the nearest blood relative, he had the power, ability, and freedom to redeem his kinsman from difficulty and danger (cf. Lev. 25:23-28). As the kinsman-redeemer, Boaz was able to redeem the property of Naomi only after a nearer redeemer waived his right of redemption (cf. Ruth 4:6).

In evangelical Christianity, the principle of redemption is intimately related to the ongoing Christian effort of spreading the gospel. In light of this relationship, the remainder of this article will seek to take the above-mentioned concepts of power, ability, and freedom, in addition to the importance of willingness, and relate them to the missionary who has been called by God to take the message of the gospel to people who are spiritually lost in their sins and in need of a Redeemer.

First, a missionary must be filled with spiritual power. This infusion of power cannot come from within the missionary himself. It comes from the Holy Spirit. Acts 1:8 states, "Ye shall receive power, after that the Holy Ghost is come upon you." The only way a missionary can gain or obtain the power necessary to fulfill his mission is to submit to the Holy Spirit.

Lost humanity exists in a state of spiritual death, a relational separation from the Lord that is maintained by the powerful control of Satan and his demonic cohorts. The only power that can infiltrate and give spiritual life to those who are spiritually dead is that of God's Holy Spirit.

Second, a missionary must possess the spiritual ability to perform his evangelistic calling. This unique ability is the result of the presence of the Holy Spirit, who sends forth the missionary with spiritual gifts and talents to engage the demonic enemies of sin and Satan (cf. Acts 13:1-13).

Ephesians 6:11 states, "Put on the whole armour of God, that ye may be able to stand against the wiles of the devil." This verse teaches us that Satan has cunning, crafty, and deceitful plans to enslave people in their sin. The missionary must counteract his demonic wiles through the use of the spiritual giftedness and abilities received from the Holy Spirit. The primary weapons the Spirit gives us are "truth," "righteousness," "the preparation of the gospel of peace," "faith," "salvation," "the word of God," and prayer (vss. 14-18). These are available to every believer, and thus God has given every believer the ability to be a minister of the gospel.

Third, the missionary must be free to exercise his spiritual gifts in the power of the Holy Spirit. This freedom has a spiritual facet—that is, the missionary must be a person who has placed his faith and trust in the Lord Jesus Christ for the forgiveness of sins. This freedom also has a financial facet—that is, the missionary must be sufficiently supported so that he is not burdened by monetary concerns.

Finally, the missionary must be willing to conduct his ministry of spreading the gospel to people in need of a Saviour. The missionary must not conduct his ministry under compulsion or guilt. He must not be a missionary simply to fulfill the wishes and demands of others. Rather, the missionary must freely desire to spread the gospel because of his great love for people and for the One who calls and sends him.

—*Thomas R. Chmura*

The Jewish Aspect

Three observations should be noted concerning Ruth 4:5. First, levirate marriage was a secondary issue. While the kinsman-redeemer was not obligated to redeem the property, if he chose to do so, he would also be obligated to perform a levirate marriage.

Second, when Elimelech died, the property went to Mahlon, and when Mahlon died, the property then included the widow Ruth. She was now part of the redemption responsibility, and the property would go to any son born to her to perpetuate the family line.

Third, this was not strictly the levirate law as spelled out in Deuteronomy 25:5-10. This text deals with the extension of the levirate law to cover a matter of clan responsibility, not just a matter of immediate family in the strict sense.

With that in mind, the sequence of events in the book of Ruth is as follows. First, Naomi was about to sell her inherited land due to her poverty. Second, it was necessary for a kinsman-redeemer to redeem the land in order to keep it in the family. By buying back the land, the redeemer "would not come into possession of the land himself, but would hold it in trust for his son by Ruth, who would inherit the name and patrimony of Mahlon" (Pfeiffer and Harrison, eds., *Wycliffe Bible Commentary,* Moody). While Naomi had prior claim on the redeemer, she surrendered it to Ruth. Third, the nearest kinsman wanted the land but not Ruth, since he would not gain by the transaction. Boaz wanted Ruth, not the land, but he had the money and willingness to redeem both.

The genealogy of Boaz (Ruth 4:18-22) began with Pharez and not with Judah. This kept the genealogy to ten generations. The tribal identity with Judah was obvious, but the genealogy identified it clearly as from the line of Pharez.

Rabbinic tradition teaches that there were two women from whom the royal seat of Judah was built and from whom descended King David, King Solomon, and King Messiah: Tamar (Gen. 38) and Ruth. Both, it is said, acted properly to do good to the dead.

Another rabbinic tradition teaches that the monarchy came through women of pagan origins so that the kings would have an element of cruelty from the mother's side in addition to compassion from the father's side, thus equipping them to exact revenge on Israel's enemies while treating Israel with compassion.

Still another rabbinic tradition notes three episodes leading to the emergence of David that involved wondrous ways dependent on split-second timing. Had the moment passed, David would never have been born. Lot's daughters sought to conceive by their father because they thought the entire world had been destroyed (Gen. 19:30-38). Had they waited, they would have discovered that was not the case, but from the older daughter's conception ultimately came the Moabites, the people of Ruth. Judah was about to pass Tamar by and continue on his way when an angel impelled him toward her. As a result, Pharez was born. And Boaz was about to die when he wed Ruth. According to the rabbis, these traditions teach that as soon as the time is ripe, the Messiah will not delay in coming.

The rabbinic tradition is that Ruth lived to see the reign of Solomon, though there is no biblical evidence. Nevertheless, the genealogical link connects the son of Judah, Pharez, with King David. This serves as a bridge between the books of Joshua and Judges and the books of I and II Samuel.

—Arnold G. Fruchtenbaum

Guiding the Superintendent

God's care for His own is wonderfully pictured for us in the actions of Boaz toward Ruth and her mother-in-law, Naomi, in this lesson.

DEVOTIONAL OUTLINE

1. Assembling a quorum (Ruth 4:1-2). Boaz was a relative of Naomi's husband's family and had the right of redemption regarding family property. The way to fulfill that right was to assemble, in essence, a court of witnesses to make the transaction legal in the eyes of the public. The only complication in the process was the fact there was one other relative even closer to Naomi, who thus had the first right to redeem—or to refuse to do so.

To settle the issue, Boaz went to the place where business and legal proceedings were handled, the gate of the city—the public square, if you will. When he saw the other kinsman come by, Boaz asked him to sit down for the transacting of business. Then Boaz asked ten of the elders of the city to also pause to hear the case Boaz wanted settled. There was no requirement in the Law for ten men to be seated, but evidently ten was sufficient to make any deal legal and binding.

2. Presenting the question (Ruth 4:3-8). With all in place to hear the reason for holding court, Boaz explained that the property that once belonged to Naomi's husband was for sale. He gave the closer kinsman the opportunity to make the purchase. At first it sounded like a great idea, and the man was agreeable since it meant expanding his property. When the rest of the story was told, however—that he would have to marry Ruth and raise up children who would in turn inherit the land one day—the situation changed, and he refused.

Had he followed through with the redemption, he would have had the added expense of supporting Ruth as his wife and raising any children of the union. In addition, he would lose the purchased land to any son born to him and Ruth. The inheritance he had for his own children could be in jeopardy too, so the deal was much less attractive than he first thought. What sounded like a good thing was not, and thus he refused. Before witnesses he told Boaz he could make the purchase if he wanted.

In today's world, when property is purchased, there is a mountain of legal paperwork to be signed. But in that day and culture, the deal was sealed before witnesses by the symbolic handing over of a shoe. Compare this with Psalm 60:8 when the Lord said His coming reign would include Edom: "Over Edom will I cast out my shoe."

3. Closing the case (Ruth 4:9-10). Boaz had fallen in love with a poor outsider to Israel and decided to make her his own. He did what he needed to do, making it legal by having witnesses to the transaction. What a wonderful picture of Christ loving us and then setting out to pay the redemption price in order to acquire a bride (cf. John 3:29; II Cor. 11:2; Rev. 21:9)! O how He cares for us!

AGE-GROUP EMPHASES

Children: Guide children to know that Jesus cares for them very much. He paid the extreme price for them on the cross.

Youths: Help the teens see that things worth having are worth following the rules to get. God will not bless those who go after what they want in ways that are wrong.

Adults: Lead the adults to think further regarding the similarities between Boaz and Christ and between Ruth and themselves. They could make a list of comparisons.

—*Darrell W. McKay*

SCRIPTURE LESSON TEXT

I SAM. 1:20 Wherefore it came to pass, when the time was come about after Hannah had conceived, that she bare a son, and called his name Samuel, *saying,* Because I have asked him of the LORD.

26 And she said, Oh my lord, *as* thy soul liveth, my lord, I *am* the woman that stood by thee here, praying unto the LORD.

27 For this child I prayed; and the LORD hath given me my petition which I asked of him:

28 Therefore also I have lent him to the LORD; as long as he liveth he shall be lent to the LORD. And he worshipped the LORD there.

2:1 And Hannah prayed, and said, My heart rejoiceth in the LORD, mine horn is exalted in the LORD: my mouth is enlarged over mine enemies; because I rejoice in thy salvation.

2 *There is* none holy as the LORD: for *there is* none beside thee: neither *is there* any rock like our God.

3 Talk no more so exceeding proudly; let *not* arrogancy come out of your mouth: for the LORD *is* a God of knowledge, and by him actions are weighed.

4 The bows of the mighty men *are* broken, and they that stumbled are girded with strength.

5 *They that were* full have hired out themselves for bread; and *they that were* hungry ceased: so that the barren hath born seven; and she that hath many children is waxed feeble.

6 The LORD killeth, and maketh alive: he bringeth down to the grave, and bringeth up.

7 The LORD maketh poor, and maketh rich: he bringeth low, and lifteth up.

8 He raiseth up the poor out of the dust, *and* lifteth up the beggar from the dunghill, to set *them* among princes, and to make them inherit the throne of glory: for the pillars of the earth *are* the LORD'S, and he hath set the world upon them.

9 He will keep the feet of his saints, and the wicked shall be silent in darkness; for by strength shall no man prevail.

10 The adversaries of the LORD shall be broken to pieces; out of heaven shall he thunder upon them: the LORD shall judge the ends of the earth; and he shall give strength unto his king, and exalt the horn of his anointed.

NOTES

Hannah Commits Her Son to God

Lesson Text: I Samuel 1:20, 26-28; 2:1-10

Related Scriptures: I Samuel 1:1-19, 21-25; 2:18-21;
Psalm 113:1-9; Luke 1:46-55, 67-80

TIMES: about 1105 B.C.; 1102 B.C.

PLACES: Ramah; Shiloh

GOLDEN TEXT—"There is none holy as the Lord: for there is none beside thee: neither is there any rock like our God" (I Samuel 2:2).

Introduction

Psalm 37:4 reads, "Delight thyself also in the Lord; and he shall give thee the desires of thine heart." A good example of this promise is the story of Hannah and her son Samuel. Often, God's people are so lax in claiming this promise, when the truth of this verse is so simple.

The American Heritage Dictionary defines "delight" as a great pleasure and joy or "something that gives great pleasure or enjoyment." Should it not be so that the Lord is our greatest source of pleasure and joy?

We must admit that while the expectation in Psalm 37:4 sounds simple, the difficulty of obeying it comes from our living in a world of temptations.

LESSON OUTLINE

I. HANNAH'S ANSWERED PRAYER—I Sam. 1:20, 26-28

II. HANNAH'S SONG OF JOY: NONE HOLY AS THE LORD—I Sam. 2:1-5

III. HANNAH'S SONG: GOD THUNDERS FROM HEAVEN—I Sam. 2:6-10

Exposition: Verse by Verse

HANNAH'S ANSWERED PRAYER

I SAM. 1:20 Wherefore it came to pass, when the time was come about after Hannah had conceived, that she bare a son, and called his name Samuel, saying, Because I have asked him of the LORD.

26 And she said, Oh my lord, as thy soul liveth, my lord, I am the woman that stood by thee here, praying unto the LORD.

27 For this child I prayed; and the LORD hath given me my petition which I asked of him:

28 Therefore also I have lent him to the LORD; as long as he liveth he shall be lent to the LORD. And he worshipped the LORD there.

Her son (I Sam. 1:20, 26). Elkanah's two wives were Hannah and Peninnah. Peninnah had children, but Hannah remained barren. Since {it was the desire of Jewish women to have at least one son (perhaps hoping he might be the Messiah),}[Q1] this was very painful for Hannah. Her pain was magnified by Peninnah's heartless reminders of her condition (vs. 6). Peninnah especially enjoyed making her cruel remarks during the annual festivals in Shiloh where the Lord's tabernacle was kept.

During one especially sorrowful time in Shiloh, Hannah wept and prayed so fervently that Eli the priest accused her of being drunk. Upon assuring him that she had not been drinking, Hannah explained that she was simply pouring out her anguished soul to God. Eli then blessed her, asking that God would grant her request (I Sam. 1:13-17). When Hannah left Eli's presence, she was no longer despondent (vs. 18), giving evidence of her faith in the God to whom she had been praying so fervently.

Sometime later Hannah conceived and gave birth to a son she named Samuel. The name Samuel in Hebrew sounds like "heard by God." The baby's name itself would testify that God hears and answers prayer.

After Samuel was weaned, Hannah took him to Shiloh and presented him to Eli.

Her response (I Sam. 1:27-28). {In I Samuel 1:11 we read that Hannah had vowed to the Lord, "O Lord of hosts, if thou wilt indeed look on the affliction of thine handmaid, and remember me, and not forget thine handmaid, but wilt give unto thine handmaid a man child, then I will give him unto the Lord all the days of his life, and there shall no razor come upon his head." This was a promise to God that she would give the son she received back to Him for a life of divine service.

When Hannah reappeared before Eli,}[Q2] she first reminded him of who she was and then presented Samuel as the answer to her prayers. Eli probably remembered that he had at first considered her to be drunk. In his position, Eli apparently had seen others in that condition. We are specifically told that his own sons were very corrupt. They cheated worshipers out of the best parts of their sacrifices (I Sam. 2:12-17) and even went so far as to be immoral with the women who came to worship (vs. 22).

In Eli's culture Hannah was a shining example of a truly godly woman. One of her greatest acts of godliness was taking place as she brought Samuel to Eli and consecrated him to serve the Lord the rest of his life. The word "lent" is unusual in this context, but its Hebrew root is the same that is found in "petition" (vss. 17 and 28) and "asked" (vs. 20), suggesting a word play. The gift given to her by God is given back to Him.

HANNAH'S SONG OF JOY: NONE HOLY AS THE LORD

2:1 And Hannah prayed, and said, My heart rejoiceth in the LORD, mine horn is exalted in the LORD: my mouth is enlarged over mine enemies; because I rejoice in thy salvation.

2 There is none holy as the LORD: for there is none beside thee: neither is there any rock like our God.

3 Talk no more so exceeding proudly; let not arrogancy come out of your mouth: for the LORD is a God of knowledge, and by him actions are weighed.

4 The bows of the mighty men are broken, and they that stumbled are girded with strength.

5 They that were full have hired

out themselves for bread; and they that were hungry ceased: so that the barren hath born seven; and she that hath many children is waxed feeble.

God's salvation (I Sam. 2:1-2). The heart attitude of Hannah is indeed amazing. God had finally given her a son, the greatest desire she had ever known; now she was giving him back to God, leaving him with the priest and knowing he would no longer live in her home. Instead of mourning and longing for things to be different, Hannah humbled her heart before God in worship.

Hannah's prayer is a remarkable expression of joy in the Lord. The song has strong verbal and conceptual connections to David's song near the end of II Samuel (22:2-51) and to Mary's song when she learned she was to give birth to the Messiah in Luke 1:46-55. Hannah began her prayer with an expression of rejoicing in the Lord. {She then acknowledged that God had exalted her to such a degree that she could smile at her enemies. A "horn" was a symbol of strength.}Q3 {God had provided salvation from the curse of barrenness and the accompanying shame heaped upon her by others, including Peninnah.}Q4

No longer was Hannah an embarrassment to her husband for not giving him a male heir. No longer could others mock and belittle her. No longer would she suffer the depression she had known. In this glorious provision, Hannah saw the working of the holy God. She celebrated God's unique holiness—there is none like Him. In referring to Him as a rock, she used a metaphor that speaks of His being strength for His own, a place of refuge for those in need, and a deliverer from trouble.

God's knowledge (I Sam. 2:3-4). Hannah's words now sound like she had experienced so much grief from others during her barren condition that {she felt compelled to warn them about brash talking.}Q5 After all, those who had belittled her now had to face the fact that they were wrong. In their pride they had ignored the fact that God can do whatever He wants and can, therefore, reverse any situation, as He had done for her.

Pride and arrogance should never come from the mouth of humans, for God is the God of knowledge and His knowledge is far superior to that of all humanity. Hannah knew that she did not need to get even with those who had persecuted her. God weighs what people do and say against His children, and He Himself determines what needs to be done to defend them.

Beginning in I Samuel 2:4, seven contrasts are listed in Hannah's prayer (or song, as many prefer to call it). This contrast is between those who are mighty and those who are weak. Reference to bows indicates weaponry used by the strong against the weak. In some cases the weapons might be words instead of physical weapons. Such was the case for Hannah, but God had broken the strength of her enemies' belittling words and given them nothing more to say against her.

At the same time, God had clothed her with new strength. She walked with her head held up and rejoiced in the Lord who had provided her salvation.

God's justice (I Sam. 2:5). Two more contrasts are mentioned in this verse. The first is between the full and the hungry, and the second is between the barren and the fertile. {As in each of the other contrasts, Hannah reflected on the fact that God can completely change any circumstance He wishes at any time.}Q6

Here is an example of how fleeting riches can be and why we should not place our trust in possessions. The one who once was full was at one time wealthy enough to never worry about food. When God removes the wealth, however, that person must work for wages in order to buy what is needed. On the other hand, when God chooses to bless someone who is poor, that person who once regularly suffered hunger now has plenty. Hannah's point was that God can easily bring about such a change whenever He determines it.

She then made a much more personal application of the principle by referring to one who was barren. After Samuel's birth Hannah eventually gave birth to five more children (vs. 21). Her mention of seven children in verse 5 is reference to the perfection this number stood for. Having Samuel made her feel complete and fulfilled. She felt strong and blessed, as opposed to others who may have given birth to many but lacked the same sense of God's blessing upon them.

HANNAH'S SONG: GOD THUNDERS FROM HEAVEN

6 The Lord killeth, and maketh alive: he bringeth down to the grave, and bringeth up.

7 The Lord maketh poor, and maketh rich: he bringeth low, and lifteth up.

8 He raiseth up the poor out of the dust, and lifteth up the beggar from the dunghill, to set them among princes, and to make them inherit the throne of glory: for the pillars of the earth are the Lord's, and he hath set the world upon them.

9 He will keep the feet of his saints, and the wicked shall be silent in darkness; for by strength shall no man prevail.

10 The adversaries of the Lord shall be broken to pieces; out of heaven shall he thunder upon them: the Lord shall judge the ends of the earth; and he shall give strength unto his king, and exalt the horn of his anointed.

God's control (I Sam. 2:6-7). It probably was not a conscious change of thought for Hannah at this point in her prayer, but she did seem to begin to reflect more seriously now than before. Her rejoicing turned to serious contemplation of exactly how God sovereignly oversees the situations people face. There is a sense in which she moved away from being very personal and began to think more generally.

{Hannah recognized that all life is in the hand of God.}[Q7] {He alone has the power and authority to give and take life (I Sam. 2:6). His power is so great that He can even resurrect those who are dead.}[Q8] The second statement of this verse is nearly synonymous with the first part but serves to heighten or intensify the Lord's sovereignty in commanding life and death.

God also has control over the status in life each person experiences, something Hannah had already mentioned in I Samuel 2:5. While people may think their success is due solely to their own ingenuity and hard work, it is really the blessing of God that makes a person rich (cf. Prov. 10:22). He likewise can cause the disappearance of riches from those who have them.

God's help (I Sam. 2:8). Hannah was particularly thankful that God helps those in need, for she had just witnessed His helping her with her great need. To illustrate this truth graphically, she spoke of how God can {raise a beggar to a position of wealth and honor. She described someone who sat in the dust and among ashes, not having a nice home or the comfort of clean and new clothing.}[Q9] This person had nothing to eat unless someone kindly gave him food or money.

God, however, sometimes reaches down to such a person and dramatically causes a change of circumstances that is almost unbelievable. Instead of begging, he may suddenly find himself seated among those who have plenty and respected by all those around him. There is no need to speculate exactly how God does such a thing, for His ways are infinite and He is able to accomplish something like this with anyone.

The reason we can maintain hope in the midst of trials is that everything in the universe is God's and under His complete control. Hannah spoke of the earth as being supported by pillars. While we know that is not literally so, her point was that everything on earth is stable because God is in control of it (Ps. 104:5). He may or may not choose to give us the wealth of princes, but no matter what, His choices are good and right.

God's power (I Sam. 2:9-10). Hannah concluded her prayer with one final contrast: God will take good care of His saints, but He will judge and destroy all those who are His wicked adversaries. She knew it was safe for saints to walk through life, for God guards their steps. At the same time, she knew it was dangerous to ignore God and His ways, for eventually those who do so will be silenced by eternal darkness and broken forever. The Lord will "thunder upon them" in judgment from His place in heaven.

Hannah also had amazing insight into the truth that "by strength shall no man prevail" (I Sam. 2:9). Psalm 33:17 reads, "An horse is a vain thing for safety: neither shall he deliver any by his great strength." A similar thought is found in Proverbs 21:31, which says, "The horse is prepared against the day of battle: but safety is of the Lord." No human army or cavalry can win against the Lord.

Hannah's final statement has a prophetic element to it: "He shall give strength unto his king, and exalt the horn of his anointed" (I Sam. 2:10). This prophetic reference to a king is important, for Samuel was born when Israel had no king. Yet this Samuel grew up to anoint David as King (the Hebrew word translated "anointed" here is *mashiach*, or messiah). David himself wrote a song with many verbal and conceptual connections with Hannah's song that is placed near the end of II Samuel (23:1-7), in the final days of his reign. {By faith, Israel could look forward to the coming of the true Messiah, Jesus.}Q10

—*Keith E. Eggert*

QUESTIONS

1. Why was the birth of Samuel so important to Hannah?

2. Why did Hannah feel it was necessary to present Samuel to Eli?

3. How did Hannah express what she felt was her exaltation?

4. In what way did she experience the salvation of the Lord (I Sam. 2:1)?

5. What were Hannah's thoughts concerning those who had spoken cruelly toward her?

6. What do we learn about the lack of security in riches from Hannah's prayer?

7. What did Hannah say about God's control over life?

8. Why could Hannah be certain that God can elevate whomever He wishes?

9. What final contrast did Hannah make to encourage God's children?

10. Who was the "anointed" (vs. 10) of whom Hannah spoke?

—*Keith E. Eggert*

Preparing to Teach the Lesson

Have you ever wondered why you are here on earth or why you were born at this particular juncture in history? We could have been born at an earlier time or at a later time, but God had a purpose in putting you and me in this world at this time. This week's lesson shows us that we are here by divine planning and purpose.

TODAY'S AIM

Facts: to show that Samuel was given as a gift in answer to prayer.

Principle: to emphasize that God of ten works in response to our prayers.

Application: to assure students that God has a special plan for each of His children.

INTRODUCING THE LESSON

Most of us take childbearing as something natural and expected, but couples who cannot have children often experience the depths of agony as they struggle to have what we consider normal. Samuel's mother, Hannah, found herself in this situation. In the depth of her pain, she discovered that God had a special plan for her in answer to her prayers.

DEVELOPING THE LESSON

1. Hannah's prayer answered (I Sam. 1:20). It must have been one of the happiest days of Hannah's life when she gave birth to a baby boy she named Samuel. She had waited a long time for her prayer to be answered. Hannah had wrestled with God in prayer about her inability to have a child for so long, and now she finally had been shown God's grace. Hannah was overjoyed.

There are two special things to note about baby Samuel's birth. First, we see that he was born "when the time was come" (vs. 20), in fulfillment of God's specific timing for his arrival in this world. Nothing happens by accident in this world for the Christian. Everything is designed by God far in advance of anything we have planned for ourselves.

This tells us something about the nature of our God. He never loses sight of us in the crowds of this world. Each of us is special in His eyes, and He has a divine plan for each of us. Samuel came at God's perfect timing for God's special purpose for his time in history. We are handpicked for His purposes.

The second is that Samuel was born in answer to his mother's prayers. It is true that Hannah longed for a baby; however, it is also significant that God works in response to our prayers. He seeks to work with us as we seek His will for our daily lives. He calls us to be partners with Him in His divine plans: God Almighty seeks us out to work with Him. Would we not be better off if we talked with Him more in prayer about our daily plans as Hannah did?

2. Hannah's response (I Sam. 1:26-28). We can learn a spiritual principle here. When we receive anything from the Lord, we are to respond in gratitude and give ourselves back to Him in His service. When Hannah went back to the tabernacle at Shiloh, which was the place of worship, she met Eli the high priest again.

You will remember that Eli was the one who thought that Hannah was drunk when she was really crying her heart out in prayer for a child (vss. 12-13). She now told Eli that she had come to give the child to the Lord in response to His goodness to her. Samuel was to be God's very own for as long as he lived. This is a picture of total dedication and surrender to God.

3. Hannah thanked her God (I Sam. 2:1). God had answered her prayer, and Hannah's response was one of praise and gratitude. When we recognize God's goodness to us, we must respond in praise, for He has done it all. Hannah recognized that God had been good to her.

Hannah's praise was also a testimony for all the world to see, especially her enemies. In Hannah's day, infertility was viewed with contempt; it was a shame to be childless. Hannah was now free from the shame of barrenness.

Encourage your students to consider the many times that God has worked wonderful things in our lives and how easy it is for us to forget that He is the One behind it all. We often forget to thank Him and praise Him for His loving-kindness to us.

4. Hannah praised her God (I Sam. 2:2-10). In her joy, Hannah also recognized the attributes of her God. He was her Rock. He is unique, for there is none like Him. He is holy, which means that He is set apart. There is none like Him in character and person. He was far different from the gods of the nations around Israel.

God knows our hearts, our thoughts, and our deeds; therefore we are to be humble before Him. This implies that we are accountable to Him for our actions. Since He is in absolute control, both the mighty and the weak are under His care. He does with them as He pleases. The hungry and the well-fed, the barren woman and the one who has many children—all are under His keeping. He has power over death and life, for He is God. He raises some up and puts others down. The rich and the poor are under His care.

God controls the earth, and the world runs under His direction. He protects the godly, and the wicked perish at His command. He is so great that it is futile to fight against Him. His voice is as thunder, and He gives strength to the king He appoints.

Clearly, God is in charge of the universe; nothing can stand against Him. He knows the troubles that afflict us and gives needed wisdom, strength, and protection. When we recognize His goodness, this wonderful God is on our side. Hannah praised God for His kindness to her.

ILLUSTRATING THE LESSON

God works His special plans in answer to our prayers. In fact, God's best for us often comes out of our desperate needs.

CONCLUDING THE LESSON

Is our lack of prayer holding up God's best for us? If He is in absolute control, we must surrender to Him.

ANTICIPATING THE NEXT LESSON

Next week we will look at how God used the faith of a young woman to intervene in the lives of His people.

—A. Koshy Muthalaly

PRACTICAL POINTS

1. We should give tangible acknowledgment when the Lord hears and answers our prayers (I Sam. 1:20).
2. It is good to give testimony to God's answers to our prayers so that others can join in our praise (vss. 26-28).
3. God's answers to our prayers are intended to increase our delight in *Him* (2:1-2).
4. Pride in one's status is foolish, for the Lord can overturn circumstances in an instant (vss. 3-5).
5. Everything we have is from the Lord's hand; there is no room for boasting or smug treatment of others (vss. 6-8).
6. The Lord strengthens the weak who wait in faith upon Him; those who are confident in their own strength will be overthrown (vss. 9-10).

—*Kenneth A. Sponsler*

RESEARCH AND DISCUSSION

1. What did it cost Hannah to dedicate her son to the Lord (I Sam. 1:26-28)? Does the Lord normally expect such a sacrifice? What does dedicating our lives cost us?
2. Why did Hannah see the Lord's answer to her prayer in terms of triumphing over enemies (2:1-2)? Is this a sentiment we ought to share?
3. What is the life lesson we should learn from the truths expressed in verses 6 through 8?
4. Of how much value are great physical strength and economic resources in the grand scheme of things? What should the foundation of our lives rest on (vss. 9-10)?

—*Kenneth A. Sponsler*

ILLUSTRATED HIGH POINTS

Given me my petition (I Sam. 1:27)

Tom and Anne were not able to have children of their own; so they attempted to adopt a child. They filled out papers and went in for interviews, but they were not given a child. At one point they were assigned two foster children with the possibility of adopting them, but they had to give the children up when the birth mother wanted them back. Tom and Anne continued to pray for a child.

One day a very excited Anne called me to tell me that a child had been found for them. In a few weeks, they were the proud parents of a beautiful baby girl. A short time later, Tom and Anne dedicated their little answer to prayer to the Lord in a service at our church.

He bringeth low, and lifteth up (2:7)

Ted was stricken with bowel cancer. The doctors fought the disease aggressively, but it eventually spread to Ted's liver. After a brave battle, this Christian brother died.

Ted's wife, Rita, stayed by his side through the whole ordeal. She waited on him, nursed him, prayed with him, and ministered to him in every way that she could. It was a devastating experience for her. When Ted died, the hopes and dreams the couple had shared for so many years died also. What would she do? Where would she go? Rita had never been so low in her whole life.

God led her to a grief support group, where she found healing and love.

In a couple of years, God placed a wonderful new man in Rita's life. Today they are serving the Lord together in a Christian organization. Christmas letters indicate that Rita and her new husband are very happy. God may allow us to be brought low, but He also lifts us up!

—*Bruce A. Tanner*

Golden Text Illuminated

"There is none holy as the Lord: for there is none beside thee: neither is there any rock like our God" (I Samuel 2:2).

Samuel was a miracle child. His mother, Hannah, had prayed that God would provide her with a son. She was heartbroken that she did not have a child while her husband's other wife, Peninnah, had many children. In fact, Peninnah belittled her because of this! If God answered her prayer, Hannah promised to dedicate her son to the Lord.

After Samuel's birth, she brought him to the house of the Lord at Shiloh to Eli the priest. She explained that Samuel was the child for whom she had prayed to the Lord. Now was the time to fulfill her promise to God to dedicate Samuel. She left him in Eli's care to raise him in God's service.

Hannah committed herself to prayer and worship throughout the entire process. Her prayers for a child were fervent. The promise to dedicate her son to the Lord resulted from an expectant hope that God was able to answer her prayer. After that answer came and she brought Samuel to Eli and to God, she worshipped and rejoiced that God had looked kindly on her.

Hannah is an excellent example of willingness to trust God. She turned to Him when she suffered inward anguish at her outward persecution. But she was also willing to trust Him with her most precious possession—her son Samuel. Hannah followed through on her promise to dedicate Samuel to the Lord for His service. Certainly, she could trust God to care for the son He Himself had provided for her.

While she was at Shiloh, Hannah praised God for His goodness to her (I Sam. 2:1-10). The backstory for the content of this praise was the suffering Hannah endured because she was childless and the subsequent reversal of events through the birth of Samuel. Unfavorable situations are no obstacle to God. He is both willing and able to turn despair into delight.

Hannah begins her prayer by recognizing that she is triumphant over her enemies because God delivered her (vs. 1). No one else could have rescued her. God is holy, separate from this world and all that is corrupt in it. He stands outside of it, untainted by its wickedness, uniquely qualified to judge and act on behalf of His people. He is the unmovable rock they trust with their lives (vs. 2). The prideful ones should be concerned because God is an all-knowing and just judge (vs. 3).

God can redeem any circumstances, just as He did for Hannah. In her prayer, she provides numerous examples of situations God can change. The strength that God provides can overcome the overwhelming might of enemy soldiers (vs. 4). The famished soul will feast, while the arrogant (and well-fed) will go hungry. And the barren woman who trusts God will have a multitude of children (vs. 5). The Lord strengthens and provides for His children, while the wicked will be debased (vss. 7-9).

No matter what obstacles we face, God wants us to turn to Him in faith, just as Hannah did. He is as powerful today as He was in Hannah's day. But He asks that we follow Hannah's example of dedication to Him. Our lives are not our own. We dedicate ourselves to serving Christ when we trust Him as our Saviour. If we can trust Him for our eternal destination, surely we can trust His daily guidance, too!

—*Glenn Weaver*

Heart of the Lesson

The virgin birth of Jesus was a tremendous miracle unlike any other. Prior to that, however, we find God sending other children whose births were also miraculous, and who pointed forward to the birth of the Messiah. One such birth was that of Samuel to Hannah, the barren wife of Elkanah, as a result of her prayer.

1. Receiving the gift (I Sam. 1:20). Hannah's joy over the birth of Samuel can be fully appreciated only by those who, having been barren, finally conceive, and are blessed with what they wanted most in marriage—a child. In Hannah's case, the child was given in response to her intense prayer, uttered in profound anguish and accompanied with a vow to give the child back to God for His use.

How different her attitude toward children was from that of many in our day who either choose to go childless because it will cramp their lifestyle or choose abortion in order not to be burdened with a child!

The name Samuel that Hannah gave to her son indicates that she had not forgotten that Samuel was given to her from God.

2. Acknowledging the Giver (I Sam. 1:26-28). So often we pray for safety before we travel and forget to thank God at the end of the journey; likewise, we pray for rain and, when it comes, neglect to thank the One who sent it, forgetting the gift was in answer to our prayer.

Even several years later, Hannah did not forget. She promised to give Samuel back to God, but she also realized this could not be done until the child was properly weaned and able to do some things on his own. There is no hint of bargaining with God to allow her to keep Samuel for even one day longer than necessary.

At the appropriate time and with various sacrifices, Hannah presented Samuel to the Lord in Shiloh. She had experienced the satisfying time of preparing for motherhood, the actual birth of a son, and the joy of nurturing the baby until he was a young lad. That was what her heart had desired. God had heard her prayer and had wonderfully answered. She could do no less than complete her vow to the One who had graciously fulfilled her dreams.

Are we negligent in acknowledging God's answer to some prayer? Is there some vow we once made to the Lord but have not kept?

3. Extolling His glories (I Sam. 2:1-10). In a manner foreshadowing a virgin in Nazareth centuries later, Hannah broke into a lyrical prayer laden with praise to God, who works on behalf of His people.

Like Mary, Hannah burst into glad recognition that the salvation of God had come to her. God is great because He deals not only with nations but also with individuals. Whether He allows the barren to give birth or is involved in the financial affairs of men, God is sovereign and will see to it that His will is done.

Hannah's prophetic prayer-song closes with the use of the word "anointed" (vs. 10), or messiah. This primarily seems to refer to Israel's great future king, David (yet to be born), whose coming would portend a greater fulfillment when the Messiah Himself would be given to Israel and the world.

Should not our hearts, especially upon reflection on God's grace, break out in similar praise as we think through God's gifts to us? A proper theology will evoke such praise and adoration.

—*Darrell W. McKay*

World Missions

Married couples without children may feel the emptiness that Hannah experienced until the Lord heard her prayer and gave her Samuel. Her testimony upon his birth was "I have asked him of the Lord" (I Sam. 1:20).

Bringing a child into the world is an incomparable joy. Bringing a child into a Christian home usually means an addition to the body of Christ. In the past thirty-five years we have witnessed the growth of the body through adoption.

After the breakup of the Eastern bloc nations of Europe, the plight of unwanted infants and children in Romania became known. Many believers considered it a challenge from the Lord and went through the arduous task of traveling to a nation in ruins, working through the red tape, and shouldering the expense of adoption in order to provide a home and an opportunity for children at risk to come to know Christ as Saviour.

Our next-door neighbors, with three young girls of their own, are adopting an eighteen-month-old boy. The home study is complete. Isaiah, a very happy little toddler, comes for short visits until the legal process is complete. Our neighbors are active, growing Christians. They prayed about adopting, and the primary element in their prayer was that they might lead a child to saving faith in Jesus Christ.

Jerry Avery and his wife are the parents of three bright, growing young people. The Averys are Caucasian. They went to a Christian adoption agency and asked for an African-American child. They now have three. The first is seven and has already trusted Christ as Saviour. The second is two and a half. She has a heart for Jesus, Jerry Avery has reported, and loves gospel songs. The youngest is a year and a half.

The Averys believe that "if abortion is wrong, we need an alternative." Jerry Avery added, "Half a million adoptable children could be won to Christ. Government administered foster care is broken."

Mrs. Donna Buzan, a pastor's wife and mother of two of her own children, prayed about adopting a child. Initially she thought of approaching a local adoption agency, but the Lord placed a burden on her heart for the sorely depressed nation of Haiti. On the Internet she found a Christian adoption agency in Port-au-Prince. The agency showed pictures of unwanted children they had taken in. There was Sami, a skinny, half-bald little girl.

"God knew the exact, perfect child for us," Mrs. Buzan testified. Pastor and Mrs. Buzan went to Haiti and brought Sami home. Sami prays, loves Christian stories, and is growing in every way. "She is extremely intelligent," Mrs. Buzan stated. "I see something special for her. She has great potential for the future. She could be a doctor in Haiti."

Sami has two sisters a Haitian is struggling to raise. The Buzans are willing to adopt these youngsters if the Lord leads in that way.

Rick and Cindy have two children of their own. When they adopted Elena, a four-year-old Russian child, she could not sit or stand. In two months she was at the appropriate weight, growing, and taking a new lease on life. Elena is saved now and growing in a Christian family.

Perhaps you, too, would consider adopting a child who needs a godly home to call their own.

—Lyle P. Murphy

The Jewish Aspect

The account of Hannah, mother of Samuel, is one of the most touching accounts of a woman totally dedicated to God. She had a hard time of it since she had no children, while her husband's other wife, Peninnah, had sons and daughters. Peninnah's taunts forced Hannah to leave the dinner table when the family was in Shiloh every year for worship at the Feast of Tabernacles (during September-October). Hannah desperately wanted children. Elkanah, her husband, tried his best to calm the circumstances, offering Hannah a double portion in offerings (I Sam. 1:5) to make up for her lack of children.

Over the years, the Jewish religious leaders developed numerous guidelines on how husbands and fathers were to care for their families. Husbands were to provide food and clothing for their wives. Obviously, Elkanah had his responsibilities to his children: having his sons circumcised, teaching them Torah as well as a trade, and providing for the special needs of his daughters. The Torah was extremely important. If the father was not fully able to teach, he had to hire teachers for his sons. Teaching a trade was also necessary; if he did not do this, it would be considered the same as teaching his sons to steal. Even those who were studying to be rabbis had to learn a trade—Paul, for example, was taught to be a tentmaker; see volume 10 of the *Jewish Encyclopedia* (Best Books) for a list of rabbis qualified in their trades.

Hannah's greatest lesson for us today is her life of prayer. Even though Peninnah's provocations greatly aggravated Hannah, she still knew whom to go and pour out her heart—none other than the Lord Himself. She thus took her place near the doorpost of the tabernacle, near where Eli, the priest and judge, sat in his appointed seat of oversight.

Though her prayer was inaudible, it was intense. She vowed to give her son to the Lord and promised God his dedication as a Nazirite (I Sam. 1:9-11; cf. Num. 6:1-5). Later, after weaning her son, she came again to Shiloh with her husband and turned the boy, Samuel ("Shemuel," meaning heard by God), over to Eli. The boy was likely only three to five years of age, but her vow had been that her son would serve the Lord all the days of his life.

Was Hannah sad as she followed through on her promise? No, she had a long-range view for her son and complete confidence in what God would do for him. She took the high road in the dedication of her son, praised God for His gift in the birth of her firstborn, and had faith that he would be called as a leader in Israel.

Prayer life is important in Judaism. In the twelfth century Maimonides emphasized prayer as removing from one's mind all thoughts of oneself as one stands before the Shekinah (the presence of God); otherwise, prayer is no prayer at all (Moore, *Judaism,* vol. 2, citing Maimonides, *Hilkot Tefillah*). No priest or rabbi need mediate in this prayer life. At certain times, specific prayer requests were formulated for people to repeat; but on numerous other occasions, people could speak in reverence from their hearts.

Hannah is a great example of how we also can proclaim in victory over our challenges, "For this I prayed," giving God all the honor and glory.

—Louis Goldberg

Guiding the Superintendent

People who are unnoticed by those around them are precious to God and may have unexpected roles to play in His plan. Hannah was such a person.

This week our discussion will center on Hannah and her son Samuel, who was born in the chaotic days of the judges, but will anoint the future King David who serves to point to the coming of King Jesus.

DEVOTIONAL OUTLINE

1. A child named (I Sam. 1:20). It all started with a wife who was unable to have children. This was a condition that many women experienced. Before the story was over, the whole history of Israel was affected.

Suddenly, there in her hands was the answer to Hannah's years of prayer (I Sam. 1:9-11). It seems only natural that she named her child "Samuel," a name that probably means "heard of God." Here was a baby who was truly an answer to prayer.

2. A child presented (I Sam. 1:26-28). A gift so precious could not be kept to herself. He had to be shared. When her child was about two or three, Hannah returned her child to the Lord. Little Samuel was brought to the high priest, Eli, and presented to the Lord.

The text tells us that Hannah "lent" (I Sam. 1:28) Samuel to the Lord. This word has the idea of returning. What an attitude she manifested! She was only returning to the Lord what He had graciously given her.

Samuel would go on to become a noteworthy leader in the nation of Israel. God would ultimately use Samuel to anoint David as the king of Israel.

3. God praised (I Sam. 2:1-10). It is only fitting that Hannah praised God for her child. Before she was done, Hannah would thank God for His Messiah, His anointed Deliverer.

Hannah saw in her experience a picture of God's dealings with the entire nation. Like her, Israel was barren. The answer to her prayer for herself and her nation was found in Samuel.

First, Hannah praised the character of God (I Sam. 2:1-3). God had come to her deliverance and exalted her over her enemies. Second, she praised God for what He had done (vss. 4-8). His actions could best be described as a great reversal. Those who were lowly were exalted; those who were mighty and high were brought low. What was true for her also would be true for the nation.

Finally, Hannah spoke prophetically, saying that in the future God would advance the cause of His children (I Sam. 2:9-10). She said God would "exalt the horn of his anointed." This is the first use in the Bible of the Hebrew word *messiah* in reference to a coming king.

God's work in Hannah's life was a picture of the far greater future work of the Messiah, or Christ. What happened to her would be played out on a much broader scale when Christ came to deliver His people.

AGE-GROUP EMPHASES

Children: This is a good lesson to emphasize to children how they are a special gift from God. Help them see how important they are in God's eyes.

Youths: Teens can learn how to be thankful to God. Even the smallest of gifts from God can have great significance.

Adults: Help adults realize that God's work in their lives is part of God's larger picture for the world.

—*Martin R. Dahlquist*

SCRIPTURE LESSON TEXT

ESTH. 3:2 And all the king's servants, that *were* in the king's gate, bowed, and reverenced Haman: for the king had so commanded concerning him. But Mordecai bowed not, nor did *him* reverence.

3 Then the king's servants, which *were* in the king's gate, said unto Mordecai, Why transgressest thou the king's commandment?

5 And when Haman saw that Mordecai bowed not, nor did him reverence, then was Haman full of wrath.

6 And he thought scorn to lay hands on Mordecai alone.

4:7 And Mordecai told him of all that had happened unto him, and of the sum of the money that Haman had promised to pay to the king's treasuries for the Jews, to destroy them.

8 Also he gave him the copy of the writing of the decree that was given at Shushan to destroy them, to shew *it* unto Esther, and to declare *it* unto her, and to charge her that she should go in unto the king, to make supplication unto him, and to make request before him for her people.

9 And Hatach came and told Esther the words of Mordecai.

10 Again Esther spake unto Hatach, and gave him commandment unto Mordecai;

11 All the king's servants, and the people of the king's provinces, do know, that whosoever, whether man or woman, shall come unto the king into the inner court, who is not called, *there is* one law of his to put *him* to death, except such to whom the king shall hold out the golden sceptre, that he may live: but I have not been called to come in unto the king these thirty days.

12 And they told to Mordecai Esther's words.

13 Then Mordecai commanded to answer Esther, Think not with thyself that thou shalt escape in the king's house, more than all the Jews.

14 For if thou altogether holdest thy peace at this time, *then* shall there enlargement and deliverance arise to the Jews from another place; but thou and thy father's house shall be destroyed: and who knoweth whether thou art come to the kingdom for *such* a time as this?

15 Then Esther bade *them* return Mordecai *this answer,*

16 Go, gather together all the Jews that are present in Shushan, and fast ye for me, and neither eat nor drink three days, night or day: I also and my maidens will fast likewise; and so will I go in unto the king, which *is* not according to the law: and if I perish, I perish.

NOTES

Esther's Bold Faith

Lesson Text: Esther 3:2-3, 5-6*a*; 4:7-16

Related Scriptures: Esther 1:1—3:1; 3:7—4:6;
Genesis 12:1-3; Daniel 3:14-28

TIME: between 478 and 474 B.C.   PLACE: Shushan

GOLDEN TEXT—"So will I go in unto the king, which is not according to the law: and if I perish, I perish" (Esther 4:16).

Introduction

The book of Esther recounts an incident in Persia that nearly resulted in the annihilation of the Jews. Historically, it fits in the same time period as the book of Ezra. One group of exiles had returned from captivity, and the temple had been rebuilt. The events of the book of Esther are set among the Jewish exiles who had not returned but had instead remained in Persia. In this context, God used Esther and her high governmental position to accomplish an unlikely deliverance for His people from their enemies.

What makes God's sovereign protection and preservation of Israel even more impressive is the fact that the Israelites in Persia were outside their homeland and thus were not able to worship according to the Mosaic Law. Those who had returned to Judah had reestablished worship in the temple. Those who remained in exile had no temple in which to carry out their system of worship with its ceremonies and animal sacrifices.

LESSON OUTLINE

I. AN EVIL PLAN—Esth. 3:2-3, 5-6*a*

II. A DANGEROUS PLAN—
Esth. 4:7-12

III. A GODLY PLAN—Esth. 4:13-16

Exposition: Verse by Verse

AN EVIL PLAN

ESTH. 3:2 And all the king's servants, that were in the king's gate, bowed, and reverenced Haman: for the king had so commanded concerning him. But Mordecai bowed not, nor did him reverence.

3 Then the king's servants, which were in the king's gate, said unto Mordecai, Why transgressest thou the king's commandment?

5 And when Haman saw that Mordecai bowed not, nor did him reverence, then was Haman full of wrath.

6 And he thought scorn to lay hands on Mordecai alone.

Mordecai's resistance (Esth. 3:2-3). After King Ahasuerus deposed Queen Vashti, he conducted an extensive search for a new queen. Since the Jewish girl Esther fit the parameters of the command for young women to appear before the king, she found herself in a most unexpected situation. The one thing her cousin Mordecai (who had taken her as his daughter) commanded her was that she not reveal her Jewish nationality (2:20).

{Many have noted that the book of Esther is not only an accurate historical account but also great literature. Short stories normally include main characters, some kind of conflict, an antagonist, a hero or heroine, tension that builds to a climax, and a resolution. All the elements of such literature are obviously present here.}[Q1] The antagonist, Haman, is first mentioned in 3:1, where we are told that the king elevated him to the position of prime minister in his government, above even his seven counselors (cf. 1:14).

Along with the promotion came a command from the king that everyone pay homage to Haman. As a result, all the king's servants sitting in the gates of the palace bowed whenever he approached. The fact that Mordecai was present there might indicate he held a judicial position of some kind. He, however, refused to bow or pay homage to Haman. It was customary even in Israel for lower-level people to show the courtesy of bowing to higher-level officials. It is not clear exactly why Mordecai had objections to doing so in this case.

The king's servants noticed Mordecai's behavior and asked him repeatedly why he was not obeying the king's command. Mordecai told them he was a Jew (3:4), and apparently that was the reason he gave for his refusal to bow to Haman. He might have viewed it as disloyalty to God to bow to a foreign dignitary. The servants finally reported him to Haman "to see whether Mordecai's matters would stand." Perhaps they wondered if an exception had been determined for the Jewish people.

Haman's wrath (Esth. 3:5-6a). "The most arrogant people are often those who must measure their self-worth by the power or influence they think they have over others. Haman was an extremely arrogant leader. He recognized the king as his superior but could not accept anyone as an equal. When one man, Mordecai, refused to bow in submission to him, Haman wanted to destroy him. He became consumed with hatred for Mordecai" (*NKJV Life Application Study Bible,* Tyndale). Haman's hatred soon extended to all Mordecai's people, the Jews.

Since God is the one who ultimately controls the hearts of kings (Prov. 21:1), we recognize that Haman was elevated to his position not just by King Ahasuerus but by God Himself. The Jews constantly lived with the potential for disaster, and they needed protection. {God already had Esther in place for her role, and now He had allowed Haman to attain his position. Although Haman thought he was plotting and carrying out his own plans, God was actually doing a most amazing thing, something that would again prove His faithfulness and sovereign protection of His people.}[Q2]

{After the king's servants told Haman about Mordecai's attitudes and actions, Haman no doubt paid special attention to Mordecai from then on. As he personally observed Mordecai's refusal to bow before him, his anger grew into wrath.}[Q3] The word for "wrath" (vs. 5) refers to forceful, vindictive anger that is ready to boil over. Haman was not just angry but also determined that he would get revenge in some way. That in itself was bad, but Haman decided on something extreme.

Haman's desire for revenge becomes more ominous when we read that he scorned the thought of merely laying hands on Mordecai alone (vs. 6). {His hatred had grown into a haughty disdain for all Jews, and he determined that Mordecai's punishment would have far-reaching consequences for all the Jewish people in the empire.}Q4 Anti-Semitism is not new. It has been in the world for many centuries. Since God chose the Jews, Satan has a deep hatred for them. He has been the moving force behind the centuries of hatred of Jews and attempts to exterminate them.

A DANGEROUS PLAN

4:7 And Mordecai told him of all that had happened unto him, and of the sum of the money that Haman had promised to pay to the king's treasuries for the Jews, to destroy them.

8 Also he gave him the copy of the writing of the decree that was given at Shushan to destroy them, to shew it unto Esther, and to declare it unto her, and to charge her that she should go in unto the king, to make supplication unto him, and to make request before him for her people.

9 And Hatach came and told Esther the words of Mordecai.

10 Again Esther spake unto Hatach, and gave him commandment unto Mordecai;

11 All the king's servants, and the people of the king's provinces, do know, that whosoever, whether man or woman, shall come unto the king into the inner court, who is not called, there is one law of his to put him to death, except such to whom the king shall hold out the golden sceptre, that he may live: but I have not been called to come in unto the king these thirty days.

12 And they told to Mordecai Esther's words.

Mordecai's report (Esth. 4:7-9). Haman knew that if he worked through the king he would have a much better opportunity to accomplish what he wanted to do, namely, annihilate the Jews. He therefore told the king that a certain group of people in his kingdom refused to obey his laws and that they were not worthy of being left alive. He added that he himself would pay ten thousand talents of silver to those who carried out the killing. Without researching the matter further, the king allowed Haman to draw up the decree to have it done (3:8-15).

Before long Mordecai learned what was happening and went into deep mourning (4:1). In every province of the kingdom, Jews were mourning, knowing their deaths had been decreed (vs. 3). {Esther was told about her cousin's mourning by her servants, and she became deeply distressed (vs. 4). She sent Hatach, a trusted royal servant, to learn what was troubling Mordecai.}Q5

Mordecai told Hatach all that had taken place, including what Haman intended to do and the amount of money being paid (vs. 7). Mordecai then gave the servant a written copy of the decree and told him to show it to Esther (vs. 8). By now Mordecai knew what would have to be done: Esther would have to appeal to the king for help. Along with the copy of the decree, he gave a command to Esther to go in to the king and plead on behalf of her people. They needed him to rescue them from the certain deaths they all faced.

We remember that Esther had obediently kept her nationality secret because Mordecai had instructed her to. This, however, was going to be a much more difficult order to follow. As the queen of the land, she certainly could have disobeyed Mordecai, and he would have been helpless to do anything about it. Her moral convictions, though, made her realize that under God she still owed him respect as her adoptive parent. We can only imagine the emotional turmoil she went through when Hatach returned with his message.

Esther's response (Esth. 4:10-12). Esther now gave a command for Hatach to give Mordecai an explanation just as serious as the one Mordecai had sent her. {It reveals the fact that no one, including her, was allowed to enter into the presence of the king without having been summoned by him. For her to do as Mordecai had commanded would require that she put her life at risk.}[Q6] The only possible reprieve was if the king held the golden scepter out toward her after her appearance.

{Esther informed Mordecai that she had not been called into the king's presence for a month. She had no idea what his attitude toward her might be; for all she knew, she was not currently being thought of favorably for some reason.}[Q7] This is what made Mordecai's plan so dangerous. If for any reason the king resented Esther's coming to him without an appointment, she would be taken out and killed. It really did not matter that she was the queen.

This was, no doubt, a security precaution on the part of Ahasuerus, not something practiced only because of certain whims. There are many historical records of kings being murdered within their palaces or throne rooms. The holding out of the golden scepter amounted to an immediate pardon from the king, thus sparing the life of the intruder.

Esther was not telling Mordecai anything he did not already know. The beginning of her response, in fact, was "All the king's servants, and the people of the king's provinces, do know" (vs. 11). Ahasuerus ruled over 127 provinces, reaching east to India and west to Ethiopia (1:1). He was a very powerful king with a multitude of subjects, and it was evidently common knowledge that one did not dare displease him. Esther was doing her best to cause Mordecai to realize what he was commanding her to do.

A GODLY PLAN

13 Then Mordecai commanded to answer Esther, Think not with thyself that thou shalt escape in the king's house, more than all the Jews.

14 For if thou altogether holdest thy peace at this time, then shall there enlargement and deliverance arise to the Jews from another place; but thou and thy father's house shall be destroyed: and who knoweth whether thou art come to the kingdom for such a time as this?

15 Then Esther bade them return Mordecai this answer,

16 Go, gather together all the Jews that are present in Shushan, and fast ye for me, and neither eat nor drink three days, night or day: I also and my maidens will fast likewise; and so will I go in unto the king, which is not according to the law: and if I perish, I perish.

Mordecai's challenge (Esth. 4:13-14). Esther may have been the queen and shared many of the privileges of royalty with the king, but she was just as much in need of God's protection as all the other Jews. This is what Mordecai reminded her in the message he sent back to her. If the killing of the Jews got started, sooner or later it would be discovered that she was one of them; then those otherwise loyal to her would turn against her.

Mordecai had faith to believe God was going to protect His children in some way—that is, that the Jews would not be completely wiped out. That did not mean, though, that many individuals would not die. Mordecai felt quite certain that both he and Esther would be among those killed if the decree was not somehow nullified. He very forcefully told Esther this. If she refused to be part of the solution for their salvation, God would accomplish it in some other way.

{Mordecai then issued the greatest challenge of all: maybe the very reason she was the queen of the land was for this time of need faced by her people (vs. 14).}[Q8] She had direct access to the king, which was not true of any other Jew. She had previously won the king's confidence and love, which no other Jew had done. She was a model of integrity, and Ahasuerus could not have helped noticing, so she was respected by him above many others in his kingdom. She was the most logical one to approach the king and appeal on behalf of all the Jews.

Mordecai was saying that Esther's advancement to royal position was the providence of God at work. She was there according to His will. While we do not see much about Mordecai's spirituality, we do see evidence that he believed in God and the covenants He had established with His people. {Mordecai knew God was not going to allow them to be annihilated, for then the covenants would be broken.}[Q9] He was confident that God would rescue His people.

Esther's determination (Esth. 4:15-16). Once again the courier took a message back to Mordecai. {Esther understood the situation completely and was willing to do whatever she could to help, even if it meant her death.}[Q10] "If I perish, I perish," she said.

One of the things that has puzzled Bible scholars is that the book of Esther never explicitly mentions God or prayer. We recognize Mordecai's faith in God and His covenants, but we wish as we read the text that there were a clearer indication of a personal relationship with God. Now that Esther was faced with the biggest challenge of her life, it would be encouraging to hear her proclaim a deep, settled faith in the Lord.

Instead, it is unclear whether Esther's statement is one of trust in God's sovereignty or one of mere fatalism. Perhaps the biblical writer intentionally leaves this ambiguity to make readers decide for themselves whether God is at work in such desperate situations. Even though we do not see Esther's relationship with God spelled out, that should not keep us from recognizing God's providence in the situation or from realizing how important such an intimate relationship with God is in times of trial.

Esther's instructions were that Mordecai gather all the Jews in Shushan together and fast for her for three days. She and her maids would be doing the same thing at the same time. After the time of fasting (and probably prayer), she would go in to the king even though it was against the law. They were about to see whether or not Mordecai's God would use her as he anticipated. She needed to be as ready as possible.

—Keith E. Eggert

QUESTIONS

1. How is Esther both a historical account and great literature?
2. How do we see God's providence at work in the promotion of Haman?
3. What was Haman's response to the report about Mordecai's actions?
4. How did Haman plan to get back at Mordecai for his refusal to bow and do homage to him?
5. What initial exchange took place between Mordecai and Esther after Haman's decree had gone out?
6. What did Esther remind Mordecai about after hearing his plan?
7. Why was Esther so uncertain how the king would receive her?
8. What did Mordecai suggest was the purpose of Esther's royal position?
9. Why was Mordecai so certain that God would not allow the Jews to be annihilated?
10. What did Esther plan to do?

—Keith E. Eggert

Preparing to Teach the Lesson

Christianity is often looked at as a religion for weaklings by those who know nothing about it. The Bible, however, is full of examples of courageous people who stood up for what they believed, even to the point of death. In this week's lesson, we explore the need for courageous Christians.

TODAY'S AIM

Facts: to show that Esther was prepared to die if need be to save the Jews from destruction.

Principle: to teach that Christians must be prepared to live for God even at the cost of extreme consequences.

Application: to urge students to boldly and consistently choose God's way rather than the way of the world.

INTRODUCING THE LESSON

Christians in certain parts of the world face persecution every day for affirming their faith in Jesus. The government of China, for example, considers Christianity a dangerous "religious cult." Chinese officials regularly threaten to take children away from their Christian parents to deter family Bible study. Pastors are routinely arrested, questioned, and detained. Recently Chinese authorities arrested 150 members of a single church ("A Family in Exile," *The Voice of the Martyrs,* September 2022).

Paul reminds us that persecution comes to all Christians at some point; it is not the exception (II Tim. 3:12). We need to count the cost of believing in Jesus and determine to follow Him whatever the price.

DEVELOPING THE LESSON

1. Mordecai disobeys the king (Esth. 3:2-3). It takes courage to go against the grain and remain faithful to God. Morde-cai found himself in this kind of situation. He did not bow down to Haman, the king's right-hand man, but challenged the king's ruling. While Mordecai's motives are unclear, he based his action on his Jewish identity (vs. 4).

As Christians we are faced with similar situations. Ask your students to share situations in which they had to decide whether they were going to obey God or man.

2. Haman reacts with rage (Esth. 3:5-6a). Sometimes the consequences of following God can be serious. Here we find Haman very angry and determined to punish Mordecai and destroy all the Jews. When we as Christians obey God, we can be sure there will be consequences not only for ourselves but for others as well. As Christians we must stand together in a common testimony for our God. This may mean facing the wrath of the world.

3. Mordecai pleads with Esther for help (Esth. 4:7-9). When we face a crisis situation, we have nowhere to turn but to God. It is amazing how God provides us with the right people at the right time when we trust in Him to help us.

In our lesson we see that Esther sent her servants to find out what was troubling Mordecai. Mordecai then sent word about Haman's actions and provided proof with copies of the documents that decreed the destruction of the Jews. Mordecai pleaded with Esther to go speak with the king about the matter.

God is always there for His people, sometimes in mysterious ways. He governs all things and always has a plan to provide in our time of need.

4. Esther expresses her fears (Esth. 4:10-12). Esther knew she had an obligation to help her own people, but she told Mordecai that she could not just go into the king's presence without being asked. It could mean death for her if she was not favorably received.

It is all right for us to express our fears in difficult situations. However, God is able to take care of our fears.

5. Mordecai challenges Esther (Esth. 4:13-14). Christians are called to encourage one another to do what is right. Here we see Mordecai challenging Esther to be bold and speak to the king about her people and Haman's evil plans, even though doing so meant risking death. Mordecai challenged her to do what was right. He suggested to her that she was God's candidate for that moment of deliverance.

God places each Christian in a strategic place, as He did Esther, for His own purposes, sometimes for great moments of crisis like this one. God has His chosen people everywhere so He can carry out His plans through them. He calls us to acts of courage and empowers us to keep at the work until it is finished. However, we must be prepared even for death if that is what it takes to do God's will for that time. Ask the class members to tell how God has used them or others in their lives in some critical situation.

6. Esther shows her courage (Esth. 4:15-16). Esther was up to the challenge. She was prepared to go to the king at the risk of her life so that her people could be saved from Haman's plot of destruction. From Esther we learn that as faithful Christians today, we may sometimes need to take risks for our Lord.

In our lesson we find Esther making preparations to walk into the king's presence. She called for Mordecai and her people to stand with her in fasting as a sign of solidarity with her as she went to the king. She knew that she was risking her life in doing this, but she was prepared to die for the deliverance of her people. Her trust in God for the outcome was strong.

We should ask ourselves how much of a risk we are willing to take for our Lord. The believers in the early church were prepared to die for their faith. For biblical examples, read Acts 5:27-42, Philippians 1:19-30, and I Peter 3:13-17. Today we often shy away from such commitment, preferring an easy and comfortable form of Christianity. In following our Lord Jesus, we are often called to walk the pathway of death. We are to take our Christian calling seriously.

ILLUSTRATING THE LESSON

Christian courage is seen in a willingness to listen to God in spite of danger and to disregard the voice of man.

COURAGE TO OBEY

VOICE OF GOD

VOICE OF MAN

CONCLUDING THE LESSON

We are called to be bold in our faith. Esther was prepared to die to save her people. We too must boldly speak up for our Lord.

ANTICIPATING THE NEXT LESSON

Our lesson next week helps us celebrate the glory of deliverance as we contemplate Esther's victory.

—A. Koshy Muthalaly

PRACTICAL POINTS

1. We are subject to authorities (cf. Rom. 13:1-7), but we need not slavishly grovel before human pride (Esth. 3:2-3).
2. When we take a stand on principle, it may affect many others for good or ill (vss. 5-6).
3. When we seek action by someone in a position of influence, it is wise to have our facts and information documented (4:7-9).
4. Even for someone in a position of great favor and influence, it can be risky to step out on behalf of others (vss. 10-12).
5. Seeking the less dangerous course of action often provides no safety; God sometimes puts us in the place of risk (vss. 13-14).
6. Supported by prayer, we can always do the right thing if we are willing to deny ourselves (Esth. 4:15-16; cf. Luke 9:23-24).

—*Kenneth A. Sponsler*

RESEARCH AND DISCUSSION

1. How do we discern when a command is right to obey and when it should be ignored (Esth. 3:2-3; cf. Acts 4:19; 5:29)?
2. Was Mordecai's refusal to honor Haman a principled stand based on God's law or a manifestation of stubborn pride? Defend your answer from Scripture.
3. Why do persons who feel affronted by an individual often take out their anger against a whole group of people (Esth. 3:5-6)? What do they usually accomplish?

—*Kenneth A. Sponsler*

ILLUSTRATED HIGH POINTS

Mordecai bowed not (Esth. 3:2)

In Eastern Europe during the days of communism, a pastor had been imprisoned and was being interrogated by the secret police. They wanted the names of other Christians so that they too could be arrested.

When beating did not achieve the desired result, the pastor's tormentors brought in his teenage son and threatened to beat him to death if names were not divulged. The pastor could not bear to see this happen and told his son that he was going to tell the police what they wanted to know. The young man insisted that the father not cooperate. He was then beaten to death before his father's eyes.

That Christian pastor and his young son, like Mordecai, stood on principle and paid the ultimate price for it.

If I perish, I perish (4:16)

Martin Luther, the great reformer, stood before the Diet of Worms in 1521. He was ordered to retract certain statements that he had issued. Luther had been assured safe conduct while he testified; however, it was understood that he would be apprehended and punished as soon as he returned home. Luther knew of the danger.

Martin Luther believed in the absolute authority of Scripture. He believed that the positions he had taken were scripturally sound. He therefore knew that he could not compromise. He challenged his accusers to prove him wrong from the Bible. Unless they could do so, he would not recant.

Queen Esther knew the risk she was taking by interceding for her people before the king. She was willing to take those risks. Doing what is right is even more important than life.

—*Bruce A. Tanner*

Golden Text Illuminated

"So will I go in unto the king, which is not according to the law: and if I perish, I perish" (Esther 4:16).

Our lesson begins with a situation that looked very bleak for the Lord's people. Haman, who had won the king's favor, was a proud man who proved himself to be dishonest and deceitful. He had been elevated to a position above all the other princes in Persia. His high status meant that all the king's servants who were in the king's gate had to bow before him and reverence him. "But Mordecai bowed not, nor did him reverence" (Esth. 3:2).

Godly principles seemed to guide the way Mordecai lived. Even though he was one among many, he was determined to abide by his principles no matter what price he had to pay. As a result, Mordecai was confronted by the servants who were in the king's gate. They said to him, "Why transgressest thou the king's commandment?" (vs. 3).

The situation in which Mordecai found himself was one that demanded true bravery. Mordecai met the test. In his faithfulness to godly principles he showed great courage.

Mordecai is an excellent example of how we should stand for the Lord in the face of opposition. Although it may not put our lives in danger as it did for Mordecai, there is only one right decision we Christians can make. We must be faithful to our God. We must keep in mind, however, that our decision to stand for God will have ramifications. In Mordecai's case it meant the possible destruction of all his people. Still, he was willing to stand for God and to trust Him for the outcome. The closer we walk with the Lord in our service for Him, the more we become the focus of Satan's attacks. Yet God maintains control even over those attacks (cf. Job 1:12).

Through Hatach, one of the king's chamberlains, Mordecai was able to send Esther a copy of the edict that put Esther and her people in great danger. He told her that she should go before the king and plead the case of the Jewish people. Esther found herself between a rock and a hard place. She did not want her people to be killed. At the same time, going before the king without being summoned could result in her death. The only hope was if the king held out the golden scepter to her. Then her life would be spared.

The situation was a very grave one for Esther and all her people. If we allow human reasoning to guide us, we are in trouble. There are times when we cannot see through the blur, but if we are obedient to the Lord, we do not have to know everything. He knows our future, so as long as we walk with Him, the outcome will be the best for us no matter what it is.

Mordecai told Esther that she should not assume she would escape in the king's house any more than the rest of the Jews would. He said that if she held her peace and kept quiet, deliverance for the Jews would arise (but not for her family) from another place. It was a moment for courage. Her task was clear. Mordecai went on to say, "And who knoweth whether thou art come to the kingdom for such a time as this?" (4:14).

Esther made her decision. She asked the people to fast with her. She said, "If I perish, I perish." Esther showed great bravery and is a wonderful example of courage for all the Lord's people.

—V. Ben Kendrick

Heart of the Lesson

Whether because of peer pressure or simply because people want to fit in with the crowd, many do what they see others doing without thinking through what their actions actually mean. Some, however, are different and do not mind if others know it. They will not compromise their beliefs.

In this week's lesson we see two people who made decisions based on what was right rather than on what was easy or convenient. One was Mordecai, and the other was Esther.

1. Courage to live one's faith (Esth. 3:2-3, 5-6a).

When the king's law demanded that the people bow and pay reverence to Haman, Mordecai refused. He could not bring himself to do it. Others, specifically non-Jews, had no problem following the command of the king to treat Haman with actions that resembled religious worship. Mordecai was of a different persuasion and stood upright whenever Haman came by.

It is not clear what Mordecai's true motives were. Some say he did what he did on religious grounds because bowing before Haman would have been honoring him as a god. Others believe Mordecai's refusal was likely due to the fact that Haman was an enemy of the Jewish people.

Mordecai may well have made his stand with both reasons in mind. Either way, it was an act of courage somewhat reminiscent of the three friends of Daniel. Their action earned them time in a fiery furnace (Dan. 3).

The apostle Paul would much later state that if one acts contrary to one's Christian faith, it is sin (Rom. 14:23). That seems to have been what was behind Mordecai's refusal.

2. Courage to do the right thing (Esth. 4:7-16).

Some are bold enough to act on their own in times of great trial, while others will act only after having received encouragement and motivation from others. Esther was the latter kind of person. She was a Jew who had become queen in Persia, but the king and many others did not know her background.

Esther found herself at a turning point forced upon her by an edict her husband had issued at the bidding of Haman, who was angered by Mordecai's refusal to pay him reverence. The edict was designed to rid the land of Mordecai's people, the Jews. When the decree became known to Mordecai, he sought to persuade Esther to intervene on behalf of her people—an action that could have resulted in her death (vs. 11).

Mordecai reminded Esther to consider why she had been placed in such a high position in the kingdom. Surely it was not by chance or accident. Perhaps she had come to the king's side for just such a time when her influence could possibly save her own people.

Esther was at first hesitant to go before the king uninvited, but Mordecai's words gave her courage to do the right thing. Her comment of submission to the will of Mordecai—"So will I go in unto the king, . . . and if I perish, I perish" (vs. 16)—prefigured what Jesus would say in Gethsemane: "Not my will, but thine, be done" (Luke 22:42).

Which kind of person are you? Are you like Mordecai or like Esther? Maybe you know of someone who needs your encouragement to take a stand for God and righteousness. Your words of encouragement may be the means God uses to help them live out their faith and do the right thing.

—Darrell W. McKay

World Missions

Mordecai spoke prophetically when he addressed a hesitant Esther, saying, "For if thou altogether holdest thy peace at this time, then shall there enlargement and deliverance arise to the Jews from another place" (Esth. 4:14). Mordecai knew that the Lord had rescued His people many times in the past. The Lord had brought them out of Egypt. They had overcome numerous enemies in their conquest in Canaan and during the time of the kings.

It was no accident that Mordecai was already known and appreciated in Shushan, the capital of Persia, and God certainly had brought about the selection of Esther to be the queen of a vast empire stretching over Asia from the Mediterranean to India.

Nevertheless, the most important "enlargement and deliverance" for the people of Israel has come from the few but fervent Christian witnesses God has raised up to love and befriend the Jews. In every age there have been faithful Gentiles willing to hazard their lives for the sorely oppressed Jews. Of these, there were always those who invested time and effort in bringing a witness for Messiah Jesus to the Jewish people.

Some Jews have come to faith in the Messiah through reading the Old and New Testaments. As early as 1600, believing Jews produced a Hebrew translation of the New Testament. John Immanuel Tremellius, a 1540 Jewish convert to Christianity, produced a Latin Old Testament and bound it with a New Testament. It became a primary means of propagating the Scriptures in a day when the Word of God was suppressed.

Christian Gerson, a Jewish pawnbroker in seventeenth-century Germany, received a New Testament pawned by a customer. Gerson said he read it "in secret so that [his] wife should not notice." Gerson felt he had to become a Christian, but it was at great cost. His wife asked him to leave her. He commented; "All my Jewish neighbors and acquaintances . . . have become implacable enemies" ("Timeline of Notable Jewish Christians of the Past Five Centuries," *World Magazine,* March 2002).

In the American colonies Jews found the soil of freedom favorable to Jewish life and prosperity. In 1954 American Jews celebrated what they called "three hundred years without tears." From the beginning there seem to have been born-again believers in the New World who were committed to sharing Christ with the Jewish people.

Rabbi Judah Monis was the first Jew to receive a college degree in America, earning a M.A. degree from Harvard. Monis was a born-again believer. He felt the call to reach out to his people and wrote three tracts entitled "The Truth," "The Whole Truth," and "Nothing but the Truth." In 1735, aided by a loan from Harvard, he published the first Hebrew grammar in America.

In 1892 Leopold Cohn, a Hungarian Jew, found that the United States offered the freedom to pursue the God of the prophetic Scriptures he had studied in secret in the Old World. As a committed believer, he ministered to his people through a medical clinic, a kosher food kitchen, and free coal delivery to poor Jews. His witness for the Messiah grew into the largest mission to the Jews in the world at the time.

—Lyle P. Murphy

The Jewish Aspect

Esther (in Hebrew, *Hadassah,* meaning "myrtle") enjoys high esteem for what she courageously did for her people. The entire book of Esther is read on the Jewish holiday of Purim, which occurs during February or March each year.

After Queen Vashti had been deposed, Ahasuerus's advisers' counsel was to hold a beauty contest of sorts to select Vashti's replacement. The king would choose whichever woman he pleased to be the next queen. Esther was selected as one who fit the parameters for the contest, which posed a real problem for the Jewish community. The young woman's cousin-guardian also likely held an important position in the government. The prospect of a Jewish girl becoming the wife of a non-Jew was offensive enough, but as queen, she would be involved in many questionable associations with pagan religious practices. As part of the selection process, she would also have to spend a night with the king. If Esther was not chosen, what would her life be like afterward? While the experience had serious moral problems, she really had no choice in the matter.

Things came to a head very quickly when Haman attained a position of prominence in the Persian court. Arrogant because of all his newfound power, he expected everyone to recognize him as the ruler, next to the king himself. Everyone was expected to bow to him. One can imagine his rage when he found out not only that Mordecai did not bow but also that he was a Jew, a people whom Haman hated. It was not long before he had schemed (without informing the king fully of his plans) to enact orders that not only Mordecai but all Jewish people should be put to death in the month to which the lots (*purim*) pointed. This would be when the slaughter would commence (cf. Esth. 3:8-15).

Who could intervene in this court intrigue to turn the threat around and spare the Jewish people? Who could gain the ear of the king himself to convince him concerning the corruption of his most trusted servant, Haman?

The call for courage would have to come to Esther, and Mordecai sent messages into the palace to inform her of what was about to happen to the Jewish people. Once her own identity was discovered, she would not be spared the fate of her people.

Although she was the queen, Esther did not have the right to walk into the king's presence anytime she wished. He had not called for her for at least thirty days, and Esther mentioned this to Mordecai through the messengers. Her cousin was adamant, however. She somehow had to get to the king to inform him of Haman's plots and bring salvation to her people. If she was unwilling to face the ordeal, the salvation of the Jewish people would come from another source, but she and all her father's house would perish.

Esther had the courage to face the challenge. She asked Jewish community to join her in fasting, and then she would go to the king. If she lived, it would be well, but she preferred to face the possibility of her own death rather than be fainthearted and desert her people. God honored her faith in Him, and her people were spared. We also face challenges to honor the Lord, and He expects us to be faithful as we serve Him.

—Louis Goldberg

Guiding the Superintendent

"I sought for a man among them, that should make up the hedge, and stand in the gap before me" (Ezek. 22:30), the Lord said. Can one person really make any difference in this world? Can one person really have any influence on what is happening around him?

From time to time it is necessary for a person to be courageous and stand up for what is right, even if that person is the only one standing. Down through the ages, numerous individuals have a made a difference by doing so. Just think of the apostles. They frequently risked persecution or death, but the result was that the gospel reached the ends of the earth (cf. Acts 4:1-22; 5:17-42; 6:8—7:60; 21:27—26:32). Never underestimate the difference one person can make in the hands of God.

The book of Esther tells of one courageous woman who stood in the gap and saved all the Jewish nation from holocaust. Our lesson this week focuses on two very determined people.

DEVOTIONAL OUTLINE

1. Bruised ego (Esth. 3:2-3, 5-6a). Our lesson begins in ancient Persia with a man named Haman. He had caught the eye of the king and been elevated to a great position in the kingdom. Wherever he went all the people, including government leaders, bowed before him. Only one Jewish man, Mordecai, refused to bow before Haman.

The reader is never told the reason for Mordecai's refusal. Perhaps bowing down represented some type of worship he could not do (cf. Dan. 3), or perhaps he just could not honor one who was a determined enemy of Israel. Whatever the reason, Haman's ego could not handle this treatment. He became angrier as the days passed and the lack of respect continued. Finally he determined to eliminate not only Mordecai but his people also.

2. Courageous spirit (Esth. 4:7-16). Mordecai was providentially placed in such a position that he learned the details of Haman's plot to execute all the Jews. He had a message delivered to Esther, his cousin, who had recently become queen. He pleaded with her to intercede with the king for the Jewish people.

Esther's first reaction was one of fear—and justifiably so. The king had shown no interest in her for thirty days, and the law allowed the king to put her to death for coming before him uninvited.

Mordecai apparently believed that God controls history and that He uses people to carry out His purposes. Mordecai was confident that relief for the Jewish people ultimately would come from somewhere. He exhorted Esther to be that channel of relief. He was convinced that Esther had come to her position for just this time. God had placed her there on purpose.

The queen agreed with her cousin and asked her fellow Jews to fast before she approached the king.

In the end, Esther's intercession brought deliverance for her people. Never underestimate the power of one.

AGE-GROUP EMPHASES

Children: Children need to know that God can use them in very special ways.

Youths: Help your teens understand that God is working in each of their lives and has a plan for each one.

Adults: Help your people understand how important they can be in the cause of Christ. God has not placed anyone where they are on accident.

—Martin R. Dahlquist

SCRIPTURE LESSON TEXT

ESTH. 8:3 And Esther spake yet again before the king, and fell down at his feet, and besought him with tears to put away the mischief of Haman the Agagite, and his device that he had devised against the Jews.

4 Then the king held out the golden sceptre toward Esther. So Esther arose, and stood before the king,

5 And said, If it please the king, and if I have found favour in his sight, and the thing *seem* right before the king, and I *be* pleasing in his eyes, let it be written to reverse the letters devised by Haman the son of Hammedatha the Agagite, which he wrote to destroy the Jews which *are* in all the king's provinces:

6 For how can I endure to see the evil that shall come unto my people? or how can I endure to see the destruction of my kindred?

7 Then the king Ahasuerus said unto Esther the queen and to Mordecai the Jew, Behold, I have given Esther the house of Haman, and him they have hanged upon the gallows, because he laid his hand upon the Jews.

8 Write ye also for the Jews, as it liketh you, in the king's name, and seal *it* with the king's ring: for the writing which is written in the king's name, and sealed with the king's ring, may no man reverse.

9:18 But the Jews that *were* at Shushan assembled together on the thirteenth *day* thereof, and on the fourteenth thereof; and on the fifteenth *day* of the same they rested, and made it a day of feasting and gladness.

19 Therefore the Jews of the villages, that dwelt in the unwalled towns, made the fourteenth day of the month Adar *a day of* gladness and feasting, and a good day, and of sending portions one to another.

20 And Mordecai wrote these things, and sent letters unto all the Jews that *were* in all the provinces of the king Ahasuerus, *both* nigh and far,

21 To stablish *this* among them, that they should keep the fourteenth day of the month Adar, and the fifteenth day of the same, yearly,

22 As the days wherein the Jews rested from their enemies, and the month which was turned unto them from sorrow to joy, and from mourning into a good day: that they should make them days of feasting and joy, and of sending portions one to another, and gifts to the poor.

23 And the Jews undertook to do as they had begun, and as Mordecai had written unto them.

NOTES

The Deliverance of the Jews

His Prudent *His Sovereinty*

Lesson Text: Esther 8:3-8; 9:18-23

Related Scriptures: Esther 5:1—7:10; 8:15—9:16; Psalm 106:1-5, 44-48

TIMES: 474 B.C.; 473 B.C.   PLACE: Shushan

GOLDEN TEXT—"Therefore the Jews of the villages, that dwelt in the unwalled towns, made the fourteenth day of the month Adar a day of gladness and feasting, and a good day, and of sending portions one to another" (Esther 9:19).

Introduction

Our lesson begins with the Jews' very existence being threatened by their enemies. Esther needed to urge the king to stop the oncoming slaughter of her people, for she had been raised to her position "for such a time as this" (Esth. 4:14). Her own life was at risk, however, for if she were to enter the king's presence uninvited, she could be summarily executed. Bravely she entered, and the king extended his golden scepter, signifying that she was welcomed to speak.

A college singing group had its annual tour scheduled well in advance. One of its key members, however, was told by a new boss at his work that he could not get the time off to tour. Everyone prayed for a change of heart.

As the group loaded the vans, at the last minute, the key member arrived, with permission from his boss to go on the tour.

LESSON OUTLINE

I. ESTHER'S PETITION— Esther 8:3-8

II. THE JEWS' JOY—Esther 9:18-23

Exposition: Verse by Verse

ESTHER'S PETITION

ESTH. 8:3 And Esther spake yet again before the king, and fell down at his feet, and besought him with tears to put away the mischief of Haman the Agagite, and his device that he had devised against the Jews.

4 Then the king held out the golden sceptre toward Esther. So Esther arose, and stood before the king,

5 And said, If it please the king, and if I have found favour in his sight, and the thing seem right before the king, and I be pleasing in his eyes, let it be written to reverse the letters devised by Haman the son of Hammedatha the Agagite, which he wrote to destroy the Jews which are in all the king's provinces:

6 For how can I endure to see the evil that shall come unto my people? or how can I endure to see the destruction of my kindred?

7 Then the king Ahasuerus said unto Esther the queen and to Mordecai the Jew, Behold, I have given Esther the house of Haman, and him they have hanged upon the gallows, because he laid his hand upon the Jews.

8 Write ye also for the Jews, as it liketh you, in the king's name, and seal it with the king's ring: for the writing which is written in the king's name, and sealed with the king's ring, may no man reverse.

Appearance (Esth. 8:3-4). This was Esther's second appearance before King Ahasuerus (this is the Persian king otherwise known as Xerxes) without being invited. Previously, when asked by the king what she wanted, she had invited him and Haman to a dinner. At the dinner the king asked again what she wanted, and she invited the two to a second banquet, promising to share her request at that time. We might wonder why the delay until we read what took place between those two dinners. {In that span of time Haman made special plans to kill Mordecai by hanging him on a gallows (chap. 5).

Also during that time King Ahasuerus had a bad case of insomnia the night before Haman was going to request permission to have Mordecai killed.}[a1] Once again the sovereign hand of God was present, for during the king's insomnia he had some historical records read and found out that Mordecai had once saved his life. When he asked how Mordecai had been rewarded, the king was told that nothing had ever been done for him. Upon Haman's arrival the king asked him what could be done to honor someone the king wanted honored (6:1-6).

Pride led Haman to wrongfully assume he was the one the king wanted to honor. It was only after he had detailed a grand plan that he found out the honoree was the hated Mordecai. When the king told Haman to do the honoring, he experienced a dramatic reversal of fortunes (vss. 7-11)! It is clear that these events saved Mordecai from death. During Esther's delay in presenting her request, God had induced the king's insomnia and put all the details for the Jews' salvation in place.

Esther soon exposed Haman's plot, and he was hanged on the gallows he had prepared for Mordecai (chap. 7). The problem was that Haman's decree against the Jews (3:13-14) was still in effect and would be carried out unless something could be done to stop it, for the law was irrevocable. Thus we find Esther again in the presence of the king pleading for her people. She approached the throne in tears, fell at the king's feet, and begged for his help. He again extended the scepter, allowing her to stand and present her request.

Appeal (Esth. 8:5-6). By this time Esther was even more respected by the king than previously, and Mordecai had been advanced in his kingdom. Nevertheless, none of this nullified the decree Haman had sealed with the signet ring of the king (3:10-12).

We understand the irrevocability of the decree from a statement in the book of Daniel. When Daniel's enemies wanted to get rid of him, they went to King Darius and suggested he establish a law that would force everyone to forgo petitions to any gods other than the king. They concluded their request by saying, "Now, O king, establish the decree, and sign the writing, that it be

(A) Give for the benefit of others

not changed, according to the law of the Medes and Persians, which altereth not" (Dan. 6:8).

In verses 12 and 15 the same principle is mentioned again. A sealed Persian law could not be altered or annulled. It had to be carried out, and there was no possible exception available. For Esther, Mordecai, and the Jews in Ahasuerus's kingdom, there was no hope of having Haman's decree overridden.

{Esther and Mordecai understood that Haman's edict could not be overturned, but she seemed to have no other choice but to ask the king to protect her people from genocide.}Q2 {Esther couched her request in reminders that the king had a moral sense of right and wrong and that he had good feelings toward her. Notice these phrases: "If it please the king, and if I have found favour in his sight, and the thing seem right before the king, and I be pleasing in his eyes" (Esther 8:5). She then specifically requested that the king override in writing the decree established by Haman to kill the Jews.}Q3

{Esther then ended her plea with a statement filled with emotion: "How can I endure to see the evil that shall come unto my people? or how can I endure to see the destruction of my kindred?" (vs. 6).}Q4 It is important to realize, however, that Esther did not rely on emotions alone. She had tactfully referred to the decree as Haman's rather than the king's, revealing some diplomatic abilities. At the same time, the king could not help seeing the hurt in her heart as she poured herself out on behalf of her people.

Answer (Esth. 8:7-8). When Haman had been revealed as the one who had plotted the destruction of Esther's people, the king had become furious (7:7). As soon as he was told about the gallows prepared for Mordecai, he ordered Haman to be hanged on it instead (vss. 9-10). When Esther disclosed her relationship with Mordecai, he gave Mordecai all the authority Haman had possessed. He gave Esther all of Haman's property, and she put Mordecai in charge of it (8:1-2). In his response, Ahasuerus reminded Esther of this change.

At some point Mordecai had been called into the presence of the king to meet with him and Esther, for both were addressed at this time. The king reviewed the facts, noting that Haman's property had been given to Esther and that Haman had been executed for plotting the genocide of the Jews. So far this was nothing new, and it did not directly address what Esther had requested (vs. 7).

{What the king was telling them, though, was that Mordecai now had the same power Haman had once had and could use it to his own advantage. The initial decree could not be revoked, but another could be written to offset it.}Q5 He then gave them permission not only to write whatever decree they wanted but also to do it in his name and seal it with his signet ring, which he had already given to Mordecai (8:2). Mordecai already had the permission, but the king was reminding him that he could now feel free to use this new authority.

In following this procedure Mordecai would also have an effective decree that could not be changed or revoked. {He proceeded to have a decree written that would allow the Jews to gather together to defend themselves against the attacks of the Persians (vs. 11).}Q6 They were specifically told they could annihilate any forces that attacked them. They did not have to spare any women or children, and they could plunder the possessions of the Persians. Copies of the decree were immediately sent to all the provinces.

THE JEWS' JOY

9:18 But the Jews that were at Shushan assembled together on the thirteenth day thereof, and on the fourteenth thereof; and on the fifteenth day of the same they rested, and made it a day of feasting and gladness.

19 Therefore the Jews of the villages, that dwelt in the unwalled towns, made the fourteenth day of the month Adar a day of gladness and feasting, and a good day, and of sending portions one to another.

20 And Mordecai wrote these things, and sent letters unto all the Jews that were in all the provinces of the king Ahasuerus, both nigh and far,

21 To stablish this among them, that they should keep the fourteenth day of the month Adar, and the fifteenth day of the same, yearly,

22 As the days wherein the Jews rested from their enemies, and the month which was turned unto them from sorrow to joy, and from mourning into a good day: that they should make them days of feasting and joy, and of sending portions one to another, and gifts to the poor.

23 And the Jews undertook to do as they had begun, and as Mordecai had written unto them.

Celebration (Esth. 9:18-19). The day finally came for Haman's decree to be carried out. The forces that had hoped for great success in getting rid of the Jews (vs. 1) met determined opposition and great defeat. Throughout the entire empire, the Jews gathered together and successfully defended themselves to the point that they were soon mightily feared (vs. 2). In a completely surprising turn of events, the governmental officials sided with the Jews and helped them in their defense (vs. 3).

That day five hundred Persian men in Shushan died, along with the ten sons of Haman (vs. 12). The king then asked Esther whether she had any further desires, promising to grant them to her. God had so completely changed the circumstances of the Jewish people, who had feared being annihilated, that they now had a significant advantage over their enemies. The Jews in Shushan hanged Haman's ten sons on gallows to deter others from persecuting the Jewish people.

The thirteenth day of Adar was the original date for Haman's decree to be carried out. {The king extended that time for the Jews in Shushan, allowing them to continue attacks on their enemies on the fourteenth day, but on the fifteenth they stopped.}[Q7] On that day they rested and spent the time in feasting and celebrating. Since it had been only in Shushan that the extension of the slaughter had been in effect, the rest of the Jews in the kingdom celebrated on the fourteenth day of the month. They felt so secure that even in unwalled villages they celebrated.

Psalm 30:5 reads, "[God's] anger endureth but a moment; in his favour is life: weeping may endure for a night, but joy cometh in the morning." That psalm of praise reminds us that although sorrowful circumstances sometimes overtake us, it is good to know the hope of deliverance and the joy that follows.

Communication (Esth. 9:20-21). Mordecai wrote a historical account of all that had taken place. He then sent letters to all the Jews in every province of the kingdom. Details of his chronicle are not divulged, but we do know {he told the Jews to establish both the fourteenth and the fifteenth days of the month of Adar as annual celebration days.}[Q8] {This newly established Jewish feast became known as the Feast of Purim, named after the word for a lot cast to determine the onslaught of Haman's genocide of the Jews (see 3:5-7).}[Q9]

"And the letters were sent by posts into all the king's provinces, to destroy, to kill, and to cause to perish, all Jews, both young and old, little children and women, in one day, even upon the thirteenth day of the twelfth month, which is the month Adar, and to take the spoil of them for a prey" (3:13). The naming of the new feast was meant to be an ironic way of recalling Haman's actions. It was probably viewed as an evidence of the Jews' victory in spite of Haman's strong and evil determination.

The Feast of Purim is not mentioned in the New Testament, although it is in Old Testament apocryphal literature and by Josephus. It was celebrated locally, that is, wherever Jews lived. It was not one of the national feasts established in the law. There were no pilgrimages to Jerusalem associated with the feast. Today Purim is still celebrated. Included in the celebration is a reading of the book of Esther. When Haman's name is read, the people hiss, boo, stamp their feet, and use noisemakers in an attempt to drown out his name!

Commemoration (Esth. 9:22-23). Mordecai explained further why he wanted this holiday. The fourteenth and fifteenth days of Adar had been days of rest from being pursued by their enemies. This was when their sorrow was turned into joy and their mourning became happiness. The feast was to celebrate God's goodness in working through a number of circumstances to deliver the Jews. Mordecai wanted it to be a time of feasting and joy, of exchanging gifts, and of giving to the poor.

The response of the Jews was positive. They accepted that from then on this was to be a customary observance (vs. 27). Verse 28 then adds that they were willing to see to it that all succeeding generations would also understand the importance of the time.

Sometime after Mordecai's letters went out, Esther and Mordecai wrote another letter about the Feast of Purim (vs. 29). This served to confirm their intentions to establish the feast. Verse 31 suggests that some amount of time was to be set aside for fasting and mourning. Reminders of trials and victories are very important.

{Esther's life should be an encouragement to all of God's children. In spite of the fact that God and prayer are not explicitly mentioned in this book, the evidence of His presence and sovereign work is clear throughout.}[Q10]

—Keith E. Eggert

QUESTIONS

1. What important events took place between Esther's two dinners?

2. Why did Esther make a second appearance before the king?

3. What was Esther's approach as she asked the king to change the decree established by Haman?

4. What was her concluding emotional appeal to the king?

5. Of what did King Ahasuerus remind Esther and Mordecai, and what was he implying they could do?

6. What decree did Mordecai write?

7. What did the king grant Esther at the conclusion of the day on which the Jews defended themselves?

8. What did Mordecai and Esther ask the Jews to establish?

9. What name was given to the feast celebrating the Jews' deliverance?

10. How does the faithfulness of God toward the Jews encourage you?

—Keith E. Eggert

Preparing to Teach the Lesson

Our lesson this week looks at celebration among the Jews. Queen Esther's courage had ushered in a time of great joy.

TODAY'S AIM

Facts: to show that God used Esther to transform the life of His people.

Principle: to illustrate that celebration in the Christian life comes only when we have first made the sacrifices.

Application: to prod believers to celebrate the victory they have in Christ.

INTRODUCING THE LESSON

We do not often get good results without hard work and commitment. When a student studies long and hard, he usually gets good grades. A good athlete trains hard for many months in order to get the results he is looking for. Celebration comes after the sacrifices have been made and the risks have been taken to achieve the goals we desire.

We see this same principle at work in the life of the Jewish people as Esther took on the risks and challenges that faced her. Her ultimate goal was to do what was right and to save her people.

DEVELOPING THE LESSON

1. Esther's bold request (Esth. 8:3-6). This was not the first time that Esther had risked her life to go into the king's presence, but each time she took that risk, it was to save her people from destruction. This time she went in asking that the king reverse evil Haman's orders to destroy her people. She fell down before the king. This was the way the king was shown respect, even by his wife.

The king reached out to Esther with his scepter. This was a sign of acceptance, indicating that she was allowed to come in and speak with the king. Esther told the king that she could not bear to see her people and members of her own family destroyed just because of one evil man's plans to kill them. It takes courage to step beyond our normal boundaries to do what is right.

As Christians we are called to be obedient to Jesus and face the consequences, for He is our Lord in all things.

2. The king's response (Esth. 8:7-8). Esther must have been a person of gentle nature with a great measure of boldness. The king could not refuse her request as she stood before him.

Ask the students what it was about Esther that must have drawn the king to respond so very favorably to her. We need to be aware of how we come across to our friends and neighbors. Do we come across as caring and compassionate or as proud and self-righteous? Victory often begins with courage combined with humility. Esther was a humble person with a mission in mind.

3. Victory for the Jews (Esth. 9:18-19). The Jews celebrated the victory over their enemies with feasting and gladness and gift giving. The Jews had a long history of great suffering. Having suffered so much as a people, any celebration was taken very seriously. They had defeated their enemies, and celebration was in order. Only a nation that has suffered can really appreciate the gift of freedom.

In our day it is easy to take our freedoms for granted because we do not remember days of bondage. Even to this day, the Jews celebrate their victory at that time during the month of March on our calendar. It was a day that they could not forget.

4. Mordecai's call for celebration (Esth. 9:20-22). Mordecai had been through it all. He was not about to let the people or their posterity forget the threat that they had endured or the victory that they had won. He took steps to ensure that it would not be forgotten.

First, we see that Mordecai recorded these events so that their descendants would know both the agony and the glorious victory of their ancestors. He also sent letters to people far and wide, telling them on what two days to celebrate their victory.

We must remember that in those days there was no postal system like ours today. Delivering such letters was a big effort because runners or people on horseback or some other means of transport had to carry them to each person, and this often took many days.

Mordecai also encouraged his people to give gifts to the poor and thus share the joy of their victory with each other. They were to keep the memory of their struggle alive forever. They dared not forget that it was a time when God delivered them from the hand of their enemies.

We also are to remember that our deliverance from sin came with a price and that we are to cherish it. Even more joyously than the people of Esther's time, we can celebrate because the price has been paid by our dear Lord Jesus.

5. The Jews' victory celebration (Esth. 9:23). The deliverance of the Jews was now etched in the annals of their history. Mordecai had made sure that it would be so. Mordecai on the outside of the palace and Esther from

within had worked hard to preserve the Jewish people. There was much danger involved in bringing those things to pass.

Mordecai made sure that the Jews would not forget by making it an annual custom to remember their deliverance at that time. They did this with the Feast of Purim (vss. 24-26), which reminded them of the casting of lots against them (3:7) and how God delivered them through the boldness of Queen Esther.

ILLUSTRATING THE LESSON

The celebration of our victory becomes more meaningful when we consider the suffering that preceded it. The resurrection came only after the cross.

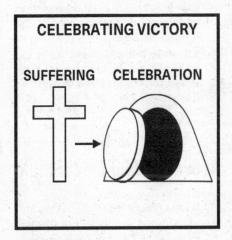

CONCLUDING THE LESSON

Because of Jesus' work on the cross, we have reason to celebrate today. Jesus paid the price for us so that we can be free. We are to accept His gift of salvation.

ANTICIPATING THE NEXT LESSON

In next week's lesson we will discuss the important interactions when a Pharisee invites Jesus to his house.

—A. Koshy Muthalaly

PRACTICAL POINTS

1. Fervent intercession, even before human authorities, is often needed to avert evils in the world (Esth. 8:3-4).
2. We should express our requests to authorities both passionately and specifically (vss. 5-6).
3. Even when an evil cannot be undone, measures for mitigating it or working around it are almost always possible (vss. 7-8).
4. It is good to set aside times to remember when we have experienced deliverance from evil or danger (9:18-19).
5. Good leaders will make sure that significant events in the life of their people are commemorated in the future (vss. 20-22).
6. We should finish those tasks we have set out to accomplish and follow the instructions of spiritual leaders (vs. 23).

—Kenneth A. Sponsler

RESEARCH AND DISCUSSION

1. If King Ahasuerus held Esther and her people in such high regard, why did he have to be begged to avert the plan for their destruction (Esth. 8:3)?
2. What did the extension of the golden scepter signify to Esther (vs. 4)? Is there any comparable situation in our day?
3. What would railing against the irrevocability of the decree have accomplished? What lessons does this have for those today who advocate for justice?

—Kenneth A. Sponsler

ILLUSTRATED HIGH POINTS

In the king's name (Esth. 8:8)

Frank and Judy were old and unable to care for themselves much longer. Their pastor contacted an agency to see what care was available.

When the social worker interviewed Frank and Judy she strongly recommended that they grant someone power of attorney. This person would be able to act on Frank and Judy's behalf. He would be able to manage their financial affairs and pay bills from the couple's account. A trusted friend was entrusted with this responsibility.

After Queen Esther had successfully approached the king on behalf of her people, Mordecai was granted a kind of power of attorney. The king allowed him to do things in his name. He was even granted the privilege of using his official signet ring.

A day of gladness and feasting (9:19)

The Pilgrims landed at Plymouth Rock in 1620. The first months in the New World were devastating to the colonists. They were ill prepared for the rigors of winter. All of them suffered, and many died.

The following spring and summer were better for the Plymouth colonists. Friendly Indians taught them to plant corn. They were able to reap a bountiful harvest and prepare themselves for the next winter.

The governor of the colony proclaimed a day of thanksgiving. The Pilgrims prepared a great feast and offered thanks to the Lord for His generous provision. Haman had nearly annihilated the Jews of Esther's time. Esther's intercession had saved their lives. They had much to be thankful for.

—Bruce A. Tanner

Golden Text Illuminated

"Therefore the Jews of the villages, that dwelt in the unwalled towns, made the fourteenth day of the month Adar a day of gladness and feasting, and a good day, and of sending portions one to another" (Esther 9:19).

The nation of Israel has a history of threats to its existence. Each time, God delivered them against seemingly impossible odds. The men and women God used to lead Israel to victory seemed larger than life.

Israel was in trouble again. The Babylonians had conquered the Jewish people years before and dispersed them throughout many foreign lands. Then the Persians conquered the Babylonians and became Israel's new rulers. King Ahasuerus of Persia promoted Haman to a position of power, second only to the king. Haman hated Mordecai, Esther's uncle. He was determined to destroy Mordecai and his people, the Jews.

Haman convinced King Ahasuerus that the Jews threatened their national security. He drafted a decree that all Jews—men, women, and children—should be killed. The date was set for when this terrible deed was to take place, and the king's swift couriers delivered the decree throughout the vast Persian empire.

The Jews did not have an army, a military commander, or a king to deliver them. But they still had an all-powerful God who cared for them. God chose a young girl, Esther, to be the conduit through which He would preserve the Israelite people.

God orchestrated the events of Israel's deliverance long before Haman's threat could be carried out. When Vashti, the queen of Persia, embarrassed King Ahasuerus at a feast, the king removed her and sought another queen. After a long process, he chose Esther to be his new queen.

Neither the king nor Haman knew Esther's ethnicity or her relationship with Mordecai. When Mordecai learned of Haman's threat, he asked Esther to appeal to the king for help. Esther responded with timidity at first. If anyone approached the king without being summoned first, that person would be killed unless the king excused the intrusion. Mordecai explained that even Esther's royal position would not save her from the decree. God would provide deliverance in another way if she was not a willing servant, but she needed to consider whether God had put her in this position for this very purpose (Esth. 4:13–14).

Esther drew courage from God and approached the king. Through Esther's pleas and the working of divine providence, Haman fell into disfavor with the king. Mordecai took his position and estate. But the king's earlier decree still stood, for no one could revoke a Persian law. Again Esther found favor with the king, and the king signed an ordinance that allowed the Jews to defend themselves against any attackers. The Jews became feared throughout the empire, effectively removing the threat. To this day, the Jews commemorate the victory with the Feast of Purim (9:19).

The Scriptures remind us that Esther played a vital role in preserving God's people. She had what all the great men and women of Scripture possessed—trust in God and a willingness to be used by Him. God doesn't need our abilities for us to serve Him. But God can save an entire nation through willing servants.

—*Glenn Weaver*

Heart of the Lesson

Celebrations need to have a reason. People do not often get together and rejoice apart from some cause. The greater the achievement or accomplishment, the greater the joy. The darker the day just past, the more gladness greets the light.

For the Jews in exile at the time of Esther, the day had been dark indeed. The light that dawned was as precious as life itself.

1. Removing the darkness (Esth. 8:3-8).

Previously Esther had gained the favor of the king, who in turn pronounced the death sentence on the perpetrator of evil against the Jews in the land. The king was in agreement with Esther, but being in agreement was not sufficient to save the Jews. The previous edict of the king at the bidding of Haman was still in effect and could not be revoked. Esther thus fell on her face in tears to get the king to issue a new order.

Her intercession on behalf of her people demonstrated that her position as queen and the status and wealth that went with it had not changed her heart. She still identified with the Jewish people, and she did everything in her power to bring deliverance to them. Her pleading touched the king's heart, and he ordered a new law that favored the Jews. The day of darkness for the Jewish people was about to end.

Similarly, Christians have come into a high and exalted position in Christ; yet many people remain lost in sin and darkness. How many more might be saved if those of us who are saved would fervently intercede on their behalf before the King of kings? We should not be content with our own deliverance but should seek the same for others.

2. Rejoicing in the light (Esth. 9:18-23).

When the Jews received the news and understood they had been saved, they celebrated. At first the Jews, scattered as they were in different provinces across a large empire feasted on different days. That was rectified by Mordecai with a letter declaring the people should celebrate together at the same time and therefore be united as a people.

Part of the celebration included the giving and receiving of gifts. Special effort was made to see that the poor received something as well.

One is reminded of the parallel between this practice and that of Christians celebrating the birth of Christ. Christians celebrate Christmas with gift giving. It is also a time when much is given to the poor as well, either directly or through various religious and civil organizations. There is something about Christmastime that opens the hearts of even nominal Christians to the plight of the needy. People are also generally more polite at that time of the year, wishing perfect strangers a merry Christmas, holding doors open for others, and being willing to give part of their wealth away. Many long to see the spirit of the Christmas season extend beyond the holiday into the new year.

Deliverance from something quite dire restores hope, brings happiness, and plants a song in the heart. It was true of the Jews saved from extinction in Esther's day, and it is true of each person newly born again today. May we who have salvation in hand not forget those who are living under a death sentence. Let us come before the King on their behalf. One day heaven will reveal how many our prayers touched, and we will celebrate that forever.

—Darrell W. McKay

World Missions

Your church, your Sunday school class, and your home Bible study could be wonderfully used by the Lord to reach out to Jewish people. A study of the annual cycle of Jewish feasts can be a time of broadening the believer's understanding of Christianity as an outgrowth of Jewish faith.

If there are Jewish people living in your community, a study of the feasts can be a valuable tool in witnessing to them. It seems clear that each of the seven major feasts in the Jewish calendar speaks of the hand of God in the history of the covenant people. In addition, the feasts give witness to the Messiah Jesus in very remarkable ways.

In our study this week we consider the occasion of the Feast of Purim, or the Feast of Esther. The Feast of Esther was ordained, in the words of Mordecai, so "that they should make them days of feasting and joy, and of sending portions one to another, and gifts to the poor" (Esth. 9:22).

The book of Esther gives the thrilling account of the escape of the Jews from threatened annihilation. The name of God is not mentioned in the text, but there is absolutely no doubt the divine hand was at work, shaping lives and events to effect another deliverance for His covenant people.

In his monumental work *The Gospel in the Feasts of Israel* (Christian Literature Crusade), Victor Buksbazen, a Hebrew Christian, wrote, "Purim is a signpost on the road of salvation, ascending from physical deliverance to the perfect redemption, which only the Lord Jesus Christ can give to those who trust His sacrifice on the cross of Calvary."

How could a local church make the Feast of Purim an evangelistic opportunity? First, the feast can be observed anytime in the month of March. The feast has special importance for Jewish children. As they do in the synagogue, you might have your children act out the book of Esther. Have the children select a classmate to be Esther and have her crowned. Select a Mordecai and an evil Haman. Relate the events with the emphasis on the hand of God.

This is an opportunity to teach that the Jews are God's chosen people and that God blesses those who bless the Jews and curses those who curse the Jews. Invite Jewish people you know or who live in your community to the play. They will be impressed and blessed.

No feast of the Jews offers the opportunity for reaching out to the Jews like the Feast of Passover. It requires sensitivity and care, however, for the history of the Jews is filled with countless atrocities across many borders and many centuries.

The celebration of Passover and Easter coincide in March or April. The Jewish people watch carefully to see whether our observances bring new charges of their responsibility for the death of Jesus.

Some Jewish missions will put on a Passover seder, the ritual meal that is the highlight of the observance. Jewish people often will come to a seder, making it a great evangelistic tool for a church.

As with any neighbor, Jewish neighbors want to be friends with people who genuinely care about them. By being friendly with them, you may have an opportunity to introduce them to Jesus.

—*Lyle P. Murphy*

The Jewish Aspect

Queen Esther planned well her audience with the king, first serving one banquet to him and Haman and then a second banquet as well. By that point, she had the king's interest so intensified that he could hardly wait to know her concerns. He promised his wife great wealth and authority. She then told him that the lives of her people were in jeopardy because of the evil intent of Haman's plans. Stunned by this abuse of power, the king immediately ordered Haman's execution on the very gallows on which he had planned to kill Mordecai.

No previous laws could be changed once enacted (Dan. 6:15); so the answer to the problem was to give the Jewish people the right to defend themselves when the day came for the confrontation with their enemies. At the end of the year, various peoples in the empire helped the Jews against those who attacked them. The number of enemies who were killed was substantial: some 500 in the major city of Shushan and 75,000 in all the empire, as well as the hanging of Haman's 10 sons. Mordecai assumed Haman's position, and Queen Esther's power in the empire was also advanced. It was a fitting end to Haman's sordid plots and the beginning of a righteous reign under the guidance of Mordecai, now the second in command in the empire.

The time for celebration and thankfulness had come; the Lord had indeed protected His people. We should remember such worthies as Mordecai and Queen Esther. In time, the occasion for celebration at the end of the Jewish year became an important freedom holiday, much like our Fourth of July, when we are thankful to God for what He has accomplished for our own country.

The time for celebration became different for various Jewish people depending on where they lived. In Persia, for those living in unwalled villages and towns, the day was set for the fourteenth of Adar (the last month), while those in the fortified cities celebrated on the fifteenth day (Esth. 9:17-18). No mourning was to occur on these days.

The practice of reading a portion of the book of Esther on this holiday became an established custom in the synagogues for all Jewish people, men as well as women and proselytes. Finally, it was decreed that the entire book be read. Eventually, its contents were put into a separate scroll. Today, as the book of Esther is read in synagogues, when the readers speak the names of Mordecai or Esther, the listeners shout their approval. When the words of Haman are read, they make noises, shouting and stomping on the floor or even using noisemakers, to make clear their disapproval of and dislike for him.

Parades are also held today. Many girls and young women dress like Esther, and everyone takes part in the joy. Food portions and money are sent to the poor, and gifts are given to those in need (vs. 19). These customs continue to this day. Frowned upon by the majority is the objectionable practice of drinking liquor until one cannot discern his right hand from his left. Clearly, this puts personal indulgence above community interests.

Celebrations are occasions for thanksgiving to God for all His blessings and goodness, both in our personal lives and for national remembrance.

—Louis Goldberg

Guiding the Superintendent

There are times in life when God wants His people to celebrate. Our time should not be consumed with grief. God expects us to deeply and passionately celebrate His good gifts to us.

Our lesson this week looks at the great time of celebration recorded for us in the final chapter of Esther.

The book of Esther revolves around a wicked man by the name of Haman and a beautiful queen named Esther. Haman developed a strong hatred for the Jews that consumed him. Unknown to Haman, Esther, the queen, was Jewish. Haman had developed a plot to have all the Jews executed on a certain date. His plans went awry, however. He ended up being hanged on the gallows he had intended for his archenemy, Mordecai, the cousin of Esther.

Our account this week records Esther's override of the edict of Haman to slaughter all the Jews and the times of joyous celebration that followed.

DEVOTIONAL OUTLINE

1. The edict overridden (Esth. 8:3-8). To begin with, something had to be done about the extermination order that was still in effect. The law of the Medes and Persians could not be revoked (cf. 1:19). Haman's edict was still in force. Mordecai arranged (through Esther) to produce a second edict that allowed the Jews to defend themselves.

Esther appeared before the king a second time. She pleaded passionately with him to end Haman's evil intentions. Although the decree could not be set aside, the law codes did allow for a second decree that in effect would make the first one invalid. Mordecai was given permission to write an edict any way he chose and put the king's stamp on it.

This was done, and the Jews through-out the empire were allowed to defend themselves.

2. The celebration (Esth. 9:18- 23). When the dreaded day arrived, the Jews defended themselves, and 75,000 Persians were killed (vs. 16). To celebrate their great deliverance, Mordecai instituted a new feast. This feast was called Purim, so named after the lots, or pur, that were cast by Haman to determine the original day of the execution of the Jews (3:7; 9:26).

Purim is a two-day celebration of God's graciousness and protection from mass murder. Mordecai made this an annual event to help keep forever before the Jews how God protected them. Purim was to be a time of giving and eating and sharing with others.

Isaiah 61:3 is a great verse to use to emphasize the key theme of this lesson: "Give unto them beauty for ashes, the oil of joy for mourning, the garment of praise for the spirit of heaviness; that they might be called trees of righteousness, the planting of the Lord, that he might be glorified."

For every follower of God there will be times of suffering, but these only make the times of joy all the greater.

AGE-GROUP EMPHASES

Children: Children naturally love to celebrate. Use this lesson to emphasize that they should celebrate the goodness of God in their lives.

Youths: Have teens think of the various reasons for worldly celebrations, and then show them that God's blessings are far more worthy of celebration.

Adults: The Feast of Purim celebrates God's protection for the Jews. Have your adults reflect on and celebrate times of divine intervention and protection in their lives.

—*Martin R. Dahlquist*

SCRIPTURE LESSON TEXT

LUKE 7:36 And one of the Pharisees desired him that he would eat with him. And he went into the Pharisee's house, and sat down to meat.

37 And, behold, a woman in the city, which was a sinner, when she knew that *Jesus* **sat at meat in the Pharisee's house, brought an alabaster box of ointment,**

38 And stood at his feet behind *him* weeping, and began to wash his feet with tears, and did wipe *them* with the hairs of her head, and kissed his feet, and anointed *them* with the ointment.

39 Now when the Pharisee which had bidden him saw *it,* **he spake within himself, saying, This man, if he were a prophet, would have known who and what manner of woman** *this is* **that toucheth him: for she is a sinner.**

40 And Jesus answering said unto him, Simon, I have somewhat to say unto thee. And he saith, Master, say on.

41 There was a certain creditor which had two debtors: the one owed five hundred pence, and the other fifty.

42 And when they had nothing to pay, he frankly forgave them both. Tell me therefore, which of them will love him most?

43 Simon answered and said, I suppose that *he,* **to whom he forgave most. And he said unto him, Thou hast rightly judged.**

44 And he turned to the woman, and said unto Simon, Seest thou this woman? I entered into thine house, thou gavest me no water for my feet: but she hath washed my feet with tears, and wiped *them* with the hairs of her head.

45 Thou gavest me no kiss: but this woman since the time I came in hath not ceased to kiss my feet.

46 My head with oil thou didst not anoint: but this woman hath anointed my feet with ointment.

47 Wherefore I say unto thee, Her sins, which are many, are forgiven; for she loved much: but to whom little is forgiven, *the same* **loveth little.**

48 And he said unto her, Thy sins are forgiven.

49 And they that sat at meat with him began to say within themselves, Who is this that forgiveth sins also?

50 And he said to the woman, Thy faith hath saved thee; go in peace.

NOTES

A Sinner Serves Christ

Lesson Text: Luke 7:36-50

Related Scriptures: John 12:1-8; Matthew 18:23-35; Luke 15:1-7; 19:1-10

TIME: A.D. 28   PLACE: Galilee

GOLDEN TEXT—"He said to the woman, Thy faith hath saved thee; go in peace" (Luke 7:50).

Introduction

Have you ever seriously overestimated your ability in something and ended up being completely embarrassed because of it? For example, did you ever issue a sports-related challenge and suffer an unexpected and thorough defeat?

King Amaziah of Judah once got overconfident and issued a challenge that ended up in a humiliating defeat (II Chr. 25:17-24). He had won a victory over Edom and, in the heat of his confidence, issued a challenge to King Joash of Israel. Joash did his best to deter him from entering into battle, but Amaziah refused to listen. He was soundly defeated and captured. Four hundred cubits (about six hundred feet) of his city wall was torn down, and all the gold and silver of his treasury was carried off to Israel.

The Pharisee in our lesson this week also had an inflated opinion of his own value and a correspondingly disparaging view of a sinful woman's worth. As we will see, he was to have his estimation abruptly overturned on both counts.

LESSON OUTLINE

I. **EATING WITH A PHARISEE—** Luke 7:36-39

II. **TEACHING THE PHARISEE—** Luke 7:40-43

III. **CONFRONTING THE PHARISEE—Luke 7:44-50**

Exposition: Verse by Verse

EATING WITH A PHARISEE

LUKE 7:36 And one of the Pharisees desired him that he would eat with him. And he went into the Pharisee's house, and sat down to meat.

37 And, behold, a woman in the city, which was a sinner, when she knew that Jesus sat at meat in the Pharisee's house, brought an alabaster box of ointment,

38 And stood at his feet behind him weeping, and began to wash his feet with tears, and did wipe them with the hairs of her head, and kissed his feet, and anointed them with the ointment.

39 Now when the Pharisee which had bidden him saw it, he spake within himself, saying, This man, if he were a prophet, would have known who and what manner of woman this is that toucheth him: for she is a sinner.

Special attention (Luke 7:36-38).
Welcome to the home of an overly confident Pharisee! He was about to look down on a sinful woman and on Jesus in the mistaken assumption that the Saviour did not know what kind of woman she was. He would soon be doubly humbled for his arrogant presumption. {Jesus had just been criticized for partying with tax collectors and sinners (vs. 34). Now, because He did not show partiality, He had accepted an invitation to eat dinner at the home of a Pharisee named Simon (cf. vs. 40).}[Q1]

The meal might have been more of a banquet than simply lunch or dinner. Jesus would have been reclining on His side on a low couch with His head near the table, the usual position for eating. As He rested on one elbow, He would have had His feet stretched out behind Him. Normally, sandals would be removed at the door and the guest's feet washed by a servant. This must not have happened, according to what Jesus said to His host later on (vs. 44).

The dinner was for invited guests, but it was not completely private. Others could enter the room and sit around the perimeter while observing and listening in on those involved. That is why this woman with a bad reputation in the city was able to enter the room. It took great courage for her to come.

{She brought an alabaster jar filled with an expensive, perfumed oil, not just ordinary olive oil.}[Q2] Alabaster jars were made from special stone from Egypt and were beautifully carved.

They usually had long necks that were broken off when the contents were to be emptied. Everything about this was expensive. {The woman went to Jesus and wept over His feet, dropping her tears on them. She wiped them with her hair, kissed them, and anointed them with the oil from the jar.}[Q3]

Critical observation (Luke 7:39).
We are now introduced more fully to the Pharisee who overestimated his own righteousness and thought of this woman in a belittling way. He did not verbally express his thoughts, but that did not keep Jesus from knowing them. {Simon also held a low opinion of Jesus, thinking that He must not be a prophet or have any special insight if He did not know what kind of woman was showering this attention upon Him. Simon concluded that Jesus was no more than a common man.}[Q4]

Few women with such a bad reputation would ever approach the home of a Pharisee, so it is likely that Simon was quite shocked to see her enter. And if it was not bad enough that she had come into the room, she then approached Jesus and immediately began to shower Him with attention. For some reason, this Teacher was special to her, giving her the boldness to come. The Pharisee, for his part, was certain that Jesus did not know her and must not have had the ability to discern the truth about her.

What seemed to scandalize Simon the most was that Jesus allowed the woman to touch Him and that the process apparently went on for a considerable length of time. Any true prophet would have put a stop to it! Notice that Simon was not at all concerned about the woman's spiritual need or interested in helping her. Rather, he mentally shoved her aside and judged her to be no more than a sinner. Surely this should be the attitude of every rabbi, so what was the matter with this Jesus?

Dwight Pentecost observed, "The

Pharisee . . . did not reprove the woman for her breach of etiquette, but rather, used the occasion as a basis for his own rejection of the person of Christ. . . . Simon wondered why Christ received demonstrations of affection from sinners" (*The Words and Works of Jesus Christ,* Zondervan).

Warren Wiersbe pointed out, "If you check a harmony of the Gospels, you will discover that just before this event, Jesus had given the gracious invitation, 'Come unto Me . . . and I will give you rest' (Matt 11:28-30). . . . Her tears, her humble attitude, and her expensive gift all spoke of a changed heart" (*The Bible Exposition Commentary,* Cook).

Note that this account bears several similarities to the anointing of Jesus by Mary of Bethany (John 12:1-8; cf. Matt. 26:6-13; Mark 14:3-9), but it may be a separate event.

TEACHING THE PHARISEE

40 And Jesus answering said unto him, Simon, I have somewhat to say unto thee. And he saith, Master, say on.

41 There was a certain creditor which had two debtors: the one owed five hundred pence, and the other fifty.

42 And when they had nothing to pay, he frankly forgave them both. Tell me therefore, which of them will love him most?

43 Simon answered and said, I suppose that he, to whom he forgave most. And he said unto him, Thou hast rightly judged.

An illustration (Luke 7:40-42). In an instructive exchange, Jesus addressed Simon by name, and the Pharisee respectfully responded by calling Him "Master." What followed revealed that Jesus did indeed know what kind of woman was showering Him with attention. He also knew Simon's heart. {Instead of verbally chastening Simon without warn-ing, Jesus used an illustration to draw out an opinion from him.}Q5 From Simon's answer, Jesus would make His point.

The illustration was in the form of a parable. {Two debtors owed a creditor some money, one owing five hundred denarii and the other owing fifty. Neither of them had the money to repay what he owed, so the lender unexpectedly forgave both of them their entire debts. The one debt was ten times greater than the other, but both of them were huge amounts, since one denarius was considered to be a day's wage. So who would love the lender more?}Q6

Since this was a parable, there was an analogy involved, though Simon would not grasp that immediately. {The creditor in Jesus' story depicts God, and the debt depicts sin. The two debtors depict different levels of sinners. The one with the smaller debt depicted Simon the Pharisee, and the one with the larger debt depicted the sinful woman.}Q7 The point of the parable is that God, in His grace, is willing to forgive all sins beyond expectation. Sinners who realize what He has done will be deeply grateful.

Without explaining this to Simon, Jesus posed the question to him about which debtor would have more love in his heart for the lender. Because he would not have understood that Jesus had read the attitudes of his heart, Simon probably had no idea that the parable had anything to do with him. It would have seemed to him that Jesus had simply come up with a story out of nowhere that had nothing to do with their meal, his hosting, or the woman who was there but not welcome.

An affirmation (Luke 7:43). Prefacing his reply with "I suppose," Simon revealed some uncertainty even though it should have been an obvious answer. "The answer to Jesus' question may have been obvious to Simon, though he seems to have known very little about forgiveness and love. However, he apparently knew that Jesus sometimes used questions to lure His critics into a trap. So he replied with uneasy reluctance allowing the possibility that the answer might not be as obvious as it appeared to be" (Constable, *Thomas Constable's Notes on the Bible,* Tyndale).

{Simon's answer was correct, of course, because the one who had been forgiven the most should have been the one who loved the creditor the most. Jesus therefore affirmed that he had answered correctly, having judged the situation accurately.}Q8

CONFRONTING THE PHARISEE

44 And he turned to the woman, and said unto Simon, Seest thou this woman? I entered into thine house, thou gavest me no water for my feet: but she hath washed my feet with tears, and wiped them with the hairs of her head.

45 Thou gavest me no kiss: but this woman since the time I came in hath not ceased to kiss my feet.

46 My head with oil thou didst not anoint: but this woman hath anointed my feet with ointment.

47 Wherefore I say unto thee, Her sins, which are many, are forgiven; for she loved much: but to whom little is forgiven, the same loveth little.

48 And he said unto her, Thy sins are forgiven.

49 And they that sat at meat with him began to say within themselves, Who is this that forgiveth sins also?

50 And he said to the woman, Thy faith hath saved thee; go in peace.

An inattentive host (Luke 7:44-46). Jesus had drawn a contrast between the two debtors in His parable, so now He applied that contrast to Simon and the woman—which no doubt was unexpected and shocking to the Pharisee. {Jesus referred to a series of socially proper activities of greeting that a host would normally show when he had a guest in his home—none of which Simon had followed.}Q9 Did Simon consider his guest to be unequal to himself? Was he elevating himself because of his religious position?

The first thing that normally happened when someone entered a home was the washing of his feet by a servant to get rid of the dust and grime accumulated from the roads. Simon had not provided this courtesy, but the woman had washed Jesus' feet with her tears and wiped them with her hair. It should be noted that the fact that her hair was hanging unbound may have been an indication of her sinful occupation and something that would have added to Simon's critical attitude toward her.

Simon had given no customary cordial kiss of greeting, but from the time she entered the room, the woman had continually kissed Jesus' feet. It was also a normal custom to anoint a guest's head with a small amount of oil, but Simon had ignored doing this as well. The woman, on the other hand, had anointed His feet with an expensive and fragrant oil. The contrast could hardly have been greater. By now, Simon may have been squirming inside and feeling regret for inviting Jesus over!

A loving worshipper (Luke 7:47). The woman's vast amount of sin had already been fully forgiven, and the evidence of that forgiveness was in the deep, expansive love she was displaying. She had evidently responded to Jesus' earlier invitation to come and find peace (cf. Matt. 11:28-30). Jesus made no comment about the spiritual condition of Simon at this point, but His statement on being forgiven little and loving little in return certainly put the spotlight on him. He had not responded to Jesus' invitation.

The Life Application Study Bible notes, "Again Luke contrasts the Pharisees with sinners—and again the sinners come out ahead. . . . In this story it is the grateful prostitute, and not the stingy religious leader, whose sins were forgiven. Although it is God's grace through faith that saves us, and not acts of love or generosity, this woman's act demonstrated her true faith, and Jesus honored her faith" (Beers, ed., Tyndale).

"This woman's act of humility and love shows that she had been forgiven. Jesus did not overlook her sins. He did, in fact, know that this woman was a sinner, and He knew her sins were many. But the fact that her many sins were forgiven caused her to overflow with much love for Jesus. The woman's love did not cause her forgiveness, for no one can earn forgiveness. Her faith in Jesus, despite her many sins, saved her" (Osborne, ed., *Life Application Bible Commentary,* Tyndale).

The contrast could not be clearer, and we must all ask ourselves where we stand in our relationship with Jesus. His invitation still stands: "Come unto me, all ye that labour and are heavy laden, and I will give you rest. Take my yoke upon you, and learn of me; for I am meek and lowly in heart: and ye shall find rest unto your souls" (Matt. 11:28-29). We are all equally loved and have no reason for feeling worthless or hopeless.

A forgiven sinner (Luke 7:48-50). {Jesus' words were right to the point: "Thy sins are forgiven." Those sitting at the table recognized the significance of Jesus' statement, thinking to themselves, "Who is this that forgiveth sins also?" They knew that God alone had the power to forgive sins (cf. Mark 2:7). Depending on how we understand this verse, they either thought Jesus was blaspheming or they were beginning to understand His true identity.}[Q10]

Jesus was not finished, however. "Thy faith hath saved thee; go in peace" (Luke 7:50). How beautiful these words must have sounded to this woman who had not known true peace in her heart for many years! Sin does that to us. There cannot be real peace in anyone's heart as long as he continues to refuse to allow Jesus into his life.

Can believers live in such a way as to miss out on that peace? Have we forgotten the greatness of Jesus' forgiveness? The problem for this Pharisee was that he did not recognize the greatness of his own sin. In Jesus' parable, even the man who owed fifty denarii was in extreme debt. When we compare ourselves to God's holiness instead of to other sinners, we will recognize the exceeding sinfulness of our sin and value the forgiveness and peace of Christ above all else.

—*Keith E. Eggert*

QUESTIONS

1. Why did Jesus accept the invitation of a Pharisee to eat at his home?

2. What did the sinful woman bring with her?

3. What did she do after entering the house?

4. What were the Pharisee's conclusions as he observed he woman's actions toward Jesus?

5. How did Jesus choose to instruct Simon?

6. What was Jesus' illustration?

7. What was the analogy in Jesus' parable that Simon did not understand?

8. How did Simon answer the concluding question of Jesus' parable?

9. How did Jesus contrast Simon—and his lack of response to Jesus—with the woman?

10. How did Jesus reassure the woman, and how did others react?

—*Keith E. Eggert*

Preparing to Teach the Lesson

Most of the adults in your class are probably professing Christians. Yet you may have an unsaved person in your class. Today's lesson is an opportunity to make the gospel clear to any unsaved person.

Even if you have no unsaved person in class, believers need to hear the gospel often. Hearing the gospel brings confidence and assurance of our faith in Christ, reminds us what Christ paid on our behalf, better equips us to share the gospel with others, and encourages us to respond to our Saviour with acts of love.

TODAY'S AIM

Facts: to gain a fresh grasp of our sinfulness and God's grace.

Principle: to put our faith in Christ as Saviour.

Application: to show our love for Christ through our actions.

INTRODUCING THE LESSON

Many in the class have likely already trusted Christ as Saviour. We should be thankful for the work that God has done in the hearts of believers. We should never tire, however, of rehearsing the truth and wonder of the gospel. Doing so reminds us of our sin and its penalty and what Christ did to save us. Take some time for a few students in the class to share their testimony of salvation.

For many of us who have been saved for some time, we may have lost a clear picture of our sinfulness and the judgment we deserve. Our study in Luke 7 will remind us of our former condition. For those who have never put their faith in Christ, this study will show the need we all have for a Saviour and the answer that is found in Him.

DEVELOPING THE LESSON

1. The invitation (Luke 7:36). Jesus had already had several confrontations with the Pharisees (5:21-26; 6:6-11; 7:30-35). Confrontation with them was nothing new, but the confrontation in our text today had a different twist. A Pharisee named Simon (cf. 7:40) invited Jesus to be his dinner guest (vs. 36)! Jesus accepted the invitation and reclined at the table to eat.

Why did Simon invite Jesus to a meal? His intentions are never made clear, but it is possible that he wanted to try to trick Jesus (cf. Matt. 22:15). If this was the case, his plan was interrupted when an uninvited guest stopped by.

2. An uninvited guest (Luke 7:37-38). The uninvited guest is identified as a "woman in the city, which was a sinner." It is possible she was a prostitute. Simon recognized her immediately as a "sinner" (vs. 39), implying either that she was well-known for her sinful lifestyle or that her appearance gave away her occupation.

This woman knew that Jesus was at Simon's house, but even at the risk of ridicule, she joined the dinner party. She brought with her an "alabaster box of ointment" (vs. 37). Both the container and the contents were expensive and represented a substantial cost to her.

Perhaps because the woman felt unworthy to anoint Jesus' head, she "stood at his feet behind him weeping, and began to wash his feet with tears, and did wipe them with the hairs of her head, and kissed his feet, and anointed them with the ointment" (vs. 38). Her actions demonstrated her love and sacrifice for the Lord.

3. The host's consternation (Luke 7:39). Simon was greatly troubled at what had transpired and thought to himself, "This man, if he were a prophet, would have known who and what manner of woman this is that toucheth him: for she is a sinner." Apparently, Simon thought such a woman should not even touch Jesus, especially at his dinner.

4. The conversation (Luke 7:40-50). The remainder of the passage is a series of interactions between Simon, Jesus, and the woman.

Jesus, sensing Simon's reaction, presented a parable. A certain man had two debtors: one owed him five hundred denarii, and the other owed him fifty. Since neither debtor had the money to repay the man, he forgave them both.

Jesus then posed the question: "Tell me therefore, which of them will love him most?" (vs. 42). Simon correctly understood the question and replied, "I suppose that he, to whom he forgave most" (vs. 43).

The Lord used Simon's response to make His point. Simon had not washed Jesus' feet, kissed Him, or anointed His head. The sinful woman had done all these things. She even washed His "feet with tears, and wiped them with the hairs of her head" (vs. 44). Jesus concluded that "her sins, which are many, are forgiven; for she loved much: but to whom little is forgiven, the same loveth little" (vs. 47). The woman had a great sense of her sinfulness and showed it through her actions. Simon thought that he was good enough, so he did not bother with expressions of love.

The woman's actions of love toward Jesus showed that she had accepted Him and was forgiven of her sins.

Simon was sinful but refused to acknowledge it. The woman was sinful and openly acknowledged it. Simon thought he had no sin to be forgiven and therefore had little love for the Lord. The woman understood how much she had been forgiven and evidenced great love for the Saviour.

ILLUSTRATING THE LESSON

We should recognize our sinfulness and realize how much we owe the Lord.

CONCLUDING THE LESSON

Invite the students in your class to examine whether they have ignored or forgotten their need for Christ. Encourage them to confess their sins and ask Jesus for forgiveness. Let them know you will be available to talk after class.

Hopefully, those who are saved have sensed in this lesson how sinful we were and how much we have been forgiven. That recognition should lead us to show acts of love toward Jesus as the woman did. Although Jesus is not physically among us today, what are some acts of love we can show to Him?

We can show acts of love to the Saviour by keeping His commandments, speaking of Him in a loving way, by giving a sacrificial gift to our church or to an individual, or by physically ministering to the helpless and needy.

ANTICIPATING THE NEXT LESSON

Next week we conclude our unit on women of faith as we look at the raising of Dorcas from the dead in Acts 9:36-43.

—Don Anderson

PRACTICAL POINTS

1. Jesus welcomes our fellowship no matter what our status in society may be (Luke 7:36-38).
2. It can be dangerous to imagine we know the Lord's thoughts on a matter (vs. 39).
3. If we think our sins are slight, we fail to adequately appreciate grace (vss. 40-43).
4. A true understanding of our sin and God's grace will bring from us an outpouring of love and devotion (vss. 44-47).
5. Jesus' assurance of forgiveness is sweet—except to those who harbor unbelief (vss. 48-49).
6. Jesus gives us peace when we come to Him in faith (vs. 50).

—*Kenneth A. Sponsler*

RESEARCH AND DISCUSSION

1. What motive might the Pharisee have had in inviting Jesus to dine in his home (Luke 7:36) when he did not plan to show the usual courtesies of the day (vss. 44-46)?
2. The woman's actions in showing love for Jesus (vss. 37-38) are alien to our society. What might some modern equivalents be?
3. What key factor failed to enter into Simon the Pharisee's calculations as he passed judgment on Jesus (vs. 39)?
4. What was Simon communicating by not providing to Jesus the customary services for guests (vss. 44-46)?
5. How can we increase our appreciation for Christ's forgiveness?

—*Kenneth A. Sponsler*

ILLUSTRATED HIGH POINTS

Washed my feet (Luke 7:44)

In Jesus' time, the sandal-shod visitor would be given a basin of water with which to wash the remnants of a dusty road from his weary feet. Though Simon had not provided this courtesy, a different kind of cleansing fluid flowed from the heart of a woman of ill repute.

It turns out that some secretions such as saliva and tears are actually germ-killing fluids. This property of mucus and tears was discovered by accident. In 1922, Alexander Fleming found that mucus from his own dripping nose was killing the bacteria in his petri dish.

Indeed, tears are cleansing, both physically and spiritually. Paul told the Corinthians that through "godly sorrow" they could find repentance and salvation (II Cor. 7:10-11).

For she loved much (vs. 47)

After an emotional cab ride on January 8, 2014, in Dallas, Iraqi war veteran and amputee J. R. Salzman posted the following on a social media site.

"Eventually my cabdriver asked about my missing arm. I told him I lost it in Iraq. . . . I asked him if he would mind telling me where he was from. He choked out the words, 'I'm a Kurd.' His voice cracked as he said, 'I can't look at you and your arm or I will start crying. I am forever grateful for what you have done for us.' . . . Eventually he turned and said, 'This cab ride is free. And I want to pay for your hotel room. I am so grateful for what you've done.'"

As with the woman who bathed Jesus' feet with tears, our gratitude is in direct proportion to our understanding of what Christ has done for us. What are we willing to do for the One who laid down His life to make us free?

—*Therese Greenberg*

Golden Text Illuminated

"He said to the woman, Thy faith hath saved thee; go in peace" (Luke 7:50).

During college, my favorite student organization was the prison ministry. Once a month, a group of students would conduct a service there. It included worship, a short message, and group prayer. I enjoyed fellowshipping with my brothers behind bars.

These men were elated to commune with us. Prayer time was especially precious to one of them. In prison he had become a follower of Christ with a passionate faith. His witness had drawn many to Jesus.

A few months after I started going, this man approached me. He looked at me and said, "Sister, I want to tell you just how Jesus saved me. Can I?"

At my nod, he proceeded to reveal his background and gang involvement. Then he said something stunning. "Sister, I killed someone."

He went on to talk about how he had been saved. "Sister," he concluded, "Jesus cleaned me up and gave me this ministry, and I love Him so much. He forgave me of everything, scoundrel that I am."

That moment I realized how little I valued God's forgiveness. I had never done anything illegal. By society's standards, I was the better person. Yet he, not I, was brimming with joy. He made my love for Jesus look like a candle flame next to a wildfire.

The same can be said about the people in this week's lesson. The woman had a reputation. People were repulsed by her appearance at the feast and even more by her actions.

Yet this woman was showing the depth of her love for Christ. By wiping Jesus' feet, she demonstrated her willingness to do the crudest of tasks for Him. In using her hair, she offered her whole heart.

The ointment was precious. In using it, she proved her readiness to give up her most costly possession. This also showed her eagerness to trust Christ for provision and turn away from her profession. She was willing to go to any extreme for the Saviour she adored. She would lay down her entire life.

Simon, though, was only half in. While he attended temple, he was not devoted to God. His heart was divided. He was self-sufficient, moral, and did not feel the need for Jesus.

It was the woman Jesus forgave. When Christ told her that God was willing to forgive the mess she had made of her life, it was huge. She had felt that she could never again be right with God.

In telling this parable, Jesus made Simon take a hard look at himself. Christ revealed that Simon was lacking in faith and love. The woman was saved because she recognized her need for Jesus, while Simon thought he could make it on his own.

There are many who think that they can get by without Jesus. Sure, we say that we love Him. But do we? A saving faith should hold nothing back. There is no room for compromise.

Moral behavior will not save us. Our good works are filthy rags next to His righteousness (Isa. 64:6). When we consider how He has rescued us, it should make us pause. Our love must be such that we are willing to place all that we have and are into His hands, for any purpose. That is the level of devotion in a saving faith and what we are called to in our daily walk.

—*Jennifer Lautermilch*

Heart of the Lesson

There is much confusion today about what true saving faith is. Millions purport to have faith, but many appear to be putting their faith in the wrong things. Many think that church attendance, or some spiritual activity, or generous giving, or doing more good than bad will enable them to enter heaven forgiven forever. But in today's lesson we see that saving faith is not something that we earn but is rather something that we receive. And having once received it, the gift blossoms into grateful and God-glorifying works.

1. A weeping woman (Luke 7:36-38). As Jesus reclined at the table in the open courtyard of His host, Simon the Pharisee, a woman came in. She was known to Simon, and most likely everyone else present, to be a great sinner. She began to wash and anoint Jesus' feet—first with her tears, then with her hair, and finally with the most expensive gift that she had, her ointment in the alabaster jar.

Although she was publicly shaming herself by touching a man, especially since He was a rabbi, and by letting her hair down in public, the woman could not help herself, shedding tears of joy for having been forgiven by Jesus. We are not told by Luke exactly when this had happened, but Jesus makes it clear in verse 47 that her actions were a result of her having been forgiven and not the reason for her forgiveness.

2. A self-righteous Simon (Luke 7:39). Simon immediately concluded that Jesus must not be the Prophet who others had considered Him to be, or else He would not allow this great sinner to touch Him.

3. A revelation about Simon (Luke 7:40-47). Jesus told a parable about two debtors who both were forgiven a great debt, although the one's debt was ten times larger than the other's. He then asked Simon which of these would be the more grateful to his master. Simon responded, "I suppose that he, to whom he forgave most" (vs. 43).

Jesus then contrasted the loving treatment by the woman with Simon's lack of even the most basic courtesies. He pronounced that because she had been forgiven much, she loved much, while Simon had shown no gratitude or love at all because he did not see himself as a sinner needing forgiveness.

Sadly, many today can easily judge those who are outwardly sinning, but they cannot or will not see their own sinfulness and need for a Saviour. The gift of salvation can be received only by those who understand that need, whether they be outwardly moral and upright or flagrantly sinful. Those who see their need, trust the Saviour, and receive forgiveness for their sins will love and serve Him in proportion to their understanding of how much they have been forgiven.

4. A forgiven woman (Luke 7:48-50). Jesus reassured the woman that her sins had been forgiven and sent her away in peace. And so the lesson ends with a reminder that those who place their faith in Jesus not only receive the assurance of the forgiveness of their sins but also are now free to live a life of peace with God, with themselves, and with others. They must regularly meditate on the words and acts of their Saviour.

—Don Kakavecos

World Missions

Each culture carries a moral code and an understanding that certain sins are not too bad while others cross the line into what is unacceptable. Those who cross that line are condemned and rejected by the rest of the society, who limit themselves to the "lesser" sins and thus feel morally superior.

This kind of rejection can be outward and obvious. It can also be subtle, meaning that the condemnation is there but not openly expressed, such as that felt by Simon toward the sinful woman. How would we behave if a drunk man staggered into our church, or a woman with a bad reputation showed up at a women's luncheon, or a man who had been openly unfaithful slipped in after the service started?

How many people who long for forgiveness have been hindered on their way to Jesus because of rejection—not from God but from His children? In other cultures it can sometimes be more easily seen. We notice the prejudices when the culture is not our own. It is sometimes harder to see the beam in our own eyes.

We could give examples of portions of society that are not welcome in some of the churches around the world. For today, however, let us take a moment and consider who is not welcome among us. Whom would we be willing to give a tract but not invite into our home? Whom would we reject (either outwardly or inwardly) as beyond the reach of forgiveness?

The woman who came into Simon's home must have had tremendous courage. She was a well-known sinner. To come into this Pharisee's home was either an act of great defiance or an act of great desperation. Her tears implied the latter. She seemed not to care about Simon's condemnation or even his presence. Her focus was entirely on Jesus.

She did not defend herself or excuse her sins. Luke does not mention her speaking at all. Her actions, however, showed her shame, repentance, and worship. Jesus accepted her rather shocking form of worship and then presented her, the sinner, as an example to the Pharisee of what real love was and what real forgiveness could do. Then He told her, "Thy faith hath saved thee; go in peace" (Luke 7:50).

She was forgiven and would never be the same again. Jesus had offered her peace. She did not say a rote prayer or fill out a card. But she confessed in a very obvious way her need of the Saviour and was given salvation, forgiveness, and something everyone longs for—peace.

We will encounter people who we might think should draw back and feel so unclean and sinful that they know they are unworthy to approach God's throne. Praise God when they do not let that or anything else stop them! Yes, those are the people who show us what grace truly is and what forgiveness can do. We should stand back and marvel when God reaches down to touch the untouchable, to accept the worship of well-known sinners, and to tell those who have lived in darkness and shame to go in peace.

Oh, the beauty of God's forgiveness and salvation!

If such people come into our midst, let us show them the way straight to the throne of heaven, where they can encounter the Jesus who forgives, offers them peace, and makes all things new.

—*Kimberly Rae*

The Jewish Aspect

Why did the sinful woman kiss the feet of Jesus (Luke 7:38)? What did her actions show about what Jesus meant to her? Even in modern times, a kiss can have a variety of meanings. For example, each year tourists visit the Blarney Castle in Ireland to kiss the Blarney stone. This supposedly will gain them the gift of eloquence. In ancient times, likewise, kissing had a variety of connotations.

The Greek word for "kiss" in Luke 7 is *kataphileo*, a word which means to kiss lovingly. It is used to describe the father's welcome of the returning prodigal son (15:20) and the Ephesian elders' farewell to Paul when he tells them they will not see him again (Acts 20:37). The sinful woman was demonstrating a strong emotion, but what did it mean to Jews at that time?

The Bible does refer to the romantic kiss of lovers (S Sol. 1:2) and a prostitute using a kiss of seduction (Prov. 7:13), but these are rare. Jews viewed the kiss more frequently as an indication of honor, and it was usually given on the cheek. In the Old Testament, for example, a son kissed his father (Gen. 27:26-27) or father-in-law (Ex. 18:7), a father kissed his children and grandchildren (Gen. 31:28), and uncles and nephews kissed (29:13). The kiss was a greeting of affection. A kiss was given between close friends (I Sam. 20:41) and to show loyal attachment for favors granted (II Sam. 19:39).

A kiss was also given at times when people separated, not expecting to see each other again (Ruth 1:14). The most poignant example of this is a kiss given at the time of death (Gen. 50:1). A kiss sometimes had ceremonial significance. Samuel kissed Saul when he anointed him king (I Sam. 10:1). In a negative example, Jews kissed the idol Baal (I Kgs. 19:18) and other idols in false worship (Hos. 13:2). In contrast, Job testified that he did not throw kisses in worship of the sun or moon (Job 31:27). Jews today still observe that "kisses can express deference, reverence, friendship, affection, love, and even betrayal" ("Kissing Kabbalists," www.myjewishlearning.com).

The Jews also believed that God Himself kissed people at death. This was an expression of covenant faithfulness. The chief example came from Moses: "So Moses the servant of the Lord died there in the land of Moab, according to the word [mouth] of the Lord" (Deut. 34:5). Jewish interpreters took the word "mouth" to mean that, at Moses' death, God "kissed Moses, and took his soul while kissing his mouth" (Midrash *Deuteronomy Rabbah* 11). The Talmud expands on this idea by saying that God made 903 forms of death, and "the mildest of them is *Neshika*—'the kiss of death'" ("With a Kiss," torah.org).

Two kissing customs were pertinent for the woman in Luke 7. Jewish custom of that time required a host to "place his hand on any guest's shoulder and give him the kiss of peace" when he entered (Bromiley, ed., "Kiss," *International Standard Bible Encyclopedia,* Eerdmans). Jesus' host, Simon the Pharisee, neglected this custom, but the woman went even further in honoring Christ. In addition, ancient Babylonian and Egyptian documents demonstrate that kissing the feet of a king was a custom to demonstrate humility and homage. In kissing the feet of Jesus, this woman may have recognized that He was the promised King of Israel (cf. Ps. 2:12). Her faith was great indeed.

—R. Larry Overstreet

Guiding the Superintendent

"Born in 1820, Fanny Crosby took ill at six weeks of age. A local 'doctor' prescribed an eye salve that soon blinded her for life. As a result, she learned to develop her other senses, including a very keen memory and sense of creativity.

"After becoming a Christian, she used her wealth of memorized Scripture to compose more than 9000 hymns! She held no animosity for the so-called doctor. She saw her blindness as a divine opportunity to impact the world for Christ, praying often that God might use her music to bring others to a saving faith in Jesus" (www.illustrationexchange.com).

In this week's lesson, we learn of the priority of saving faith in Jesus Christ. A sinner being forgiven is the most important event in this world!

DEVOTIONAL OUTLINE

1. An act of extravagant worship (Luke 7:36-39). A Pharisee named Simon invited Jesus to his home for a meal. While they were dining, a woman of sinful reputation entered the home and proceeded to approach Jesus in an act of worship. As Simon witnessed the woman's act of worship, he conducted a discussion within himself in which he questioned Jesus' knowledge and condemned the woman's character.

2. A discussion of authentic love (Luke 7:40-47). Jesus was well aware of Simon's thoughts, so He spoke a parable and taught Simon a valuable lesson about authentic love and forgiveness. After listening to Jesus' teaching and being asked a concluding question, Simon gave evidence that he had head knowledge of the parable's main lesson.

Jesus knew that Simon needed to apply the parable to himself. Using the woman as an illustration, He chastised him for not showing even minimal hospitality. The woman's worship demonstrated the immensity of her love for Jesus Christ. Simon, on the other hand, demonstrated his lack of love by refusing to serve the Lord.

Jesus' piercing conclusion declared that the woman had been forgiven much, which was evident from her profuse love. In contrast, Simon's lack of love proved his low estimation of God's forgiveness.

3. A declaration of saving faith (Luke 7:48-50). Jesus told the woman that her sins were forgiven. Hearing Jesus' declaration, the dinner guests questioned within themselves concerning Jesus' identity. Jesus then confirmed His prior statement by declaring that the woman's faith had saved her. He then conferred on her His blessing of peace.

AGE-GROUP EMPHASES

Children: Children love hearing grand stories that engage their wonderful imaginations. Try to get your children to imagine what it would have been like to be present at this event.

Youths: Young people receive a distorted view of love from the culture and their unbelieving peers. Counter this distortion with the teaching of the dynamic relationship that exists between godly love and heartfelt worship. Encourage your young people to express love for Jesus through worship, especially together with the church.

Adults: The complexities of life often cause adults to forget the simplicity of the sincere faith that resulted in their eternal salvation. Have your adults give testimonies of how God brought them to saving faith and has given them an increasing love for Jesus Christ. Spend time in prayer, asking the Holy Spirit to renew their faith and to keep them sensitive to hearing God's voice.

—*Thomas R. Chmura*

Scripture Lesson Text

ACTS 9:36 Now there was at Joppa a certain disciple named Tabitha, which by interpretation is called Dorcas: this woman was full of good works and almsdeeds which she did.

37 And it came to pass in those days, that she was sick, and died: whom when they had washed, they laid *her* in an upper chamber.

38 And forasmuch as Lydda was nigh to Joppa, and the disciples had heard that Peter was there, they sent unto him two men, desiring *him* that he would not delay to come to them.

39 Then Peter arose and went with them. When he was come, they brought him into the upper chamber: and all the widows stood by him weeping, and shewing the coats and garments which Dorcas made, while she was with them.

40 But Peter put them all forth, and kneeled down, and prayed; and turning *him* to the body said, Tabitha, arise. And she opened her eyes: and when she saw Peter, she sat up.

41 And he gave her *his* hand, and lifted her up, and when he had called the saints and widows, presented her alive.

42 And it was known throughout all Joppa; and many believed in the Lord.

43 And it came to pass, that he tarried many days in Joppa with one Simon a tanner.

NOTES

A Faithful Servant in the Church

Lesson Text: Acts 9:36-43

Related Scriptures: II Kings 4:18-37; Matthew 9:18-19, 23-26;
I Thessalonians 4:13-18

TIME: A.D. 35   PLACE: Joppa

GOLDEN TEXT—"She stretcheth out her hand to the poor; yea, she reacheth forth her hands to the needy" (Proverbs 31:20).

Introduction

Christianity grew wildly in the early years of the church. New Christians dramatically experienced forgiveness of sin and were filled with a hope and a new purpose. They eagerly shared this experience with people who were still living in darkness and hopelessness.

One of the ways they shared their faith was through ministering to those in need. Widows were especially vulnerable, often having no one to advocate for them and often in dire circumstances (Acts 6:1-2; I Tim. 5:3-16). One disciple, a woman named Tabitha, was especially known for always doing good and helping the poor (Acts 9:36).

There are many ways that the church can share its faith in Jesus Christ in our modern society. The needy and widows are still prime examples of people who need believers to share the love of Christ to their meet their needs. Tabitha provides a good model to follow.

LESSON OUTLINE

I. A FAITHFUL FRIEND—
Acts 9:36-38

II. A FAITHFUL GOD—
Acts 9:39-43

Exposition: Verse by Verse

A FAITHFUL FRIEND

ACTS 9:36 Now there was at Joppa a certain disciple named Tabitha, which by interpretation is called Dorcas: this woman was full of good works and almsdeeds which she did.

37 And it came to pass in those days, that she was sick, and died: whom when they had washed, they laid her in an upper chamber.

38 And forasmuch as Lydda was nigh to Joppa, and the disciples had heard that Peter was there, they sent unto him two men, desiring him that he would not delay to come to them.

A good woman (Acts 9:36). After detailing the conversion of Saul and his initial ministries in Damascus and Jerusalem, Luke, the author of Acts, continues Peter's story. {As Peter traveled around the country, he came to Lydda, where he healed a man named Aeneas of paralysis (vss. 32-34). The town of Joppa was about twelve miles away, where there lived "a certain disciple named Tabitha" (vs. 36), also known by her Greek name Dorcas (both meaning "gazelle").}[Q1]

Today's Jaffa, now a part of Tel-Aviv, is ancient Joppa. It was from here that Jonah tried to flee from God. In contrast, Peter went to Joppa to serve God. Joppa was a predominately Jewish town, reinforcing the depiction of Peter as following his ministerial call to the Jews (cf. Gal. 2:7-9).

{Dorcas was known for her good works and helpful deeds for others.}[Q2] She modeled the servant-heart of Christ, eager to give others a helping hand when it was needed. Luke characterized her as full of good works and charitable acts (Acts 9:36), indicating that she very willingly put aside her own needs and planned activities in order to reach out and help others who faced problems.

Dorcas's ministerial heart and loving kindness impacted many people, as indicated by the many widows who surrounded Dorcas at her time of need.

A grievous loss (Acts 9:37). {While Peter was ministering in nearby Lydda, Dorcas became sick and died. One wonders why God sometimes allows His faithful servants to die when they are eager to minister, while allowing other people to live who otherwise have no interest in serving him. Regardless, the reason why God grants life and breath to anyone is so they can serve Him.

It is always hard to accept the death of someone who is kind, active, and useful in a local church. People like Dorcas are needed everywhere, but God in His greatness accomplishes His will even through losses that are difficult to bear. He has the right to give and to take away; so even when the loss is painful, we should continue to be thankful and trust in His sovereign will and control. The death of Dorcas was truly a great loss to that congregation, but the believers in Joppa had hope in spite of it.

It was customary for the bodies of the deceased to be buried immediately (cf. Acts 5:1-10). The fact that the believers washed Dorcas's body and laid her in an upper chamber instead of having her buried immediately indicates an unusual approach. Washing the body was a common practice in many cultures, including among the Jews. Another common practice was to anoint the body with spices, but Luke doesn't mention if Tabitha's body was anointed.}[Q3]

We will soon see that her friends were aware of Peter's presence in Lydda. Although we have no record of any of the apostles previously bringing someone back to life after death, is it possible that these friends were hoping for that most unusual result?

A hopeful request (Acts 9:38). {The short distance between Joppa and Lydda allowed news of Peter's healing ministry to reach Joppa quickly. Distressed as they were over Dorcas's death, they turned to Peter for help. The Bible does not specifically record instances of the apostles raising anyone from the dead up to the time of Acts 9, but God's power was definitely at work in Peter.}[Q4]

The disciples in Joppa sent two men from their group to find Peter. Given the urgency to bury a dead body, the men likely set off at once on the three-hour southeasterly journey. Once they found Peter, the disciples implored him to come at once, without delay.

We understand the urgency of the situation when we realize that decomposition began soon in the warm climate, and since several hours of travel each way was required, time was of the essence. We are not told what Peter was doing when the two messengers arrived, but evidently he was able to leave immediately and accompany the men back to Joppa.

Those in ministry know that emergency situations require immediate attention. During such times, we must lean heavily on the Lord and ask for His guidance. Emergencies can arise in everyday life for any one of us. The only way we can be prepared to handle unexpected situations is to have a consistently close walk with God at all times. Then when the unexpected hits, we are fully aware of His presence and strengthening power.

A FAITHFUL GOD

39 Then Peter arose and went with them. When he was come, they brought him into the upper chamber: and all the widows stood by him weeping, and shewing the coats and garments which Dorcas made, while she was with them.

40 But Peter put them all forth, and kneeled down, and prayed; and turning him to the body said, Tabitha, arise. And she opened her eyes: and when she saw Peter, she sat up.

41 And he gave her his hand, and lifted her up, and when he had called the saints and widows, presented her alive.

42 And it was known throughout all Joppa; and many believed in the Lord.

43 And it came to pass, that he tarried many days in Joppa with one Simon a tanner.

Peter's arrival (Acts 9:39). Peter immediately started out with the two men. As soon as he arrived in Joppa, he was ushered into the upper chamber where Dorcas's body was lying. As was typical of death rituals in the ancient Middle East (cf. Mark 5:38-39), Peter found Dorcas's body surrounded by mourners. Dorcas was a benefactor, or patron, of many widows, and they gathered around her body to comfort one another.

{The mourners impressed upon Peter her generosity, showing him robes and other clothing she had made for them—some of which they were likely wearing at the very moment. More than an effort to convey Dorcas's competence as a seamstress, the widows were testifying to her love for people in abject poverty. No doubt Dorcas's ministry restored some measure of respect to some impoverished widows.}[Q5]

If you have a talent for sewing, use it to help others and glorify God. If your talent is automobile mechanics, you can be a great encouragement when you fix someone's broken vehicle, especially if it belongs to a widow or a single mother. If your talent is music, it should be used as a means of exalting God and pointing others to Him in worship. If you have handyman or construction skills, or computer skills, or resume writing skills, God has granted these to you so you can minister to people.

Each one of us is valuable in God's eyes and designed to minister to others, so we should never feel insignificant or unimportant.

Peter's prayer (Acts 9:40). What Peter did here closely follows Jesus' pattern in raising Jairus's daughter (Mark 5:35-42). {The first thing Peter did was send everyone else out of the room, just as Jesus had dismissed a number of people before healing the young girl.}[Q6]

{Peter then knelt down and prayed, showing that he was not relying on any power of his own but on what God could accomplish through him. We see the same attitude in the healing of Aeneas, when Peter said to him, "Aeneas, Jesus Christ maketh thee whole: arise, and make thy bed" (Acts 9:34). Peter recognized that whatever spiritual authority and power he might have came from God and was not in himself.}[Q7]

Even in the use of our gifts and talents, we should remember that what we have has been given to us by God. We have not earned or achieved such abilities on our own, so we should not take pride in the ways God uses us. All the glory belongs to Him.

Peter's words to Dorcas were "Tabitha, arise" (vs. 40). The fact that Peter used Tabitha's Aramaic name instead of her Greek name Dorcas, is a fairly strong indication that Peter was speaking with her in Aramaic.

Thomas Constable pointed out, "There is only one letter difference in what Peter said (*Tabitha qumi*) and what Jesus had said (*Talitha qumi,* lit. 'Little girl, get up'). This miracle is another evidence of Jesus' working powerfully through His witnesses in word and deed" (*Constable's Notes,* net.bible.org). {Dorcas immediately opened her eyes, saw Peter, and sat up.}[Q8] The instant response revealed both God's power and the depth of Peter's faith in Jesus' continuing presence and ability to accomplish miracles.

Peter was doing the works Jesus had previously given His apostles when He said, "Heal the sick, cleanse the lepers, raise the dead, cast out devils: freely ye have received, freely give" (Matt. 10:8).

On that occasion, Jesus sent the twelve disciples on a mission to preach the kingdom of heaven to the Israelites only. For that early mission, He prohibited them from going to the Gentiles. But now that Jesus had been crucified and risen from the dead, it was time for the mission to the Gentiles to begin. In only a few days, Peter would be instrumental in proclaiming the gospel to the Gentiles. It must have been a source of deep joy to him to see such a work of God through him, apparently restoring life for the first time.

Presentation to the saints (Acts 9:41). At Peter's command to rise, Dorcas opened her eyes and sat up. In a social context where a person is considered "unclean" if they enter a room with a dead body, Peter reaches out his hand to take Dorcas's hand. Just as was the case whenever Jesus touched an unclean person, God's power through Peter purified any "uncleanness."

It must have been with a great sense of joy that Peter called out to the believers who were there, especially to the widows who had been mourning the death of their friend, and presented her alive once again. Although Peter was being greatly used by God in unique ways, he had emotions and surely would have been moved by this miraculous event, as any of us would.

The joy the apostles felt when they did great miracles for God can be ours when we reach out and help others in need, as both Peter and Dorcas did. God does not intend for us to live only for ourselves but has given us the privilege of having relationships. He wants us to encourage and benefit others.

Prevailing message (Acts 9:42-43). {Soon the whole town had heard about the raising of Dorcas. Her own popularity surely contributed to the news spreading quickly. The miracle gave Peter and the other believers opportunities to share the gospel message, for many others became believers as a result of this one incident.}[Q9] Peter did not claim personal greatness because of what had happened but rather simply pointed people to Jesus.

To both the healing of Aeneas in Lydda and the raising of Dorcas in Joppa, there was a response of faith. Acts 9:35 reads that after Aeneas's healing, many "turned to the Lord." After Dorcas's raising, we read that "many believed in the Lord" (vs. 42). Both phrases indicate faith in Jesus as Saviour and Lord.

As was the case with Jesus' own ministry, miracles functioned to draw attention to Christ and message that He preached. Miracles had the same function for Peter and other apostles. Christianity was still in its infancy, and miraculous healings ensured that the news would spread widely and rapidly. And hearing of such amazing events brought a curiosity to learn more about Jesus and apostles who were healing in His name.

God was accomplishing the spread of the gospel through His servants, and the family of God was increasing steadily. God's plan continues to focus on spreading the good news of salvation through us.

{Peter stayed in Joppa many days as the guest of Simon the tanner. Tanners were not looked upon favorably by Jewish people because of their constant contact with the skins of dead animals, making them ceremonially unclean (cf. Lev. 11:40). In the next chapter of Acts, Peter would be sent to minister to a group of Gentiles at the home of Cornelius, so his stay with Simon served as preparation for his next assignment in ministry.}[Q10]

We have to appreciate Peter's willingness to serve in whatever way God directed, even when it might have been outside of his comfort zone. He was a faithful disciple, always eager to do what his Master wanted. He is an example we should follow.

—*Keith E. Eggert*

QUESTIONS

1. What two people and what two towns are mentioned in this account of Peter's ministry?

2. What was Dorcas's reputation among the people of Joppa?

3. What happened to Dorcas that caused sorrow in the town, and what did the people do with her?

4. To whom did Dorcas's friends reach out for help, and what made them think of doing this?

5. How did the people of Joppa let Peter know how much Dorcas had meant to them?

6. What initial action by Peter mimicked what Jesus had done?

7. Why is it important to know that Peter prayed before doing anything else?

8. What happened after his prayer?

9. What happened in Joppa as a result of this incident?

10. Where did Peter stay, and why is this significant?

—*Keith E. Eggert*

Preparing to Teach the Lesson

Faithfulness is often lived out quietly by people not recognized as glamorous or popular. Sarah Lindow was a member of our small church in upstate New York. While I was visiting her one day, she shared her daily prayer list with me. Mrs. Lindow handed me six sheets of paper containing the names of nearly two hundred individuals for whom she prayed each day. I was honored to see my name at the top of the page. I remember looking at her and stating, "Please never take my name off that list." She passed away a few years later, and I sensed the loss of her support and spiritual strength.

Christianity has succeeded throughout the centuries because of the anonymous servants of Christ behind the scenes. They are dedicated to utilizing their talents and gifts for the glory of God, uninterested in personal gain or recognition.

TODAY'S AIM

Facts: to understand the culture of discipleship in the early church.

Principle: to appreciate the position of Dorcas, the mourners, and Peter as the story unfolds.

Application: to show that God desires that we serve as faithful disciples, using the abilities He has given us.

INTRODUCING THE LESSON

Joppa was located on the eastern coast of the Mediterranean Sea. The name of the city eventually was changed to Jaffa and in modern times incorporated into the city of Tel Aviv. Modern Tel Aviv stands in stark contrast to the village of Joppa during the apostolic era.

Lydda, a smaller village nestled in the rolling hills, was about ten miles from Joppa. Peter was visiting Lydda as he went from place to place preaching the gospel.

In this lesson, we will examine the faith of a number of people. Faith caused Dorcas to use her talents for the Lord. Faith caused her friends to believe a miracle could happen. Faith encouraged Peter to attempt the impossible.

DEVELOPING THE LESSON

1. The death of Dorcas (Acts 9:36-37). Acts gives two names for the godly woman who lived at Joppa: Tabitha, her Hebrew name, and Dorcas, her Greek name. The meaning of her name in both languages is gazelle. She is not mentioned in any other portion of Scripture; however, her testimony is evident in this passage in Acts.

Dorcas is first identified as a disciple of Jesus Christ. The word "disciple" simply means one who follows the teaching of another. New Testament disciples were those who listened to the apostles and teachers relay the precepts taught to them by Jesus and then applied them to their everyday lives.

Dorcas's love for the Lord was expressed through good deeds and charitable acts (vs. 36), which involved works of mercy on behalf of the less fortunate. It seems men and women were able to have a warm coat or an outer garment because of Dorcas's labor as a seamstress (cf. vs. 39). Dorcas was faithful in fulfilling her calling.

During the time Peter was in Lydda, this godly woman passed away. The custom of the Jews was to bury the body on the day of death, but her friends placed her body in an upper room and apparently delayed burial.

2. The determination of the friends (Acts 9:38). The friends of Dorcas are also described as disciples. They also followed the teachings of Christ, and they had heard that Peter was only ten miles away. We can only imagine someone suggesting the impossible: "Call Peter. He has healed others. Maybe he can raise Dorcas." The believers decided to seek out Peter. They exercised their faith by trusting God for a miracle. Two men immediately left for Lydda to present their request to the apostle.

3. The decision of Peter (Acts 9:39-43). The average person can walk a mile in twenty minutes; therefore, it could have taken the men three hours to walk from Joppa to Lydda and another three to return. Dorcas was dead over six hours by the time Peter reached Joppa.

When Peter arrived, the disciples immediately took him to the body of Dorcas. The room was filled with widows and others who had loved her and benefited from her ministry. They were wailing loudly and sobbing openly.

Politely yet firmly, Peter requested that everyone leave the room as he sought the Lord's will. Peter had watched his Saviour bring people back from the dead. He could recall Lazarus coming out of the tomb (John 11:1-44), the widow of Nain's son (Luke 7:11-17), and the daughter of Jairus (Matt. 9:18-26). Peter personally was involved in healing a lame man (Acts 3:1-11) and a man named Aeneas (9:34) and in many other signs and wonders (5:12-16). He knew the power of God, and he knew that with faith as a grain of mustard seed he could move mountains (Matt. 17:20).

Peter knelt down and prayed. His prayer is not recorded, but perhaps he was seeking God's will in this matter or God's power. He then turned to face the dead body lying on the bed and said, "Tabitha, arise" (Acts 9:40). She immediately opened her eyes, as her spirit was quickened. Her gaze fell on Peter, and she arose to a sitting position.

Grasping her hand, Peter lifted her up from her deathbed to a renewed life.

Peter's faith had indeed been enough.

The healing of Dorcas was a powerful exhibition of the supremacy of God and the power of simple faith. The events that transpired after Dorcas's healing were as miraculous as the event itself. The writer of Acts recorded, "And many believed in the Lord" (vs. 42).

ILLUSTRATING THE LESSON

Our lesson highlights the faithfulness of true disciples of Christ. Dorcas faithfully served others, her fellow disciples believed God could raise her to life, and Peter acted in faith to do just that.

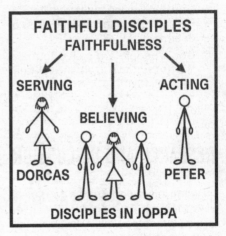

CONCLUDING THE LESSON

Not only did the Lord return Dorcas to life again, but also many people in the area were born again and given new life. Even today as we read of the miraculous raising of the seamstress, we are encouraged and our faith grows.

ANTICIPATING THE NEXT LESSON

Spiritual leaders shape our thinking and mold our character. It is essential to select godly leaders with a heart to follow God. The qualities of a godly leader may be different from the ones the world admires.

—*Phil Stamm*

PRACTICAL POINTS

1. Christians are great blessings for Christ as they lovingly serve their communities (Acts 9:36).
2. Active faith leaves a lasting impression on those we encounter (vss. 37-38).
3. Active faith attracts those seeking peace and comfort in times of crisis (vs. 39).
4. God works through those who will submit to Him in faith and rely on His power (vs. 40).
5. God is still using those who believe He can bring life into the midst of death (vs. 41).
6. God's people are called to make His truth known to all who will hear (vss. 42-43).

—Cheryl Y. Powell

RESEARCH AND DISCUSSION

1. Who have you known to impact others for Christ through service in your community? How have you been challenged or encouraged by those examples?
2. What is God's purpose for spiritual gifts? What does the life of Tabitha teach believers today about spiritual gifts (cf. Rom. 12:3-8; I Cor. 12:12-31)?
3. In what ways can believers today be helpful to those who are grieving? What do believers need to do to avoid adding to the burden of the grieving?
4. What ultimate purpose did God accomplish through bringing Tabitha back to life? How does this purpose challenge us?

—Cheryl Y. Powell

ILLUSTRATED HIGH POINTS

Full of good works and acts of charity (Acts 9:36)

After twenty-five years of false imprisonment, Michael Morton was exonerated by DNA evidence.

He did not have a tough-guy image that might impress inmates. He was, however, a believer who had found Christ all alone in his cell. Soon after, as Dorcas did, he began to notice the needs of those around him.

One inmate said, "One of the things that Mike always did was, when he went to the commissary, he always ended up buying either moon pies or ice cream cones or something . . . to distribute to those guys that didn't have anything" ("An Unreal Dream"). Morton had garnered a legacy of gentle caring that brought a prison to its feet.

But Peter put them all forth (vs. 40)

The field marshal recounted the deeds of his most impressive battle while Napoleon quietly listened. Nevertheless, as much as he elaborated, Napoleon seemed unmoved. When Napoleon finally spoke, he asked simply, "And what did you do the next day?" The war was not over, and he still had a job to do.

Granted, there was good reason to believe that Dorcas was ready for a tribute (after all, she was dead), but God was not finished with her yet. Peter had no desire to listen to her being eulogized. He turned to her and prayed. Then he called the mourners back into the room and presented her alive.

Biblical men never retire from Christ's service. No matter how it looks, your ministry is not dead. You can always follow God and serve Him.

—Therese Greenberg

Golden Text Illuminated

"She stretcheth out her hand to the poor; yea, she reacheth forth her hands to the needy" (Proverbs 31:20).

When we think of an example of a faithful servant of Christ, we often envision a famous pastor or a long-time missionary in a foreign field. These are great examples of God's servants, but emphasizing these highly visible vocations may keep us from seeing the faithful service performed by godly believers around us every day. We might even miss the opportunities God offers for us to serve Him.

Consider the example of a godly wife, as described in Proverbs 31:10-31. Her excellent character qualities flow from a heart of dedication to the Lord (vs. 30). The primary benefactor of her faithful service to God is her husband. By applying God's wisdom, she cares for the needs of her household in a way that inspires her husband's confidence in her. Her wise monetary decisions help alleviate any financial burdens they face. And through her hard work and careful attention, her children have all of their daily needs met.

The godly woman's influence extends beyond her household. She notices the poor and needy around her and strives to help them. We often do not think of caring for the poor. We have government programs established for this purpose, so we often think that our efforts are not needed. It is easy to rationalize our inactivity toward the poor by saying that the help we provide might be used for illegal drugs or that they do not want to work. But caring for the poor is a scriptural mandate. In biblical times there were no government agencies available to help the poor. The servanthood of God's people was the way this societal need was met.

Tabitha of Joppa saw the importance of serving God through various good deeds, including helping the poor (Acts 9:36). She developed a good reputation for her compassion. When she became sick and died, some of her Christian friends sent for Peter. When Peter arrived, he found many widows at Tabitha's house mourning for her. The widows displayed the many articles of clothing that Tabitha created for them. Peter sent the widows out of the room and prayed for Tabitha. Many people turned to Christ when she miraculously came back to life.

Receiving praise for doing good deeds does not diminish the glory of Christ, as long as it does not build pride. The praise for the godly wife's good works is to be proclaimed publicly (Prov. 31:31). Boaz told Ruth that everyone in Bethlehem knew about her excellent character (Ruth 3:11).

Faithful service for Christ does not require a special vocational ministry, a high-profile position, or professional training. It begins with a heart devoted to Christ. Once Jesus opens our hearts to serve Him, then He can open our eyes to the opportunities surrounding us. The best place to start is in our own household. Once we have trained ourselves to serve our family members, it will be easier for us to serve in our neighborhood, workplace, and church.

We don't serve God in order to receive praise from others. But the praise and good reputation we receive can be a testimony to God's work in our lives. Our acts of compassion that God works through us can spur other people to meet the needs of those in their own sphere of influence.

—*Glenn Weaver*

Heart of the Lesson

My former unit, the Third U.S. Infantry, "The Old Guard," has several subunits. Among them is the Honor Guard—sentinels at the Tomb of the Unknown Soldier in Arlington National Cemetery. Highly trained soldiers, they perform with precision the minutest detail from the number of steps taken, the number of degrees turned, the number of seconds of hesitation, to the "shoulder-arms" movement that places the rifle nearest the visitors, symbolizing the tomb's protection. This intricate ritual has been passed on for decades. Those guards have been discipled by their predecessors.

A disciple learns from a master and imitates his lifestyle, and this week's lesson examines a faithful disciple who did exactly that.

1. The disciple's death (Acts 9:36-38). A female disciple named Tabitha (Dorcas), who had the spiritual gift of service (Rom. 12:7; I Cor. 12:7; cf. I Pet 4:10), lived in Joppa. Luke recorded that she was full of good works and acts of charity (Acts 9:36). She became ill, however, and died. Some of the disciples, hearing that Peter was at Lydda (about ten miles away), dispatched two men requesting that he quickly come up to Joppa.

2. The apostle's actions (Acts 9:39-41). When Peter arrived, he was shown to the upper chamber where Dorcas was lying. Several widows were in attendance, weeping and showing Peter "the coats and garments which Dorcas made, while she was with them." Peter sent them out of the room, knelt, and prayed. He then commanded her to arise, and Dorcas opened her eyes and sat up. He helped her to her feet, called the believers and widows back into the room, and presented her to them—alive!

3. The resurrection's result (Acts 9:42-43). This authenticating apostolic sign had immediate results. Word of Dorcas's resurrection spread throughout the city, and "many believed in the Lord." Luke wrote that Peter stayed in Joppa many days with a tanner named Simon. That God had Peter remain in Joppa is significant because it was from there that He would dispatch him to Cornelius's house, where the gospel first went to the Gentiles (10:1-48).

Several things are noteworthy. First, Dorcas was doing what a disciple should do—imitating her Lord. Christ loved people and ministered to their needs. Likewise, Dorcas loved people and ministered to them.

Second, her life so impacted others that when she died, her friends immediately sent for an apostle. While miracles seem fairly common during the apostolic age, it is significant that this is the only time surviving friends requested an apostle's aid. Was it because they expected Peter to raise her from the dead? One would think so.

Third, throughout Acts the apostles were witnessing to the resurrection of Christ (cf. 1:8; 2:32; 3:15; 4:2). The result of this apostolic sign was not only that many came to faith, but also that Dorcas undoubtedly continued her faithful ministry as His disciple.

Are we demonstrating that we are Christ's disciples by exemplary good works? While "sitting at His feet" and learning, are we imitating the Lord Jesus by our godly service? May the world see that we are true disciples not only by our words of love but also by our ministry to others!

—Timothy L. Whitehead

World Missions

When God has a task to be done, who does He call on to do it? What are the factors that contribute to the decision God makes? Surely He does not have a heavenly dart board with names on it, awaiting random tosses to determine His choices. There are instances in Scripture, of course, that reveal that God can use anyone to accomplish His purposes. One example would be Caesar Augustus, who decreed that all the world should be taxed. That decree resulted in Joseph and Mary traveling to Bethlehem and being there when Jesus was born, thus fulfilling prophecy (cf. Mic. 5:2).

For now, however, we want to focus on believers as the people from which the Lord chooses one or more for a specific task. A speaker once remarked that God uses FAT Christians. Right away many of us perked up just a bit at the thought. It certainly caught the attention of the audience.

What the speaker meant, though, had nothing to do with one's physical condition but rather his spiritual state. FAT means that a believer should be faithful, available, and teachable. We see it when God called Philip to go south to a road leading from Jerusalem to Gaza to meet with an Ethiopian eunuch (Acts 8:26-39). We see it also in this week's text when God used Peter in ministry in Joppa. Even a casual reading of Acts, the history of the early church, will show faithful, available, and teachable believers being used by God.

What does it mean to be faithful, and how does that tie in with missions? It means that person is not only a believer in Christ but is living obediently to Him as well. Many who profess faith in Christ do not allow their knowledge to make a difference in their lives. A faithful believer makes a conscious effort to obey Scripture in each and every situation he encounters. He desires to please the Lord, even if it costs him something. This is not a compromising faith but a steadfast faith.

What does it mean to be available? It means to be willing to alter one's own plans if the Lord should ask something of him. It is placing God's agenda above one's own. It is echoing Isaiah's "Here am I; send me" (Isa. 6:8).

What does it mean to be teachable? It means that one is open to God to show him something he has not known before, even something that might change the values deeply ingrained in him from birth. A believer is supposed to be a disciple. A disciple is a learner. A learner is open to God, His Word, and His Spirit.

A respected Bible teacher and conference speaker once confessed to his audience about a moment that changed his life and ministry. While he was in Bible school, a fellow student next to him in line at the cafeteria asked him what the Lord had said to him that morning. Stunned, he realized that he had not been in the Word or listened to the Lord before heading for breakfast. He determined then and there to never meet the day without spending time in the Word. At that moment he became a more teachable person.

The accomplishing of the Great Commission will take the hands, the hearts, the feet, and the prayers of many. It begins with a person committing himself to the Word of God and living it out as the Spirit leads. It continues with that one being willing to have God change his plans in order to accomplish something He wants done. And it requires a lifelong teachable spirit, allowing the Lord to make him a better servant.

—*Darrell W. McKay*

The Jewish Aspect

The terms "apostles" and "disciples" are sometimes used interchangeably; however, the term "disciple" means "a pupil of a teacher," from the Greek word *mathetes,* while "apostle" means "a messenger." In addition to the twelve apostles, there was a much larger group of people who were identified as disciples of Jesus.

One of those who was identified as a *mathetria,* a female disciple, was Tabitha (Acts 9:36). This is the only time the New Testament uses this word. The name Tabitha is Hebrew and means "gazelle." She was also called Dorcas (Greek), which has the same meaning. Dorcas, a well-off woman, perhaps a widow, was benevolent, compassionate, and devout. She loved and served other widows in the community by making clothes for them.

Widows often had no source of income and no one to protect or watch out for them. Dorcas used her talents and exemplified the noble woman idealized in Proverbs 31:13 and 20: "She seeketh wool, and flax, and worketh willingly with her hands. . . . She stretcheth out her hand to the poor; yea, she reacheth forth her hands to the needy."

When Dorcas died, Peter was summoned from Lydda to Joppa and upon his arrival at Dorcas's home (where her body had been placed in an upper room), Peter found the other widows weeping. Not only were the widows mourning Tabitha's death, but they also had valid concerns for their own lives now that she, their patron and benefactor, was dead.

Mourning was not a restrained activity in the ancient Middle East. People showed their grief by wailing, crying, and tearing the upper part of their woven garments. Using her Hebrew name Tabitha, Peter commanded her to get up, and she was restored to life, causing many to believe in the Lord (Acts 9:41-42).

Dorcas was one of several women who played a prominent role in the first century church. Several others included Phoebe and Priscilla (Rom. 16:1, 3); Euodias and Syntyche (Phil. 4:2); and Chloe (I Cor. 1:11). Mary Magdalene accompanied Jesus during His ministry. Within the four Gospels, she is named at least twelve times, more than most of the apostles. Throughout the early church, the Bible records many women who hosted church gatherings in their homes.

In Jewish law, women faced several limitations, particularly in leadership roles. Jewish tradition forbade women from being taught or gaining education, a law countered by Paul when he commands that women are to learn (I Tim 2:11). Relatively few women were mentioned in the Old Testament or in rabbinic literature.

The New Testament contains a higher number of references to women, especially in comparison with literary works of the same era. The Gospels often mention Jesus speaking to women publicly and contending openly against the social norms of the time. One time, He was teaching in a synagogue on the Sabbath, where He had healed a woman who had been crippled by a spirit for eighteen years (Luke 13:10-13). Jesus not only faced the wrath of the Jewish leaders by healing this woman on the Sabbath; He also called her a "daughter of Abraham" (vs. 16). The idea of being a son of Abraham was common, but Jesus raised women to a new status with that single pronouncement.

—Deborah Markowitz Solan

Guiding the Superintendent

Insects follow one another without having to think about it. Ants follow chemical trails, which lead them to food and water or back to their colony. Some caterpillars travel closely, one after another in long lines, for direction. God implants this behavior in them for survival.

Humans, however, should not follow so blindly. The Bible warns us about false doctrine and false teachers for a reason. God gives us the ability to think, and therefore we can weigh everything we learn in light of Scripture. If we rely on the Bible as a plumb line, we are far less likely to follow someone blindly or to be fooled by false doctrines.

In this week's lesson, we learn that Jesus had some faithful disciples who set an example and encouraged the faith of others. We also see that God still wants us to be faithful believers for the very same reason.

DEVOTIONAL OUTLINE

1. A woman of faith (Acts 9:36-37). Dorcas gives us an example of a believer who shows the fruits of her faith. She was openly known for her good works, including charity for the poor. After an illness of unspecified duration, Tabitha died.

2. Tabitha's testimony (Acts 9:38-39). Peter was hurriedly summoned before Tabitha's burial. The testimony to her good works was apparent to Peter in the way the people lamented her passing. The widows for whom she had made clothing showed Peter some of the coats and garments they had received.

3. God working through Peter (Acts 9:40-43). The first thing Peter did was to send everyone away so that he could kneel and pray. His prayers were not a show for all to see how faithful a servant he was. Rather, they were an expression of humble obedience to God, whom Peter served gratefully. His service is evident in the passage, as Peter acted in complete submission to God. Clearly, God had His own reasons for bringing Tabitha back from the dead. Certainly, He demonstrated His supreme power in using Peter to restore her to life.

Because of this miraculous work, many believed not in Peter but in the Lord. The disciples always made it abundantly clear that they had no power of their own. Their power came from God only.

AGE-GROUP EMPHASES

Children: Children need to learn the difference between fairy tales and reality. They have probably heard a story or two about a princess being brought back to life with a kiss from a prince. This lesson presents a good opportunity to teach them about the Prince of Peace, Jesus. Just as God used one of His faithful servants to bring Tabitha back to life, faith in Jesus also brings us back to life spiritually and gives us everlasting life, even after death. Death has lost its hold on us because of Jesus' saving work on the cross.

Youths: This lesson gives young people an example of the kind of faith walk for which they should be striving. Not only was Tabitha a woman of great faith, but she was also very charitable and kind. We cannot know God's reasons for allowing her to be restored to life, but we can certainly follow her example of kindness. Likewise, Peter was a faithful, humble servant whom God used greatly.

Adults: Although we find examples of the disciples making the same mistakes we all do, this is an excellent example of how God can use adults to further His kingdom if they submit and trust in Him.

—*Paulette L. Leblanc*

SCRIPTURE LESSON TEXT

I SAM. 16:1 And the LORD said unto Samuel, How long wilt thou mourn for Saul, seeing I have rejected him from reigning over Israel? fill thine horn with oil, and go, I will send thee to Jesse the Beth-lehemite: for I have provided me a king among his sons.

2 And Samuel said, How can I go? if Saul hear *it,* **he will kill me. And the LORD said, Take an heifer with thee, and say, I am come to sacrifice to the LORD.**

3 And call Jesse to the sacrifice, and I will shew thee what thou shalt do: and thou shalt anoint unto me *him* whom I name unto thee.

4 And Samuel did that which the LORD spake, and came to Bethlehem. And the elders of the town trembled at his coming.

6 And it came to pass, when they were come, that he looked on Eliab, and said, Surely the LORD'S anointed *is* before him.

7 But the LORD said unto Samuel, Look not on his countenance, or on the height of his stature; because I have refused him: for *the* **LORD** *seeth* **not as man seeth; for man looketh on the outward ap-** pearance, but the LORD looketh on the heart.

8 Then Jesse called Abinadab, and made him pass before Samuel. And he said, Neither hath the LORD chosen this.

9 Then Jesse made Shammah to pass by. And he said, Neither hath the LORD chosen this.

10 Again, Jesse made seven of his sons to pass before Samuel. And Samuel said unto Jesse, The LORD hath not chosen these.

11 And Samuel said unto Jesse, Are here all *thy* **children? And he said, There remaineth yet the youngest, and, behold, he keepeth the sheep. And Samuel said unto Jesse, Send and fetch him: for we will not sit down till he come hither.**

12 And he sent, and brought him in. Now he *was* ruddy, *and* withal of a beautiful countenance, and goodly to look to. And the LORD said, Arise, anoint him: for this *is* he.

13 Then Samuel took the horn of oil, and anointed him in the midst of his brethren: and the Spirit of the LORD came upon David from that day forward. So Samuel rose up, and went to Ramah.

NOTES

Young David Anointed King

Lesson Text: I Samuel 16:1-4*b*, 6-13

Related Scriptures: I Samuel 13:8-14; 15:1-23;
Psalm 51:1-19; Mark 7:14-23

TIME: about 1025 B.C.   PLACE: Bethlehem

GOLDEN TEXT—"The Lord seeth not as man seeth; for man looketh on the outward appearance, but the Lord looketh on the heart" (I Samuel 16:7).

Introduction

In his book entitled *The Integrity Crisis* (Oliver Nelson), Warren Wiersbe writes, "For some reason, our ministry doesn't match our message. Something is wrong with the church's integrity.... The church is the salt of the earth, but apparently we are not salty enough to hinder corruption in government, big business, sports, or even religious ministry. The church is the light of the world, but that light is apparently too weak to have much of an influence on today's movers and shakers." Much of the blame for the church's lack of influence on the world must rest on the many leaders who are not faithful in their duties. It is a high calling to serve God in leadership over His people. Everyone so privileged should live humbly and with a sense of submission to Him.

LESSON OUTLINE

I. **GOD'S PLAN FOR FINDING A NEW KING**—I Sam. 16:1-4*b*

II. **SAMUEL'S ATTEMPTS TO FULFILL GOD'S PLAN**—I Sam. 16:6-10

III. **DAVID'S ANOINTING FOR NEW MINISTRY**—I Sam. 16:11-13

Exposition: Verse by Verse

GOD'S PLAN FOR FINDING A NEW KING

I SAM. 16:1 And the LORD said unto Samuel, How long wilt thou mourn for Saul, seeing I have rejected him from reigning over Israel? fill thine horn with oil, and go, I will send thee to Jesse the Beth-lehemite: for I have provided me a king among his sons.

2 And Samuel said, How can I go? if Saul hear it, he will kill me. And the LORD said, Take an heifer with thee, and say, I am come to sacrifice to the LORD.

3 And call Jesse to the sacrifice, and I will shew thee what thou shalt do: and thou shalt anoint unto me him whom I name unto thee.

4 And Samuel did that which the LORD spake, and came to Beth-lehem. And the elders of the town trembled at his coming.

Sending Samuel (I Sam. 16:1-2a). {Saul was the first king of Israel, but he was never wholly obedient to God. God finally announced His rejection of Saul as king when Saul played the role of priest and disobeyed God by refusing to annihilate the Amalekites.}^Q1 On that occasion Samuel exhorted him with these words: "Hath the Lord as great delight in burnt offerings and sacrifices, as in obeying the voice of the Lord? Behold, to obey is better than sacrifice, and to hearken than the fat of rams" (15:22).

Samuel then followed his challenge with an explanation and an announcement regarding Saul's future: "For rebellion is as the sin of witchcraft, and stubbornness is as iniquity and idolatry. Because thou hast rejected the word of the Lord, he hath also rejected thee from being king" (vs. 23). Samuel never saw Saul again, and he was deeply saddened by the disobedience and rejection of Saul (vs. 35). Finally, God appeared to Samuel and said it was time to stop mourning and to move ahead with His plan for the future. Saul was no longer to be considered.

{In order to accomplish the replacement of Saul, God told Samuel to make a trip to Bethlehem to the house of Jesse. There, He said, He had a replacement already chosen. Samuel was to go there, taking a horn filled with oil for the purpose of anointing him. Samuel was willing to obey, but there was one problem with the scenario. Saul knew of the movements of significant people in his kingdom, and he would surely learn about Samuel's journey. How could Samuel carry out such a mission without putting his life in jeopardy?}^Q2

Providing protection (I Sam. 16:2b-3). Since God was giving Samuel the command to make the journey to Bethlehem, it is not surprising that He had already determined how He would protect him from Saul. God had specifically said to Samuel, "I will send thee to Jesse the Beth-lehemite: for I have provided me a king among his sons" (vs. 1). David was clearly God's choice, and the Lord would see that he was installed in the position. Samuel did not need to fear for himself as he carried out this mission.

{Still, the Lord understood Samuel's concern, so He directed him to take an animal with him for sacrifice.}^Q3 Samuel was something like a circuit-riding preacher. As he went from place to place, he apparently led the people in worship through the offering of sacrifices (cf. I Sam. 7:16). It must have been common for him to take the sacrificial animals with him. Although Samuel's primary purpose in going to Bethlehem was to anoint the new king of God's choice, he would also perform a sacrifice while he was there. This arrangement would ensure that Saul did not become suspicious.

In order to further help Samuel accomplish His will, {God specifically instructed him to invite Jesse to the worship service. As Samuel carried out these instructions, God would show him what he was to do regarding the anointing of the next king.}^Q4 For Samuel it was a matter of being obedient to the known will of God as far as God revealed it to him and then trusting the Lord to continue to direct him as he followed God's instructions.

It is often this way for us as well. God does not choose to reveal immediately the entirety of His will in most matters. Rather, He expects us to be obedient to what we know and to trust Him to continually guide us through the pathways He has chosen that are at the present not revealed to us. As we are obedient to what we understand, God will be faithful to give us further guidance as we move ahead confidently and prayerfully in following Him.

Preparing the people (I Sam. 16:4a-b). Once Samuel was sure that God would go with him and protect him, he went without hesitation. He did not know the ultimate object of his search, but he knew it was God's will for him to go. He trusted the Lord to further direct him after he arrived in Bethlehem. Missionaries and others in the Lord's service will testify to the fact that there is a certain excitement to walking with God in such a day-by-day way. You never know when God may surprise you with something unexpected!

Upon Samuel's arrival in Bethlehem, however, there arose a sense of fear on the part of the people. One of Samuel's most recent acts had been the execution of King Agag of the Amalekites (15:32-33). He had done this because God had decreed Agag's demise and Saul had failed to accomplish it. Saul had purposely spared Agag's life instead of killing him as God had commanded. The people of Bethlehem were probably aware of what Samuel had done and were fearful that he had come in judgment against them.

This great sense of respect for Samuel may well have been used by God to prepare the people to follow his instructions. Not only was Saul kept from feeling threatened by Samuel's journey to Bethlehem, but the people there also were more than willing to support whatever he wanted them to do.

SAMUEL'S ATTEMPTS TO FULFILL GOD'S PLAN

6 And it came to pass, when they were come, that he looked on Eliab, and said, Surely the LORD's anointed is before him.

7 But the LORD said unto Samuel, Look not on his countenance, or on the height of his stature; because I have refused him: for the LORD seeth not as man seeth; for man looketh on the outward appearance, but the LORD looketh on the heart.

8 Then Jesse called Abinadab, and made him pass before Samuel. And he said, Neither hath the LORD chosen this.

9 Then Jesse made Shammah to pass by. And he said, Neither hath the LORD chosen this.

10 Again, Jesse made seven of his sons to pass before Samuel. And Samuel said unto Jesse, The LORD hath not chosen these.

Guidelines given (I Sam. 16:6-7). Judging from the fact that Jesse apparently had his sons appear before Samuel in the order of their age, Samuel at some point had probably explained to Jesse why he had come. Eliab was the oldest (17:28) and the first one to step before Samuel. We can deduce from God's subsequent instruction to Samuel that Eliab was tall and handsome and apparently everything one would look for physically in a leader. He made a good impression on Samuel, who instantly felt this was surely the man God had chosen.

J. Vernon McGee, in his unique way of describing things, wrote regarding God's perspective, "When God looks at us, friend, He looks at us from the inside. He is an interior decorator. He always checks the interior. Samuel looks at this well-built, handsome young man and feels this must be God's choice for the next king of Israel. . . . We are so apt to judge folk, even in Christian circles, by their looks, by their pocketbook, by their status symbol" (*Thru the Bible with J. Vernon McGee,* Thomas Nelson).

Jeremiah wrote, "The heart is deceitful above all things, and desperately wicked: who can know it? I the Lord search the heart, I try the reins, even to give every man according to his ways, and according to the fruit of his doings" (Jer. 17:9-10). {This is surely one of the most important principles in Scripture: God does not evaluate us by what we appear to be before others; He evaluates us by what He sees in our hearts. There is nothing hidden from Him.}[Q5]

{It is important for us to recognize that when we stand before God on the last Day, we will be totally without excuse. He will know what our true motives and thoughts were, and we will be stripped of all pretense at that time.}[Q6] Does it not seem right that we should endeavor to grow spiritually and become now what He wants us to be so that we will not be ashamed in His presence?

Further rejection (I Sam. 16:8-9). First Samuel 17:13 lists the three oldest sons of Jesse as Eliab, Abinadab, and Shammah. Verse 14 says that David was the youngest of Jesse's eight sons. {In ancient cultures a great deal of emphasis was placed on the birth order, especially of sons. It was logical that Eliab would appear before Samuel first and that Abinadab and Shammah would come after him in order.}[Q7] It was also logical for Jesse to think that the firstborn would probably be the one God had chosen for the important position of king over the land.

Jesse named his sons meaningfully. "Eliab" means "My God is Father" and "Abinadab" means "My father is noble." However, meaningful names do not guarantee godly living. These men did not have the spiritual depth their young brother had. When David visited them while they were in Saul's army and being challenged by Goliath, he found them to be as fearful as everybody else. Eliab actually became extremely angry over David's confidence in God (vs. 28).

God quickly informed Samuel that neither of the next two brothers was His choice. Perhaps this was not so much of a surprise to him as the refusal of Eliab, but surely he began to wonder just what God was doing. God was fulfilling His promise to guide him, so all Samuel could do was listen to Him and keep looking.

Mission unfulfilled (I Sam. 16:10). There are those who like to speculate as to exactly how God communicated with Samuel on this occasion. It is doubtful that anyone heard an audible voice. Jesse and his family members heard nothing but Samuel's conclusions. In today's society we would feel certain that personal prejudice was behind such conclusions, but Samuel had the reputation of being a God-fearing man, so he was trusted.

{God probably spoke quietly to Samuel's spirit through His Spirit. We should recognize the spiritual sensitivity in Samuel that made it possible for such communication. God can guide us in a similar way, but we must have an intimate relationship with Him for that to happen.}[Q8] In order to have that kind of relationship, we must take the time to study His Word and pray fervently on a regular basis. We live in a noisy world that easily crowds out the quiet voice of God unless we seek Him in times of submissive solitude.

One by one Jesse's seven sons stepped before Samuel and were refused by God. After the last one had appeared, Samuel turned to Jesse and said, "The Lord hath not chosen these." That announcement must have resulted in momentary confusion in the hearts of those present, but we see in Samuel a continued quiet confidence as he proceeded.

DAVID'S ANOINTING FOR NEW MINISTRY

11 And Samuel said unto Jesse, Are here all thy children? And he said, There remaineth yet the youngest, and, behold, he keepeth the sheep. And Samuel said unto Jesse, Send and fetch him: for we will not

sit down till he come hither.

12 And he sent, and brought him in. Now he was ruddy, and withal of a beautiful countenance, and goodly to look to. And the LORD said, Arise, anoint him: for this is he.

13 Then Samuel took the horn of oil, and anointed him in the midst of his brethren: and the Spirit of the LORD came upon David from that day forward. So Samuel rose up, and went to Ramah.

David presented (I Sam. 16:11-12). When Jesse told Samuel about David, the prophet immediately commanded him to send for the boy. So important was this mission that Samuel said they would not relax and be at ease until the matter was decided. David had to be considered since all the others had not been chosen by God.

{David is described as ruddy (possibly meaning red-haired), having a beautiful countenance (perhaps indicating bright, beautiful eyes), and good-looking (cf. 17:42).}Q9 Like Saul, he was a striking person, but this was not the reason God chose him.

God's direction to Samuel was very clear: "Arise, anoint him: for this is he" (16:12). He had the privilege of anointing the one chosen by God to become the next leader of His people Israel.

David anointed (I Sam. 16:13). This initial anointing of David was done in a private ceremony. Two public anointings came much later, once when he became king over Judah and again when he became king over the entire united nation of Israel (II Sam. 2:4; 5:3). {For now, Saul was still the king, but God was indicating His will for David in the future and using this to begin preparing him for the responsibility. Part of that preparation was the coming of the Spirit of the Lord upon him.}Q10 It is significant that the text says the Spirit "came upon David from that day forward" (I Sam. 16:13). A study of the ministry of the Holy Spirit in the Old Testament reveals that He usually came upon people to accomplish special purposes but did not remain in the way He does today. The constant presence of the Spirit upon David pointed to Christ's own ministry (cf. Luke 4:14-21) as well as the permanent indwelling of the Spirit in all new covenant believers (cf. Eph. 1:13-14).

Once Samuel's mission was completed, he returned to his home in Ramah. No doubt he watched subsequent events closely as he waited to see how God would accomplish the removal of Saul and the elevation of David to his position as king.

—*Keith E. Eggert*

QUESTIONS

1. Who was the first king of Israel, and what finally precipitated his rejection by God?

2. Where was Samuel told to go, and what was the potential problem he was worried about?

3. How did God provide protection for Samuel?

4. What specific directions did God give Samuel, and what did He not yet tell him?

5. What truth did God give Samuel when he was considering Eliab?

6. Why is this truth just as important for us today as it was then?

7. Why was it logical for Jesse to present his sons in order of age?

8. How was God probably communicating with Samuel, and why should this be an encouragement to us?

9. How does the text describe David?

10. What did the anointing and the coming of the Spirit do for David?

—*Keith E. Eggert*

Preparing to Teach the Lesson

We live in a day when acknowledgment of God seems to be slowly disappearing from our society. Godly leadership is therefore all the more important. Where there are godly and faithful leaders, the people will be led in the right direction.

TODAY'S AIM

Facts: to see how God chose David for faithful leadership.

Principle: to show that if we are to choose faithful leaders, we must view people from God's perspective.

Application: to encourage godly wisdom in the choosing of spiritual leaders.

INTRODUCING THE LESSON

If we look back at the history of the United States, most will remember with pride the leadership of presidents like George Washington and Abraham Lincoln. While we cannot be completely sure what their relationship with God was like, these presidents and other early American leaders at least acknowledged God. As a result, they sought to adhere to a number of Christian principles in their leadership—however imperfectly.

Today as a nation, however, our culture has tried to put God in the backseat in the name of progress and tolerance. The lesson this week helps us see the importance of a godly heart for good leadership.

DEVELOPING THE LESSON

1. Searching for the right leader (I Sam. 16:1-4b). Politically, Israel was in turmoil. God had rejected Saul as king, and He now sent Samuel the prophet to anoint the one He had chosen to be Israel's next king.

It must be remembered that in those days the prophets and the priests had a big role to play in the leadership of the kingdom. Usually they served as advisers to the king. The prophets were usually held in high regard by the people and were recognized as the representatives of God to them.

Notice how God calmed Samuel's fears and then gave very clear instructions to him at a critical time in the nation's history. God's tasks for us are not always easy, but they further His kingdom plans.

Samuel was told to fill his horn with oil. The horn was used in anointing leaders, and olive oil was plentiful in Israel. God sent Samuel to Bethlehem and to the family of Jesse to anoint one of his sons as Israel's next king. The specific son was not disclosed yet, but God's choice would be shown to Samuel.

Here the students can discuss whether God gives clear instructions today and, if so, how He does it. Encourage the class members to share their personal experiences with this. How does our situation differ from (or perhaps resemble) Samuel's (cf. Heb. 1:1-2)? How might that affect the way we should ordinarily expect God to communicate with us today?

In I Samuel 16:4 we see something else that is significant. When the prophet arrived in Bethlehem, the town's elders were concerned. A word from God was not always good. The prophets were known to bring punishment as well as blessing from God. Should we be afraid of the word of the Lord today? If so, in what sense (cf. Prov. 1:7; Rom. 8:1)?

Here we see that as Samuel was obedient to the Lord's instructions, the Lord gave him wisdom about what needed to be done. Samuel invited Jesse and his sons to the sacrifice. They ritually cleansed themselves and went with Samuel (I Sam. 16:5).

2. The Lord looks at the heart (I Sam. 16:6-7). It is easy for us to unconsciously show partiality, even in our work for the Lord. This is what happened to Samuel the prophet. He took one look at Eliab and his big physique and assumed that he must be God's choice for king. However, God nudged Samuel with a sobering thought. God does not look at the outward appearance but at the heart within. This same principle is just as true today.

One good exercise here is to remember some of the references to the heart in the Bible. Some good examples are Proverbs 23:7 and Matthew 6:21.

3. The faithful leader is anointed (I Sam. 16:8-13). One by one all of Jesse's sons were presented before Samuel, and they were rejected from being the next king. After seven had been presented, the prophet declared that the chosen one was not there and asked whether there were any more sons. Jesse said he had one more son who was watching the sheep in the fields. He was the youngest, and Jesse apparently had discounted him. Samuel asked that this son be brought before them. They would not eat until he was there.

When David came before the prophet, he probably looked shabby and dirty from his work in the fields, but he was a very handsome young man. God, however, looked within David and saw that he had a heart for Him. Samuel then anointed David's head with the oil, thus declaring him God's choice for king.

Encourage students to consider how their hearts, not just their outward actions, appear to God. Refer them to Matthew 5:21-28. When God looks within our hearts, what does He see? Right choices are made when our hearts are attuned to God's voice.

This section closes with the pronouncement that the Spirit of God came mightily upon David. With his task completed, Samuel returned to his home in Ramah. When we obey God, we will see His mighty power at work. David was ready to faithfully lead God's people.

ILLUSTRATING THE LESSON

When God chooses leaders for His kingdom purposes, He looks at people's hearts, not at their outward appearances.

GOD LOOKS ON THE HEART

GOD

MAN

CONCLUDING THE LESSON

God is looking for faithful leaders who have a heart for Him and His mission on this earth. He often uses ordinary people who, in turn, will faithfully lead others with divinely given wisdom.

ANTICIPATING THE NEXT LESSON

In our lesson next week we will see the way God worked through a young servant girl to point a foreign military leader to Him.

—*A. Koshy Muthalaly*

PRACTICAL POINTS

1. Grieving is natural, but it must not be carried to an extreme (I Sam. 16:1).
2. God always makes a way for those willing to obey Him fully (vss. 2-4b).
3. Do not judge by outward appearances alone; rather, seek God's wisdom (vss. 6-7).
4. Do not tire of the process God is taking you through. He has a purpose for it, and His timing is right (vss. 8-10).
5. True obedience requires perseverance in the task (vs. 11).
6. In His time God gives clear direction to the one who wants to obey Him (vss. 12-13).

—Don Kakavecos

RESEARCH AND DISCUSSION

1. Why do you think that Samuel grieved so deeply over God's rejection of Saul (I Sam. 16:1; cf. 12:1-25)?
2. How did God's choice of David as king differ from the anointing of Saul as king (cf. 10:24; 12:13)?
3. What do you think was the motivation for Samuel's response recorded in 16:2?
4. How would you answer those who say that God was twisting the truth in verse 2? Is it wrong not to disclose all the truth?
5. Give some examples of how people look on the "outward appearance" (vs. 7). How can one overcome this tendency?
6. How does David's absence from the proceedings of verses 4-11 encourage you to believe that God is in control of your life?

—Don Kakavecos

ILLUSTRATED HIGH POINTS

He looked on Eliab (I Sam. 16:6)

I once had the privilege of serving on my church's vacant pulpit committee. It was a position I had sought and felt strongly about.

The search went on much longer than any of us had anticipated. One of the reasons was that two of us were determined to hold out for "just the right person."

On at least two occasions, the committee felt they had found that person, only to receive a veto from Bob and me. We simply were not satisfied with answers to our questions.

Finally, we reached a decision to call a young pastor. Bob and I still had reservations, but the mounting pressure influenced us. Besides, we were not sure how many more sons Jesse had for us to consider, so to speak.

Several sermons later, we realized we had made a mistake. It's not easy to find a good leader, which makes it all the more important to evaluate leaders based on God's standards, not our own.

He keepeth the sheep (vs. 11)

My career involved frequent relocations. As a result, we worshipped with a variety of Christian congregations and pastors.

As I look back, the pastor who impressed me more than any other was the one who seemed most uncomfortable in the pulpit. He was slow of speech, and his sermons were simple. What made him unusual was his deep humility and his compassion for each of his parishioners. People often wept during his sermons. He knew us all by name, and he loved us all.

This pastor had been a carpenter by trade. When visiting the church, you could often hear a hammer pounding or a saw buzzing. He kept the church in remarkable shape.

—Albert J. Schneider

Golden Text Illuminated

"The Lord seeth not as man seeth; for man looketh on the outward appearance, but the Lord looketh on the heart" (I Samuel 16:7).

God has the ultimate X-ray vision. He not only sees the heart itself, but He can also see deeper and discern its thoughts and intents. He knows each of us from the inside out. How wonderful and terrifying to be known by the Creator of the universe!

God knew whom to choose to lead the people of Israel because He knew the character of the man He would choose. Samuel was able to see only the outer appearance and the outward accomplishments. These could not give him enough information to make a wise choice. God saw David's heart and whispered His choice in Samuel's ear.

The word "appearance" refers to what can be seen with the eyes. The principle in our golden text goes all the way back to Eden, when Adam and Eve chose the outward appearance of the fruit over God's command (Gen. 3:6). They walked by sight. Because we have this same tendency, God often works in unexpected ways so that we will depend on His grace and not our strength (cf. I Sam. 2:1-10; Luke 1:46-55), Most notably, the cross of Jesus Christ is "foolishness" to the world, but the power of God to those who believe (I Cor. 1:18-31).

When we judge by appearances only, we tend to overlook people who are just ordinary or seem to be of lesser abilities. My friend told me of a young woman in her church who sings loudly and off-key and does not know the words to the songs. People find it distracting and even annoying to sit next to her. But no one knows what beauty God sees in her heart as she makes a joyful noise to the Lord!

On the other hand, we have movie stars and fashion models as our spokespersons and role models. We make them important because they are the "beautiful people," but we often give no thought to the character they espouse. "The world is full of idolatries, but I question if any idolatry has been more extensively practiced than the idolatry of the outward appearance" (Blaikie, *The First Book of Samuel,* Klock & Klock).

The first king God chose for Israel had an imposing appearance. About Saul it was said that "there was not among the children of Israel a goodlier person than he: from his shoulders and upward he was higher than any of the people" (I Sam. 9:2). However, Saul's stature and appearance did not make him a good king. Interestingly enough, David was also good-looking, though perhaps not very tall. "Now he was ruddy, and withal of a beautiful countenance, and goodly to look to" (16:12). God did not have to choose an ugly person to make His point, but it was David's heart that made him a man after God's own heart, not his looks.

Often a person who is good-looking is well aware of it and proud of his looks. "God resisteth the proud, but giveth grace unto the humble" (Jas. 4:6). Compare this to what Isaiah says about the coming Messiah: "He hath no form nor comeliness; and when we shall see him, there is no beauty that we should desire him" (53:2). Even God's own Son did not have outward beauty to recommend Him, but He was and is the greatest of all.

—Julie Barnhart

Heart of the Lesson

It has been said that everything rises or falls on leadership. Politically, that is probably true, but it is also often true in large part in the spiritual realm. God's chosen king, Saul, had failed. A change was in the works.

1. God's decision (I Sam. 16:1-4b). God had enough of Saul. He had decided to replace him as king, and in these verses He told Samuel His plan. The bottom line was that God's mind was made up.

When God determines to do something, the best thing for us to do is accept it. He is sovereign, and what He says goes.

God told Samuel to accept the fact that He was going to ordain a new king. Still, the prophet was worried, and he was not the only one who was worried. The elders of Bethlehem knew something was going on when Samuel arrived. Samuel did not just visit such a small village for no purpose. He had to have a reason for going there. It would be somewhat like the FBI director suddenly showing up unannounced in a very small town. People would be alarmed and want to know what was going on.

To one extent or another, change is something all of us fear. Why is that? It is probably because things are easier when we keep the status quo. We get into a pattern of doing things, and we get used to it. I like the way one man defined the status quo: "It is the mess we are in." Very often that is the case. It was for Israel, and God wanted to show His people that He would fix the mess they were in with Saul as their king.

2. Mankind's choice versus God's choice (I Sam. 16:6-13). At this point, Samuel had been a prophet for many years. He had grown up around the tabernacle, and thus he knew the things of God quite well. Yet God was about to teach him a very important lesson.

As Samuel looked in turn upon each of Jesse's sons, he thought that God was going to choose one of these seven older sons. He thought he knew God's will, but he was wrong. God was going to make a change, but that change was not based on anything Samuel (or anyone else) could have predicted.

We need to be careful not to put God into a box. It is good to study the Bible, but it should always make us aware that God is God. He does not always fit into our idea of how He should act. In the case of our lesson text, God chose David, the youngest of Jesse's sons. David was not "king material" in Samuel's way of thinking—or anyone else's for that matter. Yes, Saul had been a disappointment, but no doubt people still thought the king should look like a king. Saul was head and shoulders taller than anyone else. He looked like a king! That is where we can make our greatest mistake.

Paul reminds us that "God hath chosen the foolish things of the world to confound the wise; and . . . the weak things of the world to confound the things which are mighty" (I Cor. 1:27). Why does God work this way? He does it because it glorifies Him (cf. vs. 29). God does not need the most qualified and impressive people to accomplish His will and to glorify Him. If we are not the best or most talented, we can take heart. God can still use us! Talent will not necessarily disqualify us, but the only indispensable thing is a heart open to God.

—*John Haynes*

World Missions

In this week's text we see how the Lord used Samuel to choose a son of Jesse who would become king.

Jesse first brought his older sons before Samuel to be anointed. God told Samuel that "man looketh on the outward appearance, but the Lord looketh on the heart" (I Sam. 16:7). He did not want Samuel to pick out the one who appeared to be the most likely candidate. He wanted him to choose the one whose heart was ready to serve God.

Regrettably, parents and children's ministry workers are sometimes too quick to point out the children who they believe will one day grow up to serve the Lord in a big way. Perhaps these children are the ones who can memorize Scripture most easily. We assume the pastor's children will be great missionaries or evangelists when they are older.

However, the future missionaries are not always the children who listen attentively to the lessons or even the ones who can answer all the questions after the Bible lesson is told. Sometimes the children God has chosen to serve Him on the mission field are the very ones who we leaders are sure will not amount to a hill of beans when they are older.

The little ones who are constantly trying our patience or refusing to color the water blue may be the ones who will someday lead an entire assembly to the saving knowledge of our God.

They may be the ones who now never carry their Bibles to church or are always leaving them in the pew or on top of the coatrack. Perhaps they are the children you thought never heard a word the visiting missionary had to say in children's church.

Thankfully, God can choose anyone He wishes to fulfill His purposes. He looks at the children's hearts and not at their ability to sit still in church. Perhaps the same determination of a little one who refuses to let you tell the Bible lesson is what God will one day use for His glory.

God might see awesome missionary leadership in the little one who encourages those around him to chew gum loudly instead of singing the Bible songs. God might see the adventuresome child who jumps over the pews after church on Sunday morning as one who someday will not be afraid to confront a scary, unreached tribe of people with their need to accept the Lord Jesus and His salvation.

God knows the heart. He knows which of these little, troublesome children will one day use the characteristics He has gifted them with to honor Him and to share His love with those around them.

I imagine that Jesse had a few comments for Samuel as he was checking through his family. He may have wondered why Samuel chose his youngest child.

Samuel listened carefully to God's instructions. God knew the heart He had given David to faithfully serve Him.

When everything you have tried fails to work and that little child still squirms through your Bible lesson, remember that God looks at the heart. He sees a future missionary or a successful evangelist in some of our most frustrating and anxious little believers. God sees their hearts and knows what resides there. More important, He has the power to transform their hearts.

—Elizabeth Wehman

The Jewish Aspect

Our text this week contains the significant words "the Lord looketh on the heart" (I Sam. 16:7). Knowing the end from the beginning, the Lord knew that David was the only one of Jesse's sons—indeed, the only one of all the sons of Israel—fit to be the leader of God's people.

It should be observed that Jesse seems to have been a godly man. The setting for the anointing of David is a sacrifice (vs. 3). This was apparently a ceremony appropriate for the prophet Samuel to conduct as he travelled. He did not need to be in the tabernacle, or near the ark of the covenant to make acceptable sacrifices to God.

The ceremony featured a sacrificial feast. Samuel alluded to it in the words "We will not sit down till [David] come hither" (16:11). It seems reasonable to credit Jesse—at least in part—for the strong spiritual focus of his son David.

David's devotion to God is best seen in the psalms that bear his name. In some cases, it is uncertain whether these psalms were written by David or merely to or about him. However, it seems that David authored at least seventy-three of them (Scroggie, *Psalms,* Revell).

The psalms of David reflect the heart that God saw. A practical thinker, David understood many things about God, particularly His holiness. David gave us a clear understanding of sin and the One ultimately sinned against in the words "Against thee, thee only, have I sinned, and done this evil in thy sight" (Ps. 51:4).

Sadly, many (though not all) Jewish leaders today have adopted the extreme biblical criticism formulated by liberal scholars. Jewish music scholar Alfred Sendrey wrote that the Jewish people created a "Davidic tradition," an ideal picture of the king that was different from the historical figure, by assigning the Davidic psalms to him. Sendrey quoted a liberal critic: "None of the psalms could have been written by David" (*Music in Ancient Israel,* Philosophical Library).

Downplaying the spiritual role of David and his writings is a subtle way of minimizing his part in messianic prophecy. The psalms that describe the king are patterns for fulfillment by Jesus, the ultimate Davidic king. However, Jewish scholarship does have great respect for David as a musician.

It seems clear that there was an organized profession of musicians during Saul's reign. This tells us that David must have been a very skillful player on the *kinnor,* a lyre of four to ten strings. One of Saul's servants said, "Behold, I have seen a son of Jesse the Bethlehemite, that is cunning in playing" (I Sam. 16:18). David's virtuosity in a nation of musicians brought him to the royal court (Sendrey).

David became a master musician. Although he did not live to see Solomon's temple, he did gather some of the materials for its construction and set up the organization of its choir and of its instrumentalists.

David lives on in the hearts of the Jewish people. On any Saturday, synagogue children gather for stories, playtime, and singing. One of the merriest songs is the rollicking "David, King of Israel, Rule and Reign Forever." Some may sing it in the kingdom.

—*Lyle P. Murphy.*

Guiding the Superintendent

There are many different types of leaders in today's world. Even in the spiritual realm, some are faithful to obey the Lord and others are not. Faithfulness has a lot to do with whether a person will humble himself before the Lord and obey Him. Many kings in Israel's history fell because their hearts were lifted up in pride.

David was chosen as king because he was a man after God's own heart (Acts 13:22). Being a man after God's own heart does not mean that one never sins. It means that one desires to love, know, and obey the Lord (cf. Ps. 27:4). David was not perfect, but when he sinned, he repented of it and wholeheartedly turned back to the Lord (cf. Ps. 51).

DEVOTIONAL OUTLINE

1. Samuel sent to anoint a new king (I Sam. 16:1-4b). Saul had been disobedient to the Lord's instructions concerning the Amalekites. The Lord therefore had rejected him as king and was going to replace him with a new king. Since Samuel had been used to choose Saul as king, he naturally mourned over this loss (chap. 15).

The Lord instructed Samuel where to go to look for a king but did not yet reveal to him what person was to be king. Samuel was afraid Saul would kill him if he found out that he was on his way to anoint a new king. The Lord understood his concern and told him how to handle the situation. Samuel was faithful to obey the instructions of the Lord and went to Bethlehem.

2. Samuel unable to find a king to anoint (I Sam. 16:6-10). Samuel went to the home of Jesse and apparently explained his mission. Jesse then proceeded to have his sons pass before Samuel, beginning with the oldest.

As Eliab passed by, Samuel said, "Surely the Lord's anointed is before him." However, the Lord quickly informed Samuel that He looks at the heart of a person, not at his outward appearance. Seven of Jesse's sons passed before Samuel, but none of them were chosen.

3. David anointed as king (I Sam. 16:11-13). Samuel was probably puzzled after Jesse's sons had passed before him and the Lord had not chosen any of them. The problem was solved when Samuel asked whether Jesse had any other sons. On learning that the youngest son was out in the field, Samuel promptly had him called. When David came, the Lord revealed to Samuel that this was His chosen king. David, the man who would be a faithful leader, was a man after God's own heart.

AGE-GROUP EMPHASES

Children: Children should understand that they are never too young to follow after God with all their heart. Both Samuel and David, who were faithful leaders, were faithful in their younger years (cf. I Sam. 3:1-18).

Encourage the children to be faithful in obeying their parents, and most of all in obeying their Heavenly Father.

Youths: Emphasize to young people that while man looks on the outward appearance, God looks on the heart. Although God does not set forth an ideal for outward beauty, He does for the heart. He wants a heart that loves, trusts, and obeys Him.

Adults: Adults need to understand that faithful leadership does not refer only to church leadership. Faithful leadership also refers to the leadership parents have with their children. Help them understand their role as Christian leaders not only in the church but also in the family.

—David L. Schmidt

SCRIPTURE LESSON TEXT

II KGS. 5:1 Now Naaman, captain of the host of the king of Syria, was a great man with his master, and honourable, because by him the LORD had given deliverance unto Syria: he was also a mighty man in valour, *but he was* a leper.

2 And the Syrians had gone out by companies, and had brought away captive out of the land of Israel a little maid; and she waited on Naaman's wife.

3 And she said unto her mistress, Would God my lord *were* with the prophet that *is* in Samaria! for he would recover him of his leprosy.

4 And *one* went in, and told his lord, saying, Thus and thus said the maid that *is* of the land of Israel.

5 And the king of Syria said, Go to, go, and I will send a letter unto the king of Israel. And he departed, and took with him ten talents of silver, and six thousand *pieces* of gold, and ten changes of raiment.

9 So Naaman came with his horses and with his chariot, and stood at the door of the house of Elisha.

10 And Elisha sent a messenger unto him, saying, Go and wash in Jordan seven times, and thy flesh shall come again to thee, and thou shalt be clean.

11 But Naaman was wroth, and went away, and said, Behold, I thought, He will surely come out to me, and stand, and call on the name of the LORD his God, and strike his hand over the place, and recover the leper.

12 *Are* not Abana and Pharpar, rivers of Damascus, better than all the waters of Israel? may I not wash in them, and be clean? So he turned and went away in a rage.

13 And his servants came near, and spake unto him, and said, My father, *if* the prophet had bid thee *do some* great thing, wouldest thou not have done *it?* how much rather then, when he saith to thee, Wash, and be clean?

14 Then went he down, and dipped himself seven times in Jordan, according to the saying of the man of God: and his flesh came again like unto the flesh of a little child, and he was clean.

15 And he returned to the man of God, he and all his company, and came, and stood before him: and he said, Behold, now I know that *there is* no God in all the earth, but in Israel.

NOTES

A Servant Girl Points Naaman to God

Lesson Text: II Kings 5:1-5, 9-15*a*

Related Scriptures: Leviticus 14:1-7; Matthew 8:5-13;
Luke 4:24-27; 17:11-19

TIME: between 852 and 848 B.C.　　PLACES: Syria; Samaria; Jordan River

---

GOLDEN TEXT—"Then went he down, and dipped himself seven times in Jordan, according to the saying of the man of God: and his flesh came again like unto the flesh of a little child, and he was clean" (II Kings 5:14).

Introduction

Corrie ten Boom told a story about a proud woodpecker that was tapping away at a dead tree when the sky unexpectedly turned black and the thunder began to roll. Suddenly a bolt of lightning struck the old tree, splintering it into hundreds of pieces. Startled but unhurt, the haughty bird flew off, screeching to its feathered friends, "Hey, everyone, look what I did! Look what I did!"

Sinful pride grows out of a self-centered attitude and often leads to exaggeration and deception in misleading others. None of this pleases God.

Proverbs 6:16-19 lists seven things the Lord hates, and the first thing on the list is a proud look. Proverbs 16:18 states, "Pride goeth before destruction, and an haughty spirit before a fall." Our lesson reinforces the call to humble ourselves before God's mighty hand (I Pet. 5:6)

LESSON OUTLINE

I. HURT PRIDE—II Kgs. 5:1-5

II. ANGRY PRIDE—II Kgs. 5:9-12

II. NO PRIDE—II Kgs. 5:13-15*a*

Exposition: Verse by Verse

HURT PRIDE

II KGS. 5:1 Now Naaman, captain of the host of the king of Syria, was a great man with his master, and honourable, because by him the LORD had given deliverance unto Syria: he was also a mighty man in valour, but he was a leper.

2 And the Syrians had gone out by companies, and had brought away

captive out of the land of Israel a little maid; and she waited on Naaman's wife.

3 And she said unto her mistress, Would God my lord were with the prophet that is in Samaria! for he would recover him of his leprosy.

4 And one went in, and told his lord, saying, Thus and thus said the maid that is of the land of Israel.

5 And the king of Syria said, Go to, go, and I will send a letter unto the king of Israel. And he departed, and took with him ten talents of silver, and six thousand pieces of gold, and ten changes of raiment.

A mighty man with a problem (II Kgs. 5:1-2). Just to the northeast of Israel was the nation of Syria, or Aram. King Ben-hadad I was ruling Syria, while Jehoram ruled in Israel. The main character in this incident is neither of these kings. Four phrases at the beginning of this chapter describe the importance of the man Naaman. {First, he was the captain of the army of Syria—the supreme commander of the king's military force and directly accountable to the king himself.}Q1

{Second, Naaman was "a great man." He was esteemed as a prominent person in the nation and enjoyed a high social standing among the people. Third, he was highly regarded by his master. The word "honourable" means he was lifted high in the eyes of the king. He was such a capable military leader that the king regarded him as one of the most valuable members of his administration.}Q2

Scripture clarifies that it was the Lord who gave victory to Aram through Naaman, so that Namaan's great standing was through God alone. The Lord has control over all the nations of the world. Isaiah put this in perspective: "All nations before him are as nothing; and they are counted to him less than nothing, and vanity" (Isa. 40:17). Finally, Naaman was "a mighty man in valour"

(II Kgs. 5:1). This refers to his courage and the forceful strength with which he handled himself.

All these magnificent truths were tempered by the fact that Naaman had {a skin disease—a sort of leprosy, but perhaps not Hansen's disease with its extremely debilitating effects.}Q3

It was on a military raid into Israel that {a young girl was captured and given to Naaman's wife as a servant.}Q4

A servant girl with a solution (II Kgs. 5:3-4). Naaman and his wife may have been kind to this young girl, for in the time of her master's distress, she became concerned for his welfare. Perhaps it was one of those momentary thoughts put into words, or perhaps she had been thinking about it for a while. In any event, one day she said to her mistress, "Would God my lord were with the prophet that is in Samaria! for he would recover him of his leprosy." She was referring to Elisha, the well-known prophet of Israel.

The maiden's role in the story is striking. She had seen the war crimes perpetrated by the Syrians. She was bereft of her parents—whether through military conflict or otherwise. She was, in fact, a young girl stolen from her home. Yet, this unnamed maiden felt true compassion toward her captor and master. Discerning God's call that she, a daughter of Abraham should be a blessing to the Gentiles, she dared profess that the prophet in Samaria could heal Naaman.

Naaman reported to the king what the young girl had said. The claim may have seemed wholly impossible, for there was no cure for leprosy. It was a disease that ranged anywhere from white spots on the skin to running, open sores and in some forms resulted in the gradual loss of fingers and toes and other parts of the body. At its worst, it gradually rotted away the body until the person died.

What was Naaman's attitude when he reported to the king? Was he merely passing on information? Was he hoping to be given permission to travel to Samaria? He must have had a measure of hope in his heart, and the person who could do something about it was his master, the king.

A desperate man with a letter (II Kgs. 5:5). The king immediately responded to the news positively. His commander was very valuable to him, and unless something could be done to heal him, he would eventually lose him to the increasingly devastating effects of leprosy. The king's attitude was probably similar to that of people today who are willing to try any treatment for a life-threatening illness in the hope that something might work. He made all the necessary preparations, therefore, to send Naaman to Samaria, Israel's capital.

We must remember that all this was happening because of something said by a young slave girl who was convinced that Elisha had supernatural power to heal Naaman. By this time in his ministry, Elisha had performed a number of miracles. Apparently, word about him had spread. He had, for example, cured a large pot of stew that had poisonous gourds in it (II Kings 4:38-44). Prior to that he had raised a young boy back to life (vss. 32-37) and had increased a widow's last small amount of oil, making it possible for her to get out of debt (vss. 1-7).

The international scene was volatile. Naaman could hardly march a band of soldiers into Israelite territory without serious repercussions. {So, the king wrote a diplomatic letter to the Israelite king, and sent it with an extraordinary amount of silver and other gifts.}Q5 No mention of a prophet, however, was written in the letter, and the letter supposed that the Israelite king could perform the healing.

{In response, the Israelite king thought that the letter and request for healing were nothing but a pretense for war, for the king had no power to heal. In a fit, he ceremoniously ripped his royal robes, wondering what would happen next.}Q6

Ironically, the king of Israel—the very one who should know God's prophet, did not seem to know about Elisha, although the little slave girl did. When word of the incident came to Elisha, he rebuked the king for tearing his royal garments, telling him to send Naaman to him, so that Naaman would know that there is a true prophet in Israel.

ANGRY PRIDE

9 So Naaman came with his horses and with his chariot, and stood at the door of the house of Elisha.

10 And Elisha sent a messenger unto him, saying, Go and wash in Jordan seven times, and thy flesh shall come again to thee, and thou shalt be clean.

11 But Naaman was wroth, and went away, and said, Behold, I thought, He will surely come out to me, and stand, and call on the name of the LORD his God, and strike his hand over the place, and recover the leper.

12 Are not Abana and Pharpar, rivers of Damascus, better than all the waters of Israel? may I not wash in them, and be clean? So he turned and went away in a rage.

A simple command (II Kgs. 5:9-10). Naaman had traveled in a chariot pulled by horses, probably an impressive vehicle worthy of his position and stature. Soon he arrived at Elisha's front door, and surely Naaman's heart was filled with anticipation and excitement. As he waited outside, Elisha sent a messenger with some instructions for him. The instructions were simple and were accompanied by a specific promise. {Naaman was to go wash in the Jordan River, putting himself under the water seven times.}^Q7 After doing so his flesh would be fully healed.

The fact that Elisha simply sent a messenger out to Naaman reveals that he was not overly awed by the presence of Naaman. Here was the second most powerful man of Syria at his door, but he did not even bother to go out personally to greet him. The man wanted to be healed, and Elisha had a simple means by which that could be accomplished. The important thing was to get the word to him so that he could follow through and be healed.

A furious reaction (II Kgs. 5:11-12). This is where the pride of Naaman becomes obvious. Upon receiving the message from Elisha, he became very angry and gave two reasons for his reaction. First, he expected some type of ceremony worthy of a man of his stature. How dare that prophet send a mere servant with a message instead of coming out himself and calling ceremoniously on his God! He should have waved his hands over the leprosy and performed a miraculous healing himself. Instead, he had sent a messenger!

Is it not amazing to observe the attitudes of self-importance on the part of many who are idolized by the masses? One particularly sad trend these days is the idolizing of young entertainers who are not able to handle the attention maturely. We hear repeatedly of their ruin due to the fame and fortune that comes their way. Many of them could and should be role models for those who follow their careers, but instead we read of their turn to lives of promiscuity, extravagance, and abnormal expectations of attention.

Those of us who know the Lord should remember that every good and perfect gift comes down from the Father of lights (Jas. 1:17). When we are unusually blessed, we must recognize that God is the cause and that we do not deserve any credit for ourselves. We must keep a balanced perspective even when He does see fit to give us fame and fortune.

The second reason for Naaman's anger was the fact that he had been told to wash in the Jordan River. {He acted strongly. With typical prejudice, he deemed two rivers in Syria as superior to the Jordan. Disappointed that Elisha did not wave his hand over his leprosy (or perhaps some other mystical gesture), he went off angry.}^Q8

NO PRIDE

13 And his servants came near, and spake unto him, and said, My father, if the prophet had bid thee do some great thing, wouldest thou not have done it? how much rather then, when he saith to thee, Wash, and be clean?

14 Then went he down, and dipped himself seven times in Jordan, according to the saying of the man of God: and his flesh came again like unto the flesh of a little child, and he was clean.

15 And he returned to the man of God, he and all his company, and came, and stood before him: and he said, Behold, now I know that there is no God in all the earth, but in Israel.

A reasonable suggestion (II Kgs. 5:13-14). {Naaman had servants with him who could view the situation more objectively than he could. They approached him and addressed him tenderly and respectfully, referring to him as their "father." They pointed out to him that if he had been asked to do some great, demanding deed, his healing would have been worth whatever effort that would take. Why not, then, try something that was such a simple act of obedience?}^Q9

We must give Naaman credit for at least being teachable. He listened to his subordinates and acted on their recommendation. One of the marks of pride is an unwillingness to listen to the ideas of others when they are different from our own. Sometimes other people actually do have good ideas, and maybe even better ones than ours!

Having put aside his pride, Naaman went down into the Jordan River and dunked himself under the water seven times, just as Elisha had said he should. God then honored his humble spirit and completely and instantly healed him of his leprosy. Naaman might well have felt a tinge of shame after hearing his servants' reasonable argument, but now he certainly must have had a totally different spirit. Not only did God cleanse him of his disease, but He also restored his skin to the freshness and purity of a little child's.

It is not certain whether there was a special significance to washing seven times. Seven is a number of completion or perfection in the Bible, and some consider it to be a symbolic number of the covenant God had with Israel. What is important is to see that God gave specific instructions that had to be followed completely if healing was going to take place. This is a good reminder to us that we must not pick and choose which parts of God's Word we are going to obey to the exclusion of other parts. Rather, we must obey completely.

A changed heart (II Kgs. 5:15a). We do not know how many were accompanying Naaman in his entourage, but there appears to have been a large number of companions. It was a caravan of royal proportions, and the entire caravan now returned to Elisha's house. A much different spirit was present this time, however.

The once-proud Naaman was now deeply grateful to the prophet who had not even bothered to come out to address him. This time, however, Elisha was present. It was probably the Spirit of God who had directed Elisha to re-main out of sight the first time, because God was dealing with Naaman about his pride. God knew how to get Naaman to reveal his attitudes to himself, and the Lord then gave him the grace to change them. It all resulted in a miraculous healing and led to a man with a wholly different perspective about himself.

{It also led Naaman to a different perspective of Israel's God, for he now proclaimed that he knew there was no other God on earth.}[Q10] It is sad that many people never turn to God for salvation because of the pride that causes them to think that they do not need Him.

—Keith E. Eggert

QUESTIONS

1. What important position did Naaman hold?

2. In what other ways is Naaman described, and what does each description indicate about him?

3. What marred the exalted position and reputation that Naaman enjoyed?

4. What seemingly insignificant person suddenly became significant to Naaman and his king?

5. What did the Syrian king do after hearing Naaman's report?

6. What happened after the king's request reached the king of Israel?

7. What did Elisha instruct Naaman to do?

8. How did Naaman respond, and what were his reasons for doing so?

9. How did Naaman become convinced he should do what Elisha had said, and what was the result?

10. What happened after Naaman saw he had been completely cleansed?

—Keith E. Eggert

Preparing to Teach the Lesson

It is easy for Christians to fall short of God's best because of pride. When we are proud, we discount the need for God in our lives.

TODAY'S AIM

Facts: to show the circumstances of Naaman's condition and his pride.

Principle: to explain that pride gets in the way of God's solutions for us.

Application: to exhort students to adopt a humble attitude toward God as they seek answers from Him.

INTRODUCING THE LESSON

Proud people tend to alienate others, even friends. It is the humble person who gets the respect of others around him. Deep down there is something about humility that attracts us and something about pride that makes us withdraw. Our lesson this week illustrates how pride becomes a stumbling block to receiving God's blessings. God responds to a humble heart.

DEVELOPING THE LESSON

1. Naaman's condition (II Kgs. 5:1). Naaman was commander of the Syrian army. The king of Syria certainly was pleased with Naaman's leadership, for it was through him that Syria had won many victories against her enemies. Naaman was a mighty warrior and well respected by the king.

Like many great people, however, Naaman had something that troubled him. He suffered from a terrible skin disease, here called leprosy. Leprosy could be deadly, and it was greatly feared. In Israel, it isolated one from the rest of the society. Lepers were forced to live outside the city walls. When anyone came near, they were to call out, "Unclean, unclean" (Lev. 13:45). Touching a leper rendered a person ritually unclean.

Ask the class members to imagine themselves in Naaman's shoes. What would be their greatest wish? It should become obvious that all his glory as a Syrian commander was nothing compared to his desire to be made well. Proud Naaman was brought low by his suffering.

2. The solution (II Kgs. 5:2-5). In His wisdom, God had planted an enslaved girl in Naaman's life to direct him to the much needed remedy. God often works His greatest miracles through the simplest of people. On one of their frequent raids the Syrians had brought back a young girl from Israel as a captive. She was now serving in Naaman's house, waiting on his wife. Little did Naaman know that God was about to provide him with a solution through her.

God works in fascinating ways. Sometimes He places people in our lives long before needs arise that they can help us with. Ask the students to share experiences of God's placing people in their lives in order to provide answers for them when they needed them.

The slave girl went to Naaman's wife and told her about a prophet (Elisha) in Samaria, Israel's capital, who would be able to heal him of his disease. Naaman reported the matter to his king.

The Syrian king wrote a royal letter to the king of Israel, urging him to do what he needed to do to ensure Naaman's healing. Armed with that letter of recommendation, Naaman presented himself to the king of Israel. He took with him large gifts of silver, gold, and clothing.

Naaman was very close to the solution that God had provided, but disobedience and pride can keep people from His answers.

3. The prophet's instructions (II Kgs. 5:9-10). Naaman went to Elisha's home with his entourage of chariots and horses. Elisha was not impressed with his show of outward glory. He simply sent instructions to Naaman that he was to go and wash seven times in the Jordan, and he would be healed.

4. Naaman's pride (II Kgs. 5:11-12). God is not impressed with our outward pomp and show, and He often uses unconventional methods to show us that He is absolutely sovereign. Naaman was furious. He had expected Elisha to personally make an impressive public display of his healing—waving his hands and crying out to his God—and then send him home healed. That did not happen.

Naaman also argued that the rivers Abana and Pharpar back in Syria were certainly much better than the muddy river Jordan in Israel. Proud Naaman could not condescend to wash himself in the muddy Jordan as the prophet ordered. He was angry and disappointed, and he turned away, pouting.

God is not in as much of a hurry as we often are. He waits patiently for us to acknowledge Him, and then things begin to move.

5. Naaman's humble obedience (II Kgs. 5:13-15a). God then nudged Naaman through his servants. They suggested that if Elisha had asked him to do something great, he would have obeyed. How much more should he obey when the prophet asked such a simple thing as taking a dip seven times in the river Jordan?

God's blessings come through simple obedience. Naaman obeyed and did as the prophet had commanded.

His flesh was restored to being like that of a little child. Naaman responded with humility and praised the God of Israel. He had discovered the wonder of the God of Israel. Discuss what it takes for people to discover that God is real in our lives.

ILLUSTRATING THE LESSON

Pride and disobedience can keep us from God's answers for us.

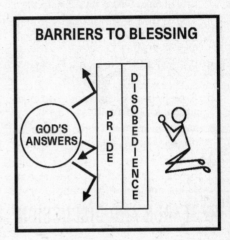

CONCLUDING THE LESSON

In our lesson this week we have learned that God often does not work the way we want Him to or when we expect Him to. Sometimes God's answers are very close to us, and all it takes is simple obedience to bring them to pass in our lives. In order to obey, we have to shed our pride and accept God's plans for us even when they do not make sense. Ultimately, He always has the best for us.

ANTICIPATING THE NEXT LESSON

In our lesson next week, we will explore how a young king's commitment to God and to fully obeying His Word changed the course of an entire nation.

—A. Koshy Muthalaly

PRACTICAL POINTS

1. All of people's worthy accomplishments come ultimately from the Lord (II Kgs. 5:1).
2. Life's apparent coincidences are in reality God's momentous movements for our good (vs. 2).
3. Even a small testimony for the Lord can lead to His great glory and praise (vss. 3-5).
4. The proud seek people's praise rather than God's pleasure and will (vss. 9-11a).
5. Pride keeps us from the full blessing of God (vss. 11b-12).
6. To really deal with our pride, we must submit to God's will (vss. 13-14).
7. Man's pride and God's glory cannot coexist (vs. 15a).

—Don Kakavecos

RESEARCH AND DISCUSSION

1. Were Naaman's accomplishments the cause of his pride? Why or why not? What other things can engender pride?
2. How does God's use of a little captured servant girl encourage you to view the circumstances and situations of your life?
3. Do you believe that there are any incidentals or coincidences with God? Explain your answer.
4. How did Elisha's actions and words help reveal Naaman's pride? Is it easy to recognize pride in our own lives? How can we lovingly challenge pride in others and ourselves?
5. If man's pride and God's glory cannot coexist, what practical steps can we take to deal with our pride?

—Don Kakavecos

ILLUSTRATED HIGH POINTS

I will send a letter unto the king (II Kgs. 5:5)

Some of us living in societies that have advanced medical technology and expertise may forget that many nations are not so well-off. Some procedures are conducted in only a few countries. Many people needing such care are unable to find help. Only those having the means to travel and to pay for such service can receive the needed treatment.

International travel seeking medical assistance still occurs, but it is unlikely that anyone is seeking a miracle.

Go and wash in Jordan seven times (vs. 10)

Many times we want to see great things accomplished for God's glory, but we fail to seek out His way to get it done.

Surely God would like His people to have a new church in which to worship. We needed a larger facility.

The problem we faced was how exactly to go about raising the necessary funds. For this we engaged a financial consultant. This expert advised us to carefully study the financial status of every family in the church. Once that was accomplished, goals were set for each family, indicating how much they should be expected to contribute.

These numbers were printed and distributed. Then, in an open forum, members were asked whether they would be faithful in doing their part to reach the overall goal. Many felt offended by these tactics.

The results were not good. Not only did the pledge amount fall far short, but several members also walked out, never to return. Plans for a new church building had to be put on hold.

—Albert J. Schneider

Golden Text Illuminated

"Then went he down, and dipped himself seven times in Jordan, according to the saying of the man of God: and his flesh came again like unto the flesh of a little child, and he was clean" (II Kings 5:14).

Most of the Old Testament focuses on the nation of Israel. Through the Scriptures, we learn of God's promises to Abraham, and we read how He fulfilled those promises by leading the Jewish people out of Egypt and into the Promised Land.

At the same time, God never ignored the other nations. A few Old Testament accounts provide a glimpse into God's thoughts concerning the world outside of the land of Israel. The account of Naaman, the commander of the army of Syria, is one such account. It says in II Kings 5:1 that the Lord gave Syria military victories through Naaman. This statement shows that God is actively working in other nations, even though they are not His chosen people.

God's most precise way to reveal His character and will is through His Scriptures. God gave the Scriptures to Israel, and He used Israel to make Himself known to other nations. It was through a young Israelite girl that Naaman learned to worship the one true God.

God used two events to reveal Himself to Naaman. First, Naaman had a skin disease. The Bible does not tell the exact nature of the skin disease, but we can deduce that he could not find a cure in Syria. Second, a Syrian raiding party captured a young Israelite girl who became a servant to Naaman's wife.

We do not know the Israelite girl's name, but we see her faith in God. She learned of Naaman's skin disease and knew that God's prophet Elisha could provide healing (vs. 3). Her faith did not depend upon good circumstances.

She was enslaved in a foreign land, taken from her family and the land of God's promised blessings, but her faith remained strong. She did not deviate from God to worship a foreign deity.

People in the Old Testament period often thought that gods were associated with specific regions. The god that the king of Syria worshipped was Rimmon, the storm god (vs. 18). Often, people thought that the gods were national. If a nation won in battle, people assumed the god of that nation must be the most powerful. In Naaman's case, he had to go to Israel for healing because Syria and its god could not provide a cure.

When Naaman went to Samaria, Elisha sent a messenger telling him to wash seven times in the Jordan River (vs. 10). Naaman became angry because after traveling all the way to Israel, Elisha did not even speak to him in person. Naaman also wondered why he couldn't wash in the "better" rivers of Syria instead of in the Jordan. After swallowing his pride and washing seven times in the Jordan River, as Elisha told him, God healed him (vs. 14). Because of his healing, he acknowledged that the God of Israel is the one true God (vs. 15).

God does not offer salvation to only one people group. Redemption is available worldwide through Jesus Christ. God places His children in specific circumstances to be faithful witnesses to the goodness of God. He used the Israelite girl in her unique situation to proclaim His goodness and open a man's heart to the one true God.

—*Glenn Weaver*

Heart of the Lesson

1. An insurmountable problem (II Kgs. 5:1-5). The top general in an army has always been held in high regard. This was certainly the case with Naaman, the commander of Syria's army. Naaman, however, had a problem: he had leprosy. In that day, having leprosy was about the worst thing that could happen to someone. This was not some political or personal problem; Naaman would not be able to continue in his job. He would waste away to almost nothing before he died.

The problems you and I face are probably not as severe as leprosy, but they are important to us nonetheless. Some may seem insurmountable. What do we do? The only thing that anyone can do is go to God with them.

In Naaman's case, he was in the right place at the right time. A servant girl from Israel had the faith in God to tell him how to be cured of his leprosy.

Children often play an important part in the plan of God. Remember the boy with five loaves of bread and two fish (John 6:9)? That was not much food for thousands of people, but this boy was willing to let his lunch be what it could be in the Master's hand. This servant girl had the information that Naaman needed, and she was not bashful about sharing it.

2. The pride of self (II Kgs. 5:9-12). Naaman went to see Elisha but was angered by what he perceived as Elisha's rebuff, not even coming out of his home to greet him. That was the first evidence of Naaman's pride. The second was his opinion of the prophet's instructions to dip in the Jordan seven times.

The word Naaman used to describe the rivers Abana and Pharpar in contrast to the Jordan ("better") is somewhat vague, but it appears that perhaps he was speaking of the cleanliness of the river. The rivers of Damascus were renowned for their beauty, unlike the often muddy Jordan. Naaman was not about to get into that nasty Jordan River. Even in his condition, he had his pride.

Are we not sometimes like Naaman? The Lord asks us to do something—maybe something simple as talking to someone about Himself—but we refuse. We have our pride, after all. Yes, that is exactly the problem. Naaman's problem was more about his pride than about his leprosy.

Unsaved people have the same kind of hang-up about God's plan of salvation. They reject it because it is too easy. "What do I have to do to earn it?" they often think. The reality is that it is not about us and what we can do. It is about Jesus and what He has done.

3. The humility that cancels pride (II Kgs. 5:13-15a). Thankfully, Naaman had some wise servants. They told him he would have done something great if the prophet had demanded it; so why not do something simple? This advice was successful partly because it was phrased in the form of a question. It has been said that while a question stirs the conscience, an accusation hardens the will. That is especially true when we explain the gospel to a lost sinner.

Sometimes people reject the gospel because of its simplicity. It seems too simple because it is all of God. Nonetheless, by humbly accepting what God has done, we benefit from His goodness.

—*John Haynes*

World Missions

The Prophet Elisha was able to heal Naaman, but there was a catch. Naaman had to obey and wash seven times in the Jordan River. He was not sure he was willing to go into the muddy waters of the Jordan. If he had not swallowed his pride, he would never have been healed of his disease.

Pride is a quiet sin. Sometimes it goes undetected among people around the sinner. With others, it stands out noticeably.

Missionaries are often trained by God to swallow their pride early in their ministries. Maybe they were raised in a wealthy family that thinks success and money go hand in hand. Possibly their background includes determined parents who raised them to believe that if they wanted anything in life, they would have to work hard for it.

Of themselves, neither of these types of families are bad, but sometimes they breed very prideful people. One of the first things a missionary needs to realize is that he does not have power to take care of himself. He needs to realize that he needs believers to help him become successful as a missionary.

From the very beginning, missionaries have needed other believers to make their mission a success. They need the prayers of others to help them learn the language. They need other believers to help them financially so that they will be free to do their job on the mission field.

That is only the beginning, though. Missionaries need everyone around them. They need to depend on a mission board to honestly receive their finances and help them settle family matters in their home country.

There are just a few missionaries who are supported by only one church or one person. Usually missionaries need to be supported by numerous churches and also by many different people. For many missionaries, this is a good thing. They appreciate the prayers and the different ways that their supporting families take care of them.

Usually missionaries work in teams. They do not enter a dangerous territory or an unknown mission field without the aid of other missionaries.

Many missionaries also struggle with a lack of finances or shortage of many needed items. They often go without the modern luxuries that many of us take for granted. The beauty that radiates from them despite not having things like a new dress or the newest tools reflects their desire to serve God, not themselves.

Many missionaries have taught me the lesson that having the best that life has to offer is not as important as we may think it is. Whenever I find myself looking to myself to supply my needs and taking my eyes off God, I learn the importance of God and other believers in my life.

Rich men, like Naaman, often have a harder time with the pride lesson. Pride can be a burden to one who will not confess sin. If we are not serious about dealing with sin, we tend to disregard it.

All of us need to accept that other Christians were given to us for encouragement and support. God did not make us beings who could survive without fellowship and encouraging words. Even Christ had help from twelve disciples in fulfilling the ministry God had called Him to do.

—Elizabeth Wehman

The Jewish Aspect

Naaman was inconsistent in his quest for a cure for his curse of leprosy. At first he seemed humble and open to advice from any quarter. He accepted the advice of a captive Hebrew girl in his own service. Then he became angry over the prophet's failure to receive him and perform a miracle of healing for him.

Naaman should have learned more from the servant girl, a true heroine of Israel. She, like the captive Daniel, had doubtless been imbued with the grace of the living God.

Melvin and I were in the same military unit. I liked Melvin. He was very intelligent and humorous, and he was a great conversationalist. Melvin was Jewish. In his hometown he said to me, "You must meet my family."

Sabbath was drawing to a close. The big house was filled with well-dressed, prosperous-looking people. Melvin led me through a maze of rooms, passing twenty or thirty adults and children. No one was introduced to me; we seemed headed for some special audience. Heads nodded in deference. We passed a huge dining room table laden with fruits and steaming casseroles of food.

Seated at the end of the table in a place of honor was a lady of great age, slightly bowed by her years, surrounded by pillows and cushions. Melvin bowed in order to be heard and said, "*Bubbe* (Grandmother), this is my friend Lyle." She smiled weakly and held out to me a bejeweled hand. I did not know what to do or quite what to say; so I said simply, "It is a pleasure to meet you." She withdrew her hand and turned a cheek for Melvin to kiss her.

Then I met Melvin's brothers and sisters and relatives spanning several generations. Melvin never explained the special audience I had received, but I took it as a special honor accorded to very special friends. I learned from other sources that the family was the center of Jewish life and that the eldest member was to be deferred to. In addition, the advice and will of the elder carry special weight in the younger person's decision making.

I believe Melvin, under similar circumstances, would have exhibited the resourcefulness of Naaman's girl captive.

One Bible scholar was quoted as saying, "We should rather expect to find [the story of Naaman] on a page of the Gospel than seek it in an Old Testament book" (Lange, *Lange's Commentary on the Holy Scriptures,* Zondervan). This point has some merit, for the Gospel went out mightily to the Gentiles, and Jesus used Naaman's example to shame and warn the Jews who were scoffing at Him (Luke 4:14-30).

The Jews needed only to look to Moses for a lesson in humility. The Midrash, a commentary of the rabbis, says Moses relinquished the leadership of the nation of Israel to Joshua in an unusual way. The story indicates Moses' essential humility. When Joshua rose in the morning, Moses was there to help him dress. Joshua balked and dressed himself.

Moses seated Joshua on the great chair he had used for many years. While Joshua resisted, Moses served in every needful way. Moses insisted that Joshua precede him on walks. The Israelites were in tears (Silverman, *The Sages Speak: Rabbinic Wisdom and Jewish Values,* Aronson).

—Lyle P. Murphy

Guiding the Superintendent

Pride is one of those natural, sinful tendencies common to people. One of the ways it manifests itself is in people not wanting anyone to tell them what to do. As a result, pride has been the downfall of many people both historically and biblically (cf. II Chr. 32:24- 26; Prov. 16:18; Jas. 4:6).

This lesson tells how a mighty man of valor named Naaman was healed because he humbled himself before the Lord. However, like Naaman, we often need others around us to point out our pride and guide us to the safe path of humility.

DEVOTIONAL OUTLINE

1. Naaman's problem (II Kgs. 5:1-5). Leprosy is a skin disease. In its most deadly form, it causes the deterioration of the body and death. God's law said that a person who had leprosy was to separate himself from the rest of society and live alone (Lev. 13:45-46).

Naaman was not of Israel, and he still dwelt among his people. He must have known the deadly, long-term effects of the disease, however. We see the significance Naaman attached to the opportunity to be cured by the large gift he took to pay for his healing.

2. Naaman's pride (II Kgs. 5:9-12). Naaman, who was a great man in Syria, expected royal treatment by the Prophet Elisha. In sending a messenger to Naaman, Elisha was making a statement about Naaman's importance. Naaman had to be taught the supremacy of the God of Israel before he could be healed.

Naaman was humiliated by being met by a servant and not even seeing the face of the prophet. His pride flared up because of the treatment he had received. As a result, he refused to follow the simple instructions that would heal his leprosy.

3. Naaman's humility (II Kgs. 5:13-15a). Many times when people are in a rage, they are blind to their own pride. God often uses the people around them to get them back on track.

This is what Naaman's servants did for him. They reasoned with him and urged him to humble himself and go wash himself in the Jordan River.

Naaman heeded the words of his servants and dipped himself seven times in the Jordan. What a glorious physical cleansing and spiritual awakening he would have missed had he continued in his pride!

Naaman returned to acknowledge the greatness of the God of Israel.

AGE-GROUP EMPHASES

Children: Urge the children to heed the warnings and instructions of their parents. They need to realize that being proud and refusing to listen will result in poverty and shame (Prov. 13:18).

Youths: Many times God gives direction to youths through their parents. Encourage the youths to humble themselves before their parents and to ask them for advice. Guide them in ways to establish good lines of communication, as well as a spirit of humility.

Adults: Warn the adults to watch out for prideful attitudes in their lives. Remind them that as believers we are to exhort one another against sin (Heb. 3:13). Help them establish a watch against pride. Exhort them to establish close friendships with other believers who can sound the alert for them when pride starts to manifest itself.

—*David L. Schmidt*

SCRIPTURE LESSON TEXT

II KGS. 22:8 And Hilkiah the high priest said unto Shaphan the scribe, I have found the book of the law in the house of the LORD. And Hilkiah gave the book to Shaphan, and he read it.

9 And Shaphan the scribe came to the king, and brought the king word again, and said, Thy servants have gathered the money that was found in the house, and have delivered it into the hand of them that do the work, that have the oversight of the house of the LORD.

10 And Shaphan the scribe shewed the king, saying, Hilkiah the priest hath delivered me a book. And Shaphan read it before the king.

23:1 And the king sent, and they gathered unto him all the elders of Judah and of Jerusalem.

2 And the king went up into the house of the LORD, and all the men of Judah and all the inhabitants of Jerusalem with him, and the priests, and the prophets, and all the people, both small and great: and he read in their ears all the words of the book of the covenant which was found in the house of the LORD.

3 And the king stood by a pillar, and made a covenant before the LORD, to walk after the LORD, and to keep his commandments and his testimonies and his statutes with all *their* heart and all *their* soul, to perform the words of this covenant that were written in this book. And all the people stood to the covenant.

21 And the king commanded all the people, saying, Keep the passover unto the LORD your God, as *it is* written in the book of this covenant.

22 Surely there was not holden such a passover from the days of the judges that judged Israel, nor in all the days of the kings of Israel, nor of the kings of Judah;

23 But in the eighteenth year of king Josiah, *wherein* this passover was holden to the LORD in Jerusalem.

NOTES

Josiah Calls the People Back to God

Lesson Text: II Kings 22:8-10; 23:1-3, 21-23

Related Scriptures: II Kings 22:1-7, 11-13; 23:4-20;
Numbers 9:1-5; I Kings 13:1-10

TIME: 622 B.C.   PLACE: Jerusalem

GOLDEN TEXT—"The king stood by a pillar, and made a covenant before the Lord, . . . to perform the words of this covenant that were written in this book. And all the people stood to the covenant" (II Kings 23:3).

Introduction

Manasseh was twelve years old when he became king in Jerusalem, and he reigned for fifty-five years (II Kgs. 21:1). He was very evil and profaned the holy land with idolatry and the shedding of innocent blood (vss. 2-18). His son Amon was no better (vss. 19-23). When he was assassinated, the people made Josiah king (vs. 24).

Things now took a turn for the better. Josiah was only eight years old when he began to reign. He "did that which was right in the sight of the Lord" (22:2). Despite his wicked predecessors and the fact that the Law of Moses had been lost, this young king put himself on the road to righteousness.

After God's law was found in the temple, it was read to Josiah. He sent a delegation to Huldah the prophetess, and she sent God's message that he would live in peace (vss. 8- 20). Josiah then brought about many reforms in the nation (23:1-24).

LESSON OUTLINE

I. DISCOVERY—II Kgs. 22:8-10

II. DETERMINATION—II Kgs. 23:1-3

II. DEVOTION—II Kgs. 23:21-23

Exposition: Verse by Verse

DISCOVERY

II KGS. 22:8 And Hilkiah the high priest said unto Shaphan the scribe, I have found the book of the law in the house of the LORD. And Hilkiah gave the book to Shaphan, and he read it.

9 And Shaphan the scribe came to the king, and brought the king word again, and said, Thy servants have gathered the money that was

found in the house, and have delivered it into the hand of them that do the work, that have the oversight of the house of the LORD.

10 And Shaphan the scribe shewed the king, saying, Hilkiah the priest hath delivered me a book. And Shaphan read it before the king.

Recovery (II Kgs. 22:8). In the eighteenth year of his reign, Josiah sent Shaphan the scribe to Hilkiah the high priest to determine the sum of silver contributions made by collectors at the door of the temple. This was to be used to repair the house of God and pay carpenters and masons for their work (vss. 3-7).

{It was while this recovery work was going on that Hilkiah found the book (scroll) of the Law of Moses in the temple.}**Q1** Many scholars think this was Deuteronomy, the fifth book of the Pentateuch. Hilkiah gave it to Shaphan the scribe, and he read it. He must have been at least somewhat aware of the importance of this lost document.

God expected His people to live by the Law given to them at Mount Sinai through Moses. The fact that it had been ignored and misplaced shows how great the spiritual decline was under Manasseh and Amon.

Report (II Kgs. 22:9). Perhaps it was a matter of doing first things first or of saving the exciting news until last, but {Shaphan made a matter-of-fact report to Josiah that the king's servants had gathered the money in the temple and given it to the tradesmen for making repairs. It was only then that the scribe brought out the scroll the priest had found as the repair work began.}**Q2**

Reading (II Kgs. 22:10). We can well imagine that Shaphan tried to remain calm and dignified as required by royal protocol, but he might have been inwardly emotional as he presented the recovered law of God to the king. As soon as he learned Hilkiah had given the scroll to Shaphan to read, Josiah instructed Shaphan to read it to him.

In those times the term "scribe" denoted a learned man. In the case of Shaphan, he was King Josiah's secretary and a greatly valued aide.

Josiah was shaken when he heard God's law read, for it was immediately clear that his nation was guilty of breaking God's covenant and that the violation of that covenant would bring God's promised judgment. {The king commanded Hilkiah the high priest and others to go visit Huldah the prophetess to see what the Lord had to say about this. Was there any way to avert divine judgment?}**Q3** Huldah told the delegates that God would bring judgment on Judah for its sins but that the tenderhearted Josiah would not see this judgment. He would be allowed to finish his reign in peace (vss. 11-20).

Josiah's reign ended abruptly in 609 B.C. when he went up against the Egyptians and was killed in battle at Megiddo. However, he died knowing that he had followed the Lord and had sought to lead his people to do the same.

DETERMINATION

23:1 And the king sent, and they gathered unto him all the elders of Judah and of Jerusalem.

2 And the king went up into the house of the LORD, and all the men of Judah and all the inhabitants of Jerusalem with him, and the priests, and the prophets, and all the people, both small and great: and he read in their ears all the words of the book of the covenant which was found in the house of the LORD.

3 And the king stood by a pillar, and made a covenant before the LORD, to walk after the LORD, and to keep his commandments and his

testimonies and his statutes with all their heart and all their soul, to perform the words of this covenant that were written in this book. And all the people stood to the covenant.

Covenant read (II Kgs. 23:1-2). Josiah had been eight years old when his reign began. He was twenty-six years old when God's law was read to him. He would live thirteen years more before being slain at Megiddo at the age of thirty-nine (22:1; 23:29). During those thirteen years, God used him to bring about many improvements in the spiritual life of Judah. This period was the last stretch of religious revival and political independence before the return to apostasy and the onset of the Babylonian Captivity in 586 B.C.

{This time of spiritual resurgence began with a great convocation ordered by King Josiah. He sent messengers throughout Judah and Jerusalem to tell the nation's elders (leaders) to gather before him in the capital.}^{Q4} The setting for this assembly was the temple. {The king went to the temple, along with the elders from outlying areas. They were joined by the inhabitants of the city, priests, prophets, and anyone else who wanted to attend.}^{Q5} It must have made quite an impressive parade of people. They probably gathered in the temple's large courtyard.

We do not know how many people were involved, and it makes us wonder how everyone could hear the king when he stood up to read the law of God. Some open-air speakers had powerful voices; if the acoustics were right, they could make themselves heard by a large crowd. It has also been suggested that the one leading the meeting could have had other speakers strategically located among the multitude. They would hear him speak and relay the message part by part to outlying members of the congregation.

Covenant made (II Kgs. 23:3). There are two parts to this verse that describe what happened after Josiah finished reading God's law to the crowd. The first has to do with the king himself as he spoke about what he intended to do. The second has to do with the people giving assent to what he said.

{Josiah stood by a pillar of the temple and made a solemn covenant with the Lord, promising to walk in His way and keep His "commandments," "testimonies," and "statutes."}^{Q6} We are not sure how to clearly distinguish these terms now, but together they refer to all of God's laws. The king said he would keep all of the Law's instructions, and he intended to do this with all his heart and soul. He meant to carry out all the demands contained in the sacred scroll.

In the original, there is no "his" or "their" before "heart" and "soul." The translation probably supplies "their" in anticipation of the last part of the verse, which shows the common assent on the part of the people. Most likely, Josiah was indicating his own intention of keeping the Law while exhorting the people to follow his example. When a king of Israel or Judah sinned, he also "made Israel to sin" (cf. I Kgs. 14:16; 16:2). Now, Josiah was reversing that pattern, causing Israel to obey by his own obedience.

The intention of the congregation that day was to go along with Josiah in his determination to keep God's covenant. {They stood to show they agreed with him and had the same desire to keep the covenant.}^{Q7}

The custom of standing to show approval of what is happening on stage still persists. Although people most often use applause to express satisfaction and some in the audience may even cheer, whenever a performance is especially noteworthy, it is rewarded with a standing ovation.

Standing is also customary as a form of respect or etiquette in certain situations. People in a courtroom are ordered to stand as the judge enters and sits at the bench. We might sometimes stands when being introduced to an older person. Everyone stands as the bride comes down the aisle on her father's arm.

It was on the basis of the people's promise to follow God's law that the king initiated a series of spiritual reforms in Judah in the years that followed. These are described in verses 4-24.

Josiah was adamant about destroying the trappings of paganism and idolatry. {He destroyed the pagan shrines and brought to an end the work of idolatrous priests. The heathen altars built by Solomon were destroyed. Members of occult groups were put away, along with other abominations.}Q8 This illustrates what just one person can do to bring glory to God if he is in the right position and is willing to take a strong stand for the Lord and His commandments.

Christians have often been told not to become involved in politics. However, that opinion has seemingly undergone a change. Decent, God-fearing, Bible-believing, churchgoing people can make a difference in national life. Josiah did not shy away from using his position and influence to call his people to the path of righteousness.

DEVOTION

21 And the king commanded all the people, saying, Keep the passover unto the LORD your God, as it is written in the book of this covenant.

22 Surely there was not holden such a passover from the days of the judges that judged Israel, nor in all the days of the kings of Israel, nor of the kings of Judah;

23 But in the eighteenth year of king Josiah, wherein this passover was holden to the LORD in Jerusalem.

Passover commanded (II Kgs. 23:21). An integral part of the Mosaic Law was the celebration of various religious festivals throughout the year. {One of the most important of these was Passover, which commemorated God's deliverance of Israel from bondage in the land of Egypt.}Q9 It was held on the fourteenth day of the Jewish month of Nisan (our March or April). It was followed by the seven-day Feast of Unleavened Bread (Lev. 23:5-6). The entire eight-day festival eventually became known as Passover (cf. Luke 22:1). This feast, along with the Feast of Weeks (Pentecost) and the Feast of Tabernacles, was a pilgrimage festival. According to Deuteronomy 16:16, all healthy and ceremonially clean male Jews were expected to "appear before the Lord" in Jerusalem each year for these three feasts.

Since the people of Judah had ignored the Law, it was natural that they would also neglect the religious festivals or just go through the motions in a perfunctory manner. When the book of the law was discovered, it led to renewed interest in the festivals. Josiah did not just suggest that they be celebrated again, however. He commanded this to be done.

Celebrations among believers in the current age of grace also serve as educational tools. We attach great significance to communion services, baptisms, weddings, dedications of new structures, ordinations, graduations, and other events. Even funerals can be celebratory if viewed as the transition of saints to their heavenly rewards.

We cannot command people to attend Christian celebrations as Josiah did with his Jewish subjects, but we can promote these occasions and use them to show the hand of God at work among His people in the world.

Passover held (II Kgs. 23:22-23). These verses declare that the Passover held in the eighteenth year of Josiah's reign was unlike any that had been held since the time of the judges and during all the days that the kings of Israel and Judah reigned.

This raises the question of how elaborate a religious event ought to be. Some groups feel justified in spending a great deal of money, time, and effort to put on a spectacular display. They may think that they should outdo unbelievers in their efforts in order to prove that they are serious about their faith. Others believe that a religious event should be as simple and unpretentious as possible in order to show humility and frugality. Usually their desire is to use the funds they have for more practical ministry projects.

It is easy to see value in both sides of this matter. Decisions have to be made on the basis of careful thought, prayer, and the leading of the Holy Spirit. Sometimes only experience will teach what should be done the next time.

It would certainly appear that the Lord approved of Josiah's outstanding celebration of Passover as the king reinstituted this festival in Judah. The Lord also must have been very pleased when Josiah put away all the mediums and spiritists, as well as the household idols, found in Judah and Jerusalem (vs. 24). We are not given a definition for "put away," but this could have ranged from banishment to execution.

In verse 25 we find an extremely favorable evaluation of King Josiah. {This young man was declared to be a better king than any before or after him, the comparison probably being to all the kings of Judah and Israel. He was best when it came to devotion to the law of God that was given to Israel at Mount Sinai.}Q10

We would do well to leave a similar legacy behind us. We are often concerned about the material things our children will inherit from us. Sometimes we are equally concerned about how to pass on our reputation, position, or power.

The greatest gift we can leave behind, though, is that of a life devoted to God and His kingdom. Conferring such a legacy actually begins before our children are born, or in the case of other family members and friends, before our initial contact with them.

—Gordon Talbot

QUESTIONS

1. Who found the book of the law of God in the temple?

2. How was King Josiah notified of the law scroll's discovery?

3. Why did Josiah send a delegation to Huldah the prophetess?

4. What was Josiah's first act as he sought revival for the nation?

5. What kinds of people joined Josiah and the elders at the temple?

6. What promise did Josiah make after reading the Law to the people?

7. How did the congregation show their assent to the decision made by Josiah?

8. What types of reforms did Josiah make following his commitment to the covenant?

9. Why was reinstitution of the Passover important?

10. What kind of legacy did Josiah leave behind him?

—Gordon Talbot

Preparing to Teach the Lesson

When a nation ignores the law of God, utter destruction is the inevitable end. It is common knowledge today that, for the most part, the mention of God has been taken out of our public school system. We are living in a secular society.

Our lesson this week shows us the powerful way God can use one person who submits to His will in the midst of a disobedient people.

TODAY'S AIM

Facts: to study how Josiah brought the law of God back into focus in the life of God's people.

Principle: to show that one person's commitment to God can turn the tide of evil for a nation.

Application: to demonstrate that when we as Christians submit to the laws of God, we will find God's blessing.

INTRODUCING THE LESSON

Have you ever wondered where the downhill trend of discarding God from our society will ultimately end? How will it change our society? What effect will it have on our children and their generation? Will our children be able to worship the Lord without being persecuted? It is time we gave some thought to these very serious issues in our time.

We also need to ask ourselves what witness God calls us to give in the midst of a crooked generation (cf. Phil. 2:15). This week's lesson shows us how a young king named Josiah with a heart for God brought the law of God back into focus for God's people. We have an example to follow.

DEVELOPING THE LESSON

1. The book of the law discovered (II Kgs. 22:8-10). Josiah was a king who came to the throne at the tender age of eight. When he was sixteen, God began a work in his heart that would help him turn Judah back toward God (cf. II Chr. 34:3).

Our lesson begins at the point when Hilkiah the high priest found the book of the law in the ruins when the temple was being repaired. Shaphan the scribe then read it to the king. The book of the law may have been the first five books of the Bible (the Pentateuch) or just the book of Deuteronomy. The book of the law had been absent from the life of God's people for too long. Now it was in the hands of a good king who knew what to do with it.

When a leader of God's people commits himself to the Word of God, the people who follow him will go in the right direction.

2. The book of the covenant read (II Kgs. 23:1-2). Young Josiah was so interested in the Law that had been found that he called all the leaders of Judah and Jerusalem together to let them listen to the reading of the Law firsthand. The priests, the prophets, and all the people gathered at the temple grounds at the command of the king. Notice that it was the king who took the initiative in this. Here is an example for Christian leaders to follow. Notice also that the king read the whole book of the law to them. The people listened carefully and attentively.

Discuss what happens when the leaders of God's people have as their authority the infallible Word of God.

3. The king and the people pledge to keep the law (II Kgs. 23:3). Josiah was so moved by the reading of the law of God that he pledged publicly to obey all the laws and regulations found in the book with all his heart and soul. The people then reciprocated by committing themselves equally to the laws of God to which Josiah had committed himself.

One must not get the idea that it was easier to put God first in the days of Josiah. The people were influenced very strongly by the pagan cultures around them and often adopted their practices and false worship.

The struggle to stay true to the laws of God was just as hard in the days of Josiah as it is today. It meant going against the grain of the dominant culture. In every generation, one will have to take a stand for God in this wicked world.

Discuss with the class what happens when a Christian leader takes the initiative to follow God's law today. What response does such a leader usually receive from the secular culture? From the church (cf. I Tim. 4:12-16)?

4. The Passover renewed (II Kgs. 23:21-23). One of the first things that Josiah did to indicate that he was following the Law was to reinstate the celebration of the Passover. It is important to remember that the Passover was the celebration of the deliverance of the Israelites from the Egyptians. Every firstborn of the Egyptians, both man and beast, was killed by God. By celebrating the Passover, the people were recognizing that God alone was their Deliverer. The nation's relationship with God was renewed.

Many countries that have historically been centers of Christianity have fallen into secularism and atheism today. They have relegated God to the sidelines and only nominally acknowledged Him. When we see this, we need to recognize the calling God has on us to be lights in the midst of a dark world. Josiah understood that calling and chose to obey God rather than the practices of his day. He brought the people back to God and showed the importance of following the law of God.

ILLUSTRATING THE LESSON

Godly leaders who live by the Word of God do things God's way, and those who follow them are blessed by God.

WHEN LEADERS OBEY GOD

GOD

THE PEOPLE ARE BLESSED

CONCLUDING THE LESSON

From the very beginning of his reign, King Josiah wanted to follow what was right in God's sight. He had a tender heart for God. We must not get the idea that he had an easy time. He probably faced opposition from some people, but we see that he stood firm to the end and was known to be one of the righteous kings of Judah. God blessed everything he did (cf. Ps. 1:1-3).

King Josiah also led his people down the pathway of righteousness as they sought to live by the book of the law that they had found. This applies even today. We are called to live by the Bible and therefore stay close to God's laws. We cannot go wrong when we do this, for it is God's truth for us today.

ANTICIPATING THE NEXT LESSON

Next week begins a new quarter in which we will study one faithful prophet (Daniel) and one resistant prophet (Jonah). Read Daniel 1:8-21 for next time.

—A. Koshy Muthalaly

PRACTICAL POINTS

1. God's Word is not something that should have to be found (II Kgs. 22:8).
2. If the Bible has been missing from our lives, we would do well to begin reading it immediately (vss. 9-10).
3. If we have neglected our walk with God, a public commitment of renewed fidelity is a good way to get back on track (23:1-3).
4. A leader who encourages faithfulness to the Lord is a blessing to his followers (vs. 21).
5. Even if we have neglected our obligations for a long time, it is worthwhile to begin observing them again (vss. 22-23).

—Kenneth A. Sponsler

RESEARCH AND DISCUSSION

1. Why might Shaphan have told the king about the collection of money before mentioning the newly found book of the law (II Kgs. 22:9-10)?
2. Do you get the impression that the Law had not been greatly missed prior to its being found? What might account for this?
3. What was the king apparently hoping to accomplish by having the entire book of the law read to the assembled crowd (23:1-2)?
4. How sincere do you think the people were in their pledge to follow everything they had heard in the Law (vs. 3)? Explain your answer.
5. What can account for the fact that the Passover had not been properly held since the time of the judges (vss. 21-23)?

—Kenneth A. Sponsler

ILLUSTRATED HIGH POINTS

Delivered me a book (II Kgs. 22:10)

There are books, and then there are *books*. Every now and then a book comes along that is extraordinary and has a powerful impact. The impact of one book by Michael Hawley would be frightful if it was dropped in your lap. The 118-page work called *Bhutan: A Visual Odyssey Across the Last Himalayan Kingdom* weighs 133 pounds and measures five by seven feet. A roll of paper more than one hundred yards long goes into one copy.

When Hilkiah the high priest delivered the book of the law to Shaphan and he gave it to King Josiah, the impact was felt all across the kingdom of Judah. Would that the Scriptures could have as weighty an impact on our nation today!

All their heart (23:3)

Rebekha, a Muslim girl, became impressed by the kindness of a Christian girl. After reading the Bible, Rebekha was saved. When an illness brought her near death, she was miraculously healed. She told her family and the incredulous doctor that she was healthy now because of her faith in Christ.

Although her mother slapped her and her uncle beat her in an attempt to persuade her to return to Islam, Rebekha's faith was not weakened. One day her father's brothers held a gun to her head and ordered her to return to Islam. When she refused, they threw her in a canal in hopes that a nearby black cobra would kill her. She got away, but hid from family members who still wanted to kill her.

Regarding the persecution she has suffered, Rebekha remarked, "Jesus was crucified for us. Can we not endure some of the same for the sake of the Great Commission?" (Lane, "Robes of White," *The Voice of the Martyrs,* March 2005).

—Todd Williams

Golden Text Illuminated

"The king stood by a pillar, and made a covenant before the Lord, . . . to perform the words of this covenant that were written in this book. And all the people stood to the covenant" (II Kings 23:3).

Josiah's reign was a breath of fresh air in Judah. Even though he ascended to the throne at the age of eight, the young king was of a different character from some of the other kings who preceded him. The difference was striking. The young monarch loved the Lord and set out at an early age to refurbish the temple in Jerusalem. It was during that campaign that the book of the law was discovered in the house of the Lord.

One sees that God was working in the king's life even before he came in contact with the Law, indicating that God was enacting a unique plan He had for Josiah, as He did for other leaders like Moses, Jeremiah, and Paul.

When the Word of God was read to King Josiah, it penetrated deeply. He became painfully aware of how far the nation had strayed from the Lord. He determined to bring reform to the land, and he knew it had to begin with him. He therefore summoned the people to the temple in Jerusalem so that they too could hear the Word and respond to it.

Our text tells us the king read the Word to his subjects and stood to make a covenant. One can only imagine God's pleasure at seeing a young king take such an interest in spiritual matters and have such a burden for others. Any godly parent would be overjoyed to see his child do such a thing, so it is easy to recognize why God would be pleased with Josiah. Perhaps we need to examine how passionate we are for the things of God and for the salvation of the lost.

The king made a covenant with God before all the people. He took a public stand for God and His Word. It is safe to say he acted not only or his own sake but also to set the example for others. One cannot say too much good about how Josiah started out in ruling Judah and in bringing religious reform to the land.

The people who had responded to the call to assemble at the temple heard the words Josiah read to them, and it made a deep impression on them. Like the king, they desired a closer relationship with God, and seeing their king make a covenant with God was all the impetus they needed to do as he did. The sight surely was one to behold, with the king and the people standing as one and promising to live according to what God's law said.

None of us will ever have the same leadership role Josiah did, but that does not mean we will never have any influence. The first priority, of course, is to make sure our relationship with God is what it should be. We will not be ashamed to communicate God's Word to others when we know its power and purpose in our own lives. We should never be ashamed to stand before others when we make a promise to God. Not only does it set an example, but it helps with accountability too.

God is a gracious God who out of love has entered into covenant with us. We live possessing His promises. The very least we can do in light of this is to make every effort to live as God's covenant people. When we do, we will please God, touch the lives of others, and make a difference in the world.

—Darrell W. McKay

Heart of the Lesson

How important is a good leader? If you have ever been involved in a project, you know that it is necessary to have someone in charge in order to get the project done. Perhaps you have been part of a group working toward a goal, but your leader was ineffective for whatever reason. It is much more difficult to get the work done when no one is in charge.

In the Old Testament we often see Israel in such a state. After King Solomon's death, the kingdom was divided. God allowed weak leaders to be in charge as a consequence of the people's sin.

In this week's text we meet a king who truly wanted to lead as God would have him lead.

1. The Law found (II Kgs. 22:8-10). Josiah was only eight years old when he became king. His family background was horrible. His grandfather was one of the worst kings of Judah until he repented near the end of his life (cf. II Chr. 33). Josiah's father was such an evil man that his own officials conspired against him and killed him after he had been king only two years!

Josiah, however, was godly. After reigning as king for eighteen years, he ordered the temple repaired. Because of their sin, Israel had allowed this holy temple, lovingly built by King Solomon, to become dirty and run-down.

Hilkiah the high priest made an amazing discovery during the renovations. He found the book of law. We do not know why it was hidden all this time or when it had been lost. Hilkiah gave the book to the secretary to read, and he reported this find to the king.

When the secretary read the book of the law to Josiah, the king realized right away how sinful they had been as a people. He repented immediately and told these leaders to ask for God's words, knowing that the Lord was extremely angry with His people.

2. The covenant renewed (II Kgs. 23:1-3). Huldah the prophetess told the men about God's plan to allow Judah to be destroyed. Because of Josiah's humility and repentance, though, this punishment would be postponed until after his death (22:14-20). Deeply moved by this prophecy, the king called all the people together so that they could hear the Law read.

King Josiah showed good leadership again as he renewed his covenant to follow God's laws with all his heart. The people all pledged to follow the Lord too.

To show their repentance, the people did a massive housecleaning. They destroyed the idols that were in the temple. They got rid of the accumulated trappings of paganism: human sacrifice, altars and shrines to heathen gods, wizards, and idolatrous priests. Is it any wonder God had been furious with His people?

3. The Passover revived (II Kgs. 23:21-23). Now that he knew more of the Law, King Josiah ordered that the Passover be revived. This important feast had not been celebrated so grandly since the judges, five hundred years before, not even during the reigns of Saul, David, or Solomon. The king revived this memorial to remind his people of God's protection in leading Israel out of Egypt. He knew it was a tangible way for the people to remember God's provision.

Because he followed God's guidance, King Josiah made a big difference in his country. Although you probably are not a king, you have a sphere of influence that can bring others to faith.

—*Judy Carlsen*

World Missions

Covenants are formal agreements that are binding for the participants. The people of Judah had violated the everlasting covenant their ancestors had entered into with the Lord. Now the book of the covenant had been found, and Josiah read it to all the leaders of the nation. Then and there they recommitted themselves to being obedient to the covenant.

Native American tribes have been involved in many agreements and have been given many promises that were broken by the people and government of the United States. Treaties were made and boundaries drawn that guaranteed protections and privileges for them, but the U.S. violated virtually all of the nearly 370 agreements.

The American church today often seems to forget how integrally Christianity was connected with the immigrant takeover of native territories. The Massachusetts General Council and Governor John Winthrop sanctioned the work of John Eliot, the "Apostle to the Indians," in establishing Christian Indian towns starting in 1646. Not long after the Revolutionary War, the U.S. federal government created a "civilization fund" for the support of missionary schools among the Native Americans (Hoxie, ed., *Encyclopedia of North American Indians,* Houghton Mifflin).

Much of the strategy behind this nation's westward expansion called specifically for the "pacification" of indigenous populations through the work of Christian missionaries. This is clearly seen in President Grant's "peace policy" that replaced civil servants in the Bureau of Indian Affairs with missionaries nominated by various Christian denominations.

From the perspective of the Native Americans, therefore, the United States' government cannot be separated from the Christian religion. Because of the numerous treaties and agreements that our "Christian" government has broken, they generally display a strong distrust when missionaries come to help in the name of Christ. They also remember the many other mistreatments and atrocities they have suffered at the hands of "Christians."

This is not to say that there have not been wise, spiritual Christians who have helped, defended, and gained the respect of Native Americans over the years. Roger Williams, David Brainerd, and the Quakers are all early examples of people who developed strong relationships with them. Indeed, true Christian people have been about the only ones to bring moderation, compassion, and understanding to Native American-white relations, however imperfect this appears in history.

There is a new generation of believers, however, that hopes to succeed in presenting the gospel of the new covenant to the Native Americans. Those involved in this new effort include mostly Native American believers, because they are not viewed with the same suspicion that white missionaries are. Please pray for these precious ambassadors of the new covenant.

The words "as long as the grass grows and the rivers flow" were often used in U.S. treaties with native tribes to show the agreements' enduring nature, and yet these were broken. Native Americans instead need to hear these words: "The mountains shall depart, and the hills be removed; but my kindness shall not depart from thee, neither shall the covenant of my peace be removed, saith the Lord that hath mercy on thee" (Isa. 54:10). Only God's covenant will never be broken, for His gifts and call are irrevocable (cf. Rom. 11:29).

—*Lyle P. Murphy*

The Jewish Aspect

The book that Hilkiah the high priest found in the temple may have been the book of Deuteronomy. When Shaphan the scribe read it to Josiah, the king tore his clothes (II Kgs. 22:11), probably in response to the curses against idolatry found in Deuteronomy. Josiah knew that many of the Jews in Judea practiced idolatry and that the nation was in jeopardy of being cursed by God and expelled from the Land of Promise.

Deuteronomy 28 declares specific blessings and curses on Israel based on their obedience or disobedience to the Lord. One of the curses says, "And the Lord shall bring thee into Egypt again with ships, by the way whereof I spake unto thee, Thou shalt see it no more again: and there ye shall be sold unto your enemies for bondmen and bondwomen, and no man shall buy you" (vs. 68).

This prophecy says that the Lord would send the idolatrous Israelites back to Egypt, probably in slave ships (though the translation of the phrase "in ships" has been debated). In Egypt, there would be no one to buy them. This could refer either to an actual absence of any Egyptians to buy them (having been taken into captivity themselves) or to an innumerable supply of Jewish slaves that outweighs the demand for them.

Scripture confirms that the curses of Deuteronomy 28, including verse 68, fell on the Jewish people during and after the fall of Jerusalem in 586 B.C. When the Babylonians invaded Judah, many of the people fled to Egypt despite the warnings of the prophets (II Kgs. 25:26; cf. Jer. 42—44). Their plan was apparently to sell themselves to the Egyptians in return for food (Lam. 5:6). However, God did not allow that to happen, because before they could enact their plan, He sent Nebuchadnezzar to take Egypt captive as well (Jer. 43:7-13; 44:26-30).

As with many of the Bible's prophecies, this initial fulfillment foreshadowed a further fulfillment as well. Jesus Himself foretold the destruction of Jerusalem and the second temple based on the disobedience of Israel's leaders (Matt. 23:1—24:2). Therefore, we should not be surprised to find in that destruction a second fulfillment of many of the curses of Deuteronomy 28.

When the Jewish revolt against the Roman Empire began around A.D. 66, the Jews initially destroyed the Roman garrison in Jerusalem. Then they defeated a poorly trained Roman army that came down from Syria. After those two defeats, the Romans sent their best legions into Judea and systematically vanquished the Jews, sacking Jerusalem and razing the second temple in A.D. 70. Josephus reports that at that time the Romans put many of the Jews "into bonds, and sent them to the Egyptian mines" (*The Wars of the Jews*, vi.9.2). After a later revolt around A.D. 130, Jewish slaves were also sent to Egypt in ships. Their numbers were so great that in some places the price of slaves crashed. The similarity of these events to the prophecy of Deuteronomy 28:68 cannot be overlooked.

These frightening displays of God's judgment should cause us, like Josiah, to respond to the Lord in reverential fear. That same judgment is what every one of us—both Jew and Gentile—deserves. Let us therefore set our hope fully on Jesus, who bore God's wrath for us on the cross so that all who believe in Him would never have to experience it.

—James Coffey

Guiding the Superintendent

In the United States of America, specific qualifications exist for someone who wants to become president. Article II, section 1 of the United States Constitution states, "No Person except a natural born Citizen, or a Citizen of the United States, at the time of the Adoption of this Constitution, shall be eligible to the Office of President."

Additionally, someone who aspires to the presidency must be at least thirty-five years old and have resided within the United States for fourteen years. On February 27, 1951, a term limit amendment to the Constitution was ratified, stating, in essence, that no person can hold the office of president for more than two four-year terms.

In this week's lesson text we learn of a unique child-king whom God used to lead His people. This child, Josiah, seemingly broke the primary qualification that we normally associate with rulers. Because of this, his righteous reign testified strongly to the fact that God was the true Sovereign in Judah.

DEVOTIONAL OUTLINE

1. The reading of God's Word to King Josiah (II Kgs. 22:8-10). King Josiah was eight years old when he began his God-pleasing reign over Judah. When he was twenty-six years old, King Josiah commanded that God's house be repaired with money that had been given by the people.

While this repair work was going on, Hilkiah the high priest discovered the book of God's law. He gave the book to a scribe named Shaphan, who proceeded to read it. Shaphan reported to King Josiah about the repair work and the discovery of the book. Then Shaphan read the Word to him.

2. The reaffirmation of God's covenant and the enactment of godly reforms (II Kgs. 23:1-3, 21-23). King Josiah gathered together everyone, small and great, who dwelt in Judah and Jerusalem and read to them "all the words of the book of the covenant" (vs. 2). The king then made a promise to God that he and all God's people would commit their hearts and souls to obeying His Word.

One of God's requirements that His people had neglected was the observance of Passover. This significant occasion had not been observed rightly since before the period of the judges (vs. 22). But when King Josiah was twenty-six years old, God's people obediently observed the Passover according to his command.

AGE-GROUP EMPHASES

Children: Even though children may have little say or influence over what goes on around them, God can still use them to testify of His love. The truth is that humble, childlike faith is necessary to enter into God's kingdom (cf. Matt. 18:1-6).

Youths: Many young people believe that serving God can wait until they are older. They believe adolescence entitles them to have a good time and even to indulge in youthful rebellion.

Encourage your teachers to use this week's lesson text to challenge that mindset. God deeply desires that His people, no matter what age they are, serve Him obediently and humbly. Help the young people not to waste their youth on the things of the world.

Adults: Adults often believe that they alone are the repositories of wisdom and knowledge. Remind your adults that even Jesus used children to teach adults valuable lessons about eternal life.

—*Thomas R. Chmura*

able members of the church, and they have gifts and wisdom to share (cf. Acts 2:17-18). In settings outside of the church publicly gathering for worship, women are free to teach. In fact, Paul encourages older women to teach (cf. Titus 2:3-5).

In the New Testament, both men and women are valued and have personal rights. In I Corinthians 7:3-4, Paul talks about husbands and wives having rights to each other's bodies in a way that would have been absolutely unheard of in the first-century Roman world. A husband would have had conjugal rights, but that a wife also had them was a shocking, radical idea at the time.

In the New Testament, as in the Old, we see the idea that men are the head of a household (Eph. 5:22-33; Col. 3:18-19; I Pet. 3:1-7). This does *not* mean that men and women are of differing value before God. Paul writes, "There is neither Jew nor Greek, there is neither bond nor free, there is neither male nor female: for ye are all one in Christ Jesus" (Gal. 3:28). Clearly, he is not saying that these categories do not exist. Instead, he is emphasizing that we are all equal before God through Jesus, regardless of ethnicity, status, or gender.

An important aside: we have talked about roles in marriage a fair amount here, so it is important to emphasize that single women have value, dignity, and worth. In Acts there are "four daughters, virgins, which did prophesy" (21:9) and Paul commends singleness (I Cor. 7:7-8). Different people are called to different things, and we should not demean someone who may be called to something different from us.

It is also important to point out that although wives are called to submit to husbands, and although both men and women are called to submit to church leadership, absolutely nowhere does the Bible teach that all women should submit to all men. That idea is foreign to the Bible and can lead to serious problems and hurt.

Women are made in the image of God, are equally loved by God, and have equal dignity and worth as men, despite distinct callings in the home and church. We will study a judge, a wife, a queen, and a mother this quarter, among others. To belittle any woman's calling is wrong, whether it be to marriage or singleness, to be a stay-at-home mom or to work in an office. As Christians, we should respect and honor women more, not less, than the world around us.

Let the Little Children Come

TOM GREENE

It can be easy to grow tired of working with children day in and day out and wonder if you are accomplishing anything. Let me encourage you: according to polls, over 80 percent of American Christians first trusted in Jesus before they were eighteen. Your work

with children—whether your own or students in your church—is important! All children are made in the image of God and deserve our time and respect.

Encourage children you know that there are kids in the Bible who did really important things. Sometimes they did not consider themselves capable. When the prophet Jeremiah was called by God, for example, he at first thought he could not do it and said: "Ah, Lord God! behold, I cannot speak: for I am a child. But the Lord said unto me, Say not, I am a child: for thou shalt go to all that I shall send thee. . . . Be not afraid of their faces: for I am with thee" (Jer. 1:6-8). Jeremiah felt small, but God was with him. If your children feel too young to do anything meaningful, point them to examples like this one!

It is important for kids to understand that before we can do anything for God, we need to be right with Him. God created all things in heaven and on earth, visible and invisible (Col. 1:16). God made people very good, and He made them to obey and enjoy Him.

Unfortunately, the very first people, Adam and Eve, sinned by disobeying God. Now people disobey God and do terrible things to each other. Sin ruins things, and the world is no longer the way it should be. But God is going to fix it one day.

Because God is perfect, He expects people to be perfect too (cf. Matt. 5:18). Children are usually willing to admit that they are not perfect; none of us are. We all sometimes do things we shouldn't, say things we shouldn't, and think nasty things about other people. Remind children that God even cares about the way we think (cf. Matt. 5:21-22).

The good news is, God sent His Son Jesus to pay the penalty for our sins on the cross so that we would not have to. Jesus was perfect, but the Father treated Him as if He had done all the bad things we ever did. Now those sins are completely taken care of, and we are set free from having to pay for them.

God promises that whoever calls on the name of the Lord will be saved (Rom. 10:14). Further, "if we confess our sins, he is faithful and just to forgive us our sins, and to cleanse us from all unrighteousness" (I John 1:9).

What amazing news! If we ask, He will forgive us everything wrong we have ever done, forever!

This promise is *not* just for adults. Jesus told His disciples to let little children come to Him (Matt. 19:14). God's love is a gift; we never have to earn it by being good or smart or strong. In fact, Jesus told some adults: "Whosoever shall not receive the kingdom of God as a little child, he shall not enter therein" (Mark 10:15). Think of how babies eat. Do they go to the kitchen, stand on top of a chair, and start chopping things up to make a fancy dinner? Ridiculous! They just sit in a high-chair and eat what they are given. That is the way we receive God's love like a little child—as gift we never worked for.

No one is ever too young to come to Jesus. Does that sound unrealistic? John the Baptist, Jesus' older cousin, leaped for joy *before he was even born* at the voice of Mary, Jesus' mother (cf. Luke 1:44). OK, that is unusual (John was a miracle baby), but it shows that no one is too young to believe in Jesus, He welcomes people of all ages. Encourage your children that if they have never asked Jesus to forgive them of their sins, they can do that today!

Children who have already asked Jesus to forgive their sins may ask what comes next. Lots of exciting things! God likes to use people who are small to do big things so that it will be obvious to everyone that the power comes from Him, not from us (cf. I Cor. 1:26-29).

God uses people who are young, like Timothy, who was told, "Let no man despise thy youth; but be thou an example of the believers, in word, in conversation, in charity, in spirit, in faith, in purity" (I Tim. 4:12).

Paul's words to Timothy hint strongly at something important. Timothy is told to be a good example. Jesus said: "If ye love me, keep my commandments" (John 14:15). One of the best ways to show God that we love Him is doing what He tells us. It is our way of saying that we trust Him, and we believe He knows the way things should be.

As we grow, we sometimes do things that are wrong. Thankfully, God forgives us. As adults, we have made more mistakes than children, simply because we are older. Hopefully we have learned and grown over time! Point this out to children, as they can sometimes feel inferior to adults.

God commands: "Children, obey your parents in the Lord: for this is right. Honour thy father and mother" (Eph. 6:1-2). This is no arbitrary rule. Because parents have lived longer, they have learned more. We naturally know more about how the world works, and children should learn from our mistakes so they can avoid repeating them.

Because God is good, the world is an exciting place. God has used lots of kids in the past—kids like David, a small servant girl, and Josiah, whose stories we will be looking at this quarter. The Bible also tells of many other people God used when they were young—people like Daniel or his three friends Shadrach, Meshach, and Abednego, or Samuel or Jonathan or Miriam or—well, you get the idea. God loves kids!

TOPICS FOR NEXT QUARTER

PARAGRAPHS ON PLACES AND PEOPLE

NAOMI

Ruth understandably gets much of the attention when we talk about the book of Ruth, but what about Naomi? Her husband, Elimelech, led her family outside of the land of Israel, where she watched him and her two sons, Mahlon and Chilion, die. It's not too surprising that when she moved back to Israel as a widow, she wanted to change her name from Naomi, which means "pleasant," to Mara, meaning "bitter." The Bible realistically portrays her bitterness as she attributes her affliction to God's testimony against her.

But despite Naomi's bitterness toward God at the beginning of the book, God is faithful and blesses her. After Ruth and Boaz marry in the final chapter, they have a son named Obed, who becomes the grandfather of King David. We can rejoice that even when we are bitter, God is faithful and good.

HANNAH

Hannah is the fifth woman recorded in the Bible to struggle with infertility, after Sarah, Rebekah, Rachel, and the mother of Samson. Yet unlike some of those who preceded her, she did not try to take matters into her own hands or retaliate against her taunting rival. Instead, she took her deep pain and sorrow before the Lord.

For years, Peninnah provoked Hannah because she was childless (I Sam. 1:6). Yet when she finally has a son, we have no record of Hannah gloating. Instead, she thanks God and keeps the vow that she made to dedicate her son to the Lord's service.

MOAB

When Naomi's family moved to Moab, it was no small thing. Moab was located east of the Dead Sea in modern-day Jordan. God had promised the land of Israel to Abraham, and Moab was clearly outside of this land.

The Moabites were descendants of Lot and his oldest daughter (cf. Gen. 19:30-38). Their king had hired a prophet to curse Israel (cf. Num. 22—24), and they had oppressed Israel as recently as the days of Eglon (cf. Judg. 3:12-14).

The Israelites were forbidden from marrying foreigners who might lead them away from worshipping God (cf. Deut. 7:3-4). Although the list in Deuteronomy 7 does not explicitly name Moab as one of the forbidden foreign peoples, the command does extend to the Moabites and Ammonites (Neh. 13:1-3, 23-27; cf. Deut. 23:3-6).

MEDIA-PERSIA

The Persian King Cyrus II conquered Media in 550 B.C., uniting two separate kingdoms. Together, the Medes and Persians controlled a massive empire. This included the land of Israel until they were conquered by Greece in 331 B.C.

Israel was allowed to return from exile to the land of promise under the rule of King Cyrus, who even helped finance the rebuilding of the temple (cf. Ezra 6:1-5). The books of Ezra, Nehemiah, Esther, Haggai, Zechariah, and Malachi all take place in this time period.

Susa, the capital city where much of the book of Esther takes place, was located in modern-day Iran.

—Tom Greene.

Daily Bible Readings for Home Study and Worship

(Readings are for the week previous to the lesson topics.)

1. June 2. The Creation of Woman

M —Everything Made Was Very Good. Gen. 1:26-31.
T —Fallen Relationship. Gen. 3:9-20.
W —Wise Women. Prov. 11:16; 14:1; 31:30-31.
T —The Woman Was Deceived. I Tim. 2:12-15.
F —Training Young Women. Titus 2:3-5.
S —A Beautiful Setting for the First Marriage. Gen. 2:8-17.
S —Fashioned with Purpose. Gen. 2:18-25.

2. June 9. Deborah Encourages Barak

M —The Lord Fights for Israel. Ex. 14:23-28.
T —Miriam's Song. Ex. 15:20-21.
W —Huldah the Prophetess. II Kgs. 22:14-20.
T —Jael and Sisera. Judg. 4:17-21.
F —Deborah's Song. Judg. 5:1-12.
S —Tribute to Jael. Judg. 5:24-31.
S —Deborah the Prophetess. Judg. 4:4-10, 12-16.

3. June 16. Ruth Follows Naomi

M —Origin of Moab. Gen. 19:29-38.
T —A Husband for Tamar. Gen. 38:1-11.
W —The Lord Protects Moab. Deut. 2:8-22.
T —Honor Godly Widows. I Tim. 5:3-8.
F —Leaving All Behind. Matt. 19:27-30.
S —Released to Find New Husbands. Ruth 1:10-13.
S —Marriage and Death in Moab. Ruth 1:1-9, 14b, 16.

4. June 23. Ruth Meets Boaz

M —Providing for the Poor. Lev. 19:9-10; Deut. 24:19-22.
T —You Will Be Fed. Ps. 37:1-6.
W —Assignment for the Rich. I Tim. 6:17-19.
T —Kindness to the Poor. Prov. 14:26-27, 30-31.
F —Return to Bethlehem. Ruth 1:19-22.
S —Gathering Grain. Ruth 2:1-7.
S —Welcome and Protection. Ruth 2:8-18.

5. June 30. Ruth Marries Boaz

M —Levirate Marriage. Deut. 25:7-10.
T —Redeeming Property. Jer. 32:6-15.
W —Moabite Prohibition. Deut. 23:2-6.
T —Blessing of Children. Ps. 127:1-5.
F —Waiting for Redemption. Ruth 3:11-18.
S —David's Ancestor. Ruth 4:15-22.
S —Marriage and Blessing. Ruth 4:1-10.

6. July 7. Hannah Commits Her Son to God

M —Mary's Song of Praise. Luke 1:46-55.
T —Hope in God Brings Strength. Isa. 40:25-31.
W —Zechariah's Song of Praise. Luke 1:67-79.
T —Who Is Like the Lord? Ps. 113:1-9.
F —Vows Fulfilled to a Faithful God. Ps. 66:13-20.
S —Hannah's Vow. I Sam. 1:9-18.
S —Hannah's Song of Praise. I Sam. 1:20, 26-28; 2:1-10.

7. July 14. Esther's Bravery

M —God's Promise to Abraham. Gen. 12:1-3.
T —Confidence in the Lord. Ps. 27:1-14.
W —Anger Blinds. Dan. 3:13-28.
T —A Decree for Annihilation. Esth. 3:8-15.

F —A Fasting People. Jonah 3:5-10.
S —Mordecai Mourns. Esth. 4:1-5.
S —Wicked Scheme of Haman. Esth. 3:2-3, 5-6a; 4:7-16.

8. July 21. The Deliverance of the Jews

M —Saved for His Name's Sake. Ps. 106:1-5.
T —The Lovingkindness of the Lord. Ps. 107:33-43.
W —Petition for Deliverance. Ps. 32:6-11.
T —The Lord Will Judge the Nations. Obad. 1:15-21.
F —Elevation of Mordecai. Esth. 8:15-17.
S —Defense for the Jews. Esth. 9:1-17.
S —Purim Instituted. Esth. 8:3-8; 9:18-23.

9. July 28. Great Forgiveness and Great Love

M —Ungrateful and Unmerciful. Matt. 18:23-35.
T —Acceptance Leads to Repentance. Luke 19:1-10.
W —Beautiful Are the Feet that Bring Good News. Isa. 52:7-10.
T —Heaven Rejoices When Sinners Repent. Luke 15:1-7.
F —Hypocritical Judgment. Rom. 2:1-5.
S —Humility Brings Mercy. Luke 18:9-14.
S —Love Poured Out on Jesus. Luke 7:36-50.

10. August 4. A Faithful Servant in the Church

M —Faithful Care Reciprocated. I Tim. 5:9-10.
T —A People Eager to Do Good. Titus 2:11-14.
W —The Dead in Christ Will Rise. I Thess. 4:13-18.
T —God Hears Our Cries. Ps. 145:14-20.
F —Elisha Raises the Dead. II Kgs. 4:18-37.
S —Let Your Light Shine. Matt. 5:14-16.
S —Tabitha Restored to Life. Acts 9:36-43.

11. August 11. Young David Anointed King

M —Provision for Those Who Fear the Lord. Ps. 147:7-11.
T —Promise of David's Kingdom. Ps. 89:19-37.
W —Corruption Comes from the Heart. Mark 7:14-23.
T —A Pure Heart Brings Blessing. Ps. 24:1-10.
F —Saul's Disobedience. I Sam. 13:8-14.
S —God's Rejection of Saul. I Sam. 15:17-23.
S —God's Chosen King. I Sam. 16:1-4, 6-13.

12. August 18. A Servant Girl Points Naaman to God

M —Outstanding Faith of a Roman. Matt. 8:5-13.
T —Determined Faith of a Gentile Woman. Mark 7:24-30.
W —The Lord Exalted by a Pagan King. Dan. 4:34-37.
T —The Lord's Concern for Those Outside Israel. Luke 4:24-27.
F —Laws for the Cleansing of Lepers. Lev. 14:1-7.
S —The Samaritan Returned to Give Thanks. Luke 17:11-19.
S —Naaman Obeys—God Brings Healing. II Kgs. 5:1-5, 9-15a.

13. August 25. Josiah Calls the People Back to God

M —Passover in the Wilderness. Num. 9:1-5.
T —Care Taken for the Temple's Upkeep. II Kgs. 12:4-16.
W —Kings Should Study the Law Daily. Deut. 17:14-20.
T —Prophecy About Josiah. I Kgs. 13:1-6.
F —Josiah's Temple Project. II Kgs. 22:1-7.
S —Judgment Will Come. II Kgs. 22:11-20.
S —Passover Celebrated. II Kgs. 22:8-10; 23:1-3, 21-23.

REVIEW

What have you learned this quarter?

Can you answer these questions?

**God's Work Through
Women and Youths**

UNIT I: Women of Faith

June 2

The Creation of Woman

1. What does Genesis 1 repeatedly say about Creation, and what was different in Genesis 2?
2. How does God's view of women differ from many cultures today?
3. What does the term "help meet" tell us about Eve in relation to Adam?
4. How was the creation of Eve different from that of Adam?
5. What are the implications of the command to "leave" and "cleave"?

June 9

Deborah Encourages Barak

1. What two ministries did Deborah perform?
2. Why did people from all over Israel come to Deborah in Ephraim?
3. What message did Deborah convey to Barak in Kedesh-naphtali?
4. What advantage did Deborah indicate that Israel had over Sisera?
5. How did Jael fulfill the prophecy made in Judges 4:9?

June 16

Ruth Follows Naomi

1. How does the portrayal of life differ in the books of Judges and Ruth?
2. Who were the Moabites? How had they dealt with Israel?
3. What kind of future did Naomi face after her husband and sons died?
4. How did Naomi urge her daughters-in-law to do? How did they respond?
5. What level of commitment is ex-seen in Ruth's "cleaving" to Naomi?

June 23

Ruth Meets Boaz

1. What had Boaz already heard about Ruth before he met her?
2. What did Boaz tell Ruth about where to glean, and what advantage did this give her?
3. How do we explain being under God's wings (Ruth 2:12)?
4. What surprising events happened for Ruth at lunchtime?
5. What did Boaz command his reapers, and why was this unexpected?

June 30

Ruth Marries Boaz

1. Why did Boaz go to the city gate? What did he do after he arrived?
2. What was Boaz's initial proposal to the other kinsman?
3. Why did the kinsman to rescind his offer to redeem Naomi's land?
4. How was the transaction sealed?
5. What were the two transactions that took place that day?

July 7

Hannah Commits Her Son to God

1. Why was the birth of Samuel so important to Hannah?
2. Why did Hannah feel it was necessary to present Samuel to Eli?
3. In what way did Hannah experience the salvation of the Lord (I Sam. 2:1).
4. What did Hannah say about God's control over her life?
5. Who was the "anointed" (I Sam. 2:10) of whom Hannah spoke?

July 14

Esther's Bold Faith

1. How do we see God's providence at work in the promotion of Haman?

2. How did Haman plan to punish Mordecai for his refusal to bow?

3. What did Esther remind Mordecai about after hearing his plan?

4. What did Mordecai suggest was the purpose of Esther's royal position?

5. Why was Mordecai so certain that the Jews would not be annihilated?

July 21

The Deliverance of the Jews

1. What important events took place between Esther's two dinners?

2. Why did Esther make a second appearance before the king?

3. What was Esther's concluding emotional appeal to the king?

4. What did the king grant Esther at the conclusion of the day on which the Jews defended themselves?

5. What name was given to the feast celebrating the Jews' deliverance?

July 28

A Sinner Serves Christ

1. Why did Jesus accept the invitation of a Pharisee to eat at his home?

2. What were the Pharisee's conclusions as he observed the woman's actions toward Jesus?

3. How did Jesus choose to instruct Simon?

4. What analogy in Jesus' parable did Simon not understand?

5. How did Jesus reassure the woman, and how did others react?

August 4

A Faithful Servant in the Church

1. What was Dorcas's reputation among the people of Joppa?

2. How did the people convey how much Dorcas had meant to them?

3. What initial action by Peter mimicked what Jesus had done?

4. Why is it important to know that Peter prayed before doing anything else when he raised Dorcas?

5. Why is it significant where Peter stayed in Joppa?

UNIT II: Young People of Faith

August 11

Young David Anointed King

1. Who was the first king of Israel, and what led to his rejection by God?

2. What directions did God give Samuel, and what did He not tell him?

3. What truth did God give Samuel when he was considering Eliab?

4. Why was it logical for Jesse to present his sons in order of age?

5. What did the anointing and the coming of the Spirit do for David?

August 18

A Servant Girl Points Naaman to God

1. What important position did Naaman hold?

2. How is Naaman described, and what does that tell us about him?

3. What insignificant person became significant to Naaman?

4. How did Naaman become convinced he should do what Elisha had said, and what was the result?

5. What happened after Naaman saw he had been completely cleansed?

August 25

Josiah Calls the People Back to God

1. Who found the book of the law of God in the temple?

2. Why did Josiah send a delegation to Huldah the prophetess?

3. What promise did Josiah make after reading the Law to the people?

4. What types of reforms did Josiah make following his commitment to the covenant?

5. Why was the reinstitution of the Passover important?